THIS WOODEN 'O'

A pre-publication first paperback edition generously donated by
McCann-Erickson Europe

12th June 1997

BARRY DAY

THIS WOODEN 'O'

SHAKESPEARE'S GLOBE REBORN

PUBLISHED IN ASSOCIATION WITH THE SHAKESPEARE GLOBE TRUST

OBERON BOOKS
LONDON

To Sam and Theo
Who Made it Happen

Twixt such friends as we
Few words suffice

The Taming of the Shrew Act 1 Sc.ii

❖

This work first published in 1996 by Oberon Books Limited,
521 Caledonian Road, London N7 9RH
Tel: 0171-607-3637 Fax: 0171-607-3629

Reprinted in paperback 1997

Published in association with The Shakespeare Globe Trust.

ISBN 1 870259 99 8

Cover and book design: Andrzej Klimowski and Richard Doust

Cover: 'Globe Theatre' *The Times* photograph by Marc Aspland
Frontispiece: 'The new Globe under construction 1996' photograph by Tom Doust

ACKNOWLEDGEMENTS

The Shakespeare's Globe Project has enjoyed a supporting cast of hundreds, if not thousands, throughout its 35 year run to date. Some have played major roles, many more have carried metaphorical spears – all have been important. It was impossible to give everyone proper credit in the narrative but I have tried to remember them in the list that follows. There will inevitably be names I have forgotten – or didn't know about. To them my apologies. They will certainly be added to the "cast list" in any subsequent edition...

This book bears one name but it is a true collaboration in every sense. I could not have written it without the wholehearted support of many people, particularly those with knowledge of the more specialised aspects of the Globe project. I am especially grateful to Professors Glynne Wickham, Andrew Gurr and John Orrell for their help with the academic and historical aspects of the story; to the late Theo Crosby, Jon Greenfield and Peter McCurdy for the sections on designing and building the Globe, a process in which John Orrell was also deeply involved; to Simon Blatherwick, Harvey Sheldon and Robin Densem for advice on the archaeology of the Rose and the Globe; to Ann Ward for untangling the political and social threads of life in Southwark.

On matters theatrical I was greatly helped by Michael Holden, Lord (Michael) Birkett, Sir Peter Hall, Mark Rylance, Patrick Tucker, Dame Judi Dench, Rosemary Harris.

On more matters than I now care to recall I was helped by the wisdom of those who had helped guide the project through bad times to good... Alan Butland, Diana Devlin, Jackie Haighton, Siri Fisher Hansen, Elizabeth Herbert, Jean Jayer, Jane Lepotaire, James Lister, Sandra Moretto, Sir David Orr, Barry O'Sullivan, Roger Parry, Sir Michael Perry, Barry Shaw, Patrick Spottiswoode and Lyn Williams in the UK... Jerry Link and Elspeth Udzarhelyi in the US.

Guiding me though much of the maze – as she guided Sam – was the invaluable Marina Blodget and, of course, I could never have gained a fraction of retrospective insight into the private Sam without the help, freely and fondly given, of brother Bill and Charlotte and Zoë Wanamaker.

Finally, I now know the true meaning of the phrase – "This book would not have been possible without ..." In my case there were two people. The first was my researcher. Subsidised by the generosity of Guy Walker and Van den Bergh Foods and Andrew Seth and Lever Brothers (UK), she dug and delved and charmed her way into archives and memories. My advice to anyone contemplating a book of this complexity is – first find yourself a Kate Hinze! The second was my assistant, Rosalind Fayne, who typed and re-typed uncomplainingly – and actually seemed anxious to discover how the plot was going to turn out...!

Last, first and always – in this as in every endeavour – thanks to my wife, Lynne, who always sees the glass as half full, when I could have sworn it was almost empty.

Barry Day is a director of the International Shakespeare Globe Centre. His previous publications include a collaboration with Graham Payn on My Life With Noël Coward [Applause]. He is currently editing and annotating Coward's Complete Lyrics for publication next year. A graduate of Balliol College, Oxford he has long been a leading figure in international advertising, serving as worldwide Creative Director for the McCann-Erickson and Lintas agencies. He is currently Director of Creative Communications for their parent company, Interpublic.

CONTENTS

FOREWORD

This book is a fitting tribute to the remarkable Sam Wanamaker and a fascinating detailed account of the trials and tribulations, despairs and triumphs which led to the extraordinary accomplishment of his dream theatre in London.

I never knew him at all, though we corresponded several times and waved cheerfully at one another on one or two official occasions. But I am ashamed now to have made no suggestion that we should meet privately, and when the Prime Minister was gracious enough to host a dinner at Downing Street to help raise funds for the enterprise, neither Sam nor his wife were well enough to grace the occasion, though his charming and talented daughters were able to fill their places.

Sam had persuaded me to let him use my name as Honorary Vice President by very persuasive letters, but I had strong misgivings, knowing I should no longer be young and energetic enough to take much active part in seeing the plans through to completion and it did seem rather ironic that the conception and its funding should be American, although the Stratford Theatre had faced much the same problem when it was rebuilt in the 1930's with American funding. Now that the opening of the new Globe is a concrete reality, I can only marvel at Sam's incredible perseverance and magnificently courageous enthusiasm, sacrificing his own stage career, his own house and his physical constitution with unbelievable tenacity to the very end.

I can only wish that the final building will fulfil his wildest hopes and that in Mark Rylance a successor has been found to bring Shakespeare once again to the very centre of our City.

John Gielgud

Sir John Gielgud
May 1996

AUTHOR'S NOTE

There are a number of logistical problems in telling the story of the rebuilding of Shakespeare's Globe for a general audience. It covers a period of many years from the time that Sam Wanamaker made his personal commitment and it proceeded in fits and starts. Also it involved a number of separate but interwoven activities, many of which followed their own parallel paths and individual time scales but had little to do with each other day to day. Some of these activities are likely to interest the general reader more than others, yet each of them is integral to the whole story.

I have tried to tell it on two planes, so to speak, and to inter-relate them as best I can as we go along. Thus, the chronology is interrupted periodically by a series of "Tales" in which we take a closer look at the more specialised aspects – academic disputes, architectural, archaeological, political considerations and so on. In these chapters I have attempted to provide a simple overview of the whole project, greatly aided by specialists, many of whom will no doubt be publishing their own detailed stories later. In doing so, I have tried to keep duplication down to the minimum. And before anyone says – "But surely the 'Tales' was Chaucer not Shakespeare?" – I would argue that a good idea doesn't care who has it (or how often). And, in any case, wasn't Chaucer also connected with Southwark?

The other problems are legion – the legion of different people who played a part. To mention all or even most of them, let alone assess their contribution to the eventual success of the project is impossible, I hope. Without them it would never have happened... If the story emerges as essentially the story of one man – then *mea culpa!* Even the most critical observers of the Globe project would accept that, in true Shakespearean fashion, this was indeed a story with one towering hero and a supporting cast of thousands...

PREFACE

We'd been looking round the bays. It was a warm evening in late summer and the wooden beams stood there against the sky like giant soldiers at attention waiting to be issued with their uniforms. But the miracle was – they finally stood there.

I lost sight of him for a moment then I came upon him standing motionless, looking across the river to where the dome of Wren's St. Paul's caught the light, a building that had come into being with a lot less pain than this one.

He was in profile to me and it struck me – not for the first time – that this was a face, craggy and characterful, that belonged on a coin or carved into the side of a mountain. It also struck me that it was nearly forty years since I first saw it, bringing a London stage to life as The Rainmaker – the man who brings something out of nothing.

For once that active face was in repose. What was he thinking of at this precise moment?

If this were a movie, he'd been seeing in his mind's eye the footbridge that one day will link the Globe site with the steps of St. Paul's, teeming with people, newly summoned by the Globe's trumpeter to see the play... or perhaps, turning, he'd piece out the imperfections of the present and fill our Wooden 'O' with a throng of Elizabethan ladies and gentlemen, conversing in ghostly voices as they awaited the Prologue.

Or perhaps, more realistically, he was simply remembering how the whole adventure began on a day in 1949 in a bomb-blasted South London street, as an eager young American actor came across a tarnished bronze plaque on a brewery wall – the only memorial to the greatest theatre the world has ever seen – and decided to take matters into his own hands.

And, then again, perhaps I was projecting on to him the thoughts that were in my own mind.

As he sensed my presence, he turned. I'd never thought of him as serene but no other word describes the smile as he indicated the collection of concrete and timber that was changing before our eyes.

"It's really going to happen, isn't it?" he said, more of a statement than a question. "Yes, Sam," I said, "it's really going to happen..."

Barry Day 1996

O for a Muse of fire, that would ascend
The brightest heaven of invention!
A kingdom for a stage, princes to act,
And monarchs to behold the swelling scene!
...

But pardon, gentles all,
The flat unraised spirit that hath dar'd
On this unworthy scaffold to bring forth
So great an object: can this cockpit hold
The vasty fields of France? or may we cram
Within this wooden O the very casques
That did affright the air at Agincourt?
O pardon! since a crooked figure may
Attest in little place a million;
And let us, ciphers to this great accompt,
On your imaginary forces work.
Suppose within the girdle of these walls
Are now confin'd two mighty monarchies,
Whose high upreared and abutting fronts
The perilous narrow ocean parts asunder:
Piece out our imperfections with your thoughts:
Into a thousand parts divide one man,
And make imaginary puissance;
Think, when we talk of horses, that you see them
Printing their proud hoof i' the receiving earth;
For 'tis your thoughts that now must deck our kings,
Carry them here and there; jumping o'er times,
Turning the accomplishment of many years
Into an hour-glass: for the which supply,
Admit me Chorus to this history;
Who, prologue-like, your humble patience pray,
Gently to hear, kindly to judge, our play.

Chorus
Henry V

PROLOGUE

In a BBC TV documentary covering the history of the Globe project up to the Dedication ceremony of 1983, Derek Jacobi played a latterday Chorus. Standing by the blackened plaque which had started Sam's quest ...

"This lonely plaque, this empty wall
Is set in Britain's cold and steely land,
Where Dreams must stand in line
With hard-press'd Enterprise.
Bold Wanamaker saw this Wooden 'O' alive again
With sound of verse and song,
With players and plaudits — the Bard reborn.
But opposition's hard —
This land, the people cry, is steeped enough in culture.
Tis homes we need — not art!"

Southwark Cathedral – March 2nd, 1994

On the day they came in their hundreds to honour him for an achievement that was still to be achieved – the great and the good and many who aspired to be neither. Side by side on the front rows crowded the Establishments, social and theatrical. Behind them clustered the Groundlings, brought here to Southwark Cathedral on this bright March morning of 1994 by the rumour that today was the chance to hear the Prologue to a play that had been waiting many years to open. While outside with the paparazzi waited the crowd that always materialises at the sound of a bandwagon passing.

To most people sitting there, quietly star-spotting, the re-creation of Shakespeare's Globe was probably no more than a perfectly good idea whose time had come. Come to think of it, what had taken them so long? Thirty-five years?

A few others with longer memories and closer connections looked at the crowded seats and remembered the time when the band of pilgrims could be counted on one hand. Members of the Board recalled those monthly meetings – not too long ago – when the first item of business was to look at the balance sheet and see whether the project could legally afford to go on trading for another month.

On the way in, warm greetings were exchanged between people who a decade earlier had been on opposite ideological sides in Southwark Council's bitter fight to take back the site from these elitist artists.

On the way out – as the flash bulbs made the bright day brighter – famous faces that had opposed each other not too long ago in the media battle between 'Shakespeare's Rose' and 'Wanamaker's Globe' were now seen enjoying a joke.

Today, as the sun shone unseasonably warm, all the brightest swords were put up and all the differences put aside.

A year from now the new Globe would be built, as near as made a damn. And even before that another plaque would be erected. Not, this time, destined to tarnish unseen on a brewery wall, but to shine proudly next to Shakespeare's statue on the cathedral wall with the legend:

In Thanksgiving for Sam Wanamaker, CBE (1919-1993). Actor. Director. Producer.

Whose Vision Rebuilt Shakespeare's Theatre on Bankside in This Parish.

And when once the play was again the thing that drew the crowds to Bankside for the first time since 1644, no one would remember or care why it had taken so much time or angst to achieve something that most countries would have taken care of in months.

In fact, the story of the rebuilding of Shakespeare's Globe is a peculiarly British story – a story of theatrical rivalry comparable to anything since Elizabethan times, a story of political advantage and apathy at national and local level and of a national ennui which takes heritage for granted, until and unless the spotlight of the media makes an issue impossible to ignore.

Above all – threading through plot and sub-plot, like the hero of a series of epic plays – this is the story of how one man, the 'onlie begetter' of the dream, became at a point both inspiration and obstacle, a fact he fully realised. And how, when things were looking their worst, the God came down from the Machine – as he does in all the best dramas – and pointed a path.

But that is to jump some forty years – or, more accurately, four hundred years. Before the how came the what.

Precisely what was the social and theatrical experience that was so unique that it continued to intrigue people over successive centuries and finally brought a very diverse group of individuals together in the determination to make the theatre of Shakespeare and his contemporaries finally live again?

Sam Wanamaker with a bust of William Shakespeare

A ferry (or wherry) on the Thames, a method of transport many people used to cross the river in order to 'hear a play.' *Edinburgh University Library*

CHAPTER ONE

THE SHAKESPEAREAN THEATRICAL EXPERIENCE

(1564 – 1644)

*The purpose of playing... was and is, to hold, as
'twere, the mirror up to nature...*

Hamlet to the Players, *Hamlet*, Act III Sc. ii

Rebuilding Shakespeare's Globe in the 20th century has generated more heated controversy than the construction of the original building. Opponents have publicly voiced objections again and again, while dedicated supporters have soldiered on regardless. It might have been a unique project in theatre history, but for the fact that Shakespeare lovers in other parts of the world, Japan and USA have beaten the Bard's compatriots to it. Yet, despite bureaucratic obstacles, partisan detractors, and chronic cash shortage, the day has finally come when the Globe has been magnificently reborn.

Shakespeare's genius, of course, has been the driving force. No other playwright has said more about the nature of the world we live in, or illuminated humanity and inhumanity with more perception, clarity and compelling language. But there is more to it than that. The rebirth of Shakespeare's Globe was due to an effort of will on the part of one man, Sam Wanamaker and, subsequently through the dedication of those who shared his dream and pursued his cause up to and since his death in 1993. The question the rest of the world has asked throughout this 25 year project has always been: What did Wanamaker and all who share his vision see in a Globe theatre for our times? What was he trying to achieve? What does a replica of an old wooden theatre that stood for a mere 14 years before it burned down have to say to our times?

Part of the answer may be in what the original Globe meant to its seventeenth century audience.

When Shakespeare was born in 1564, there *were* no theatres to write for. Had things turned out otherwise, if we remembered him at all, it might have been as one of the many minor poets of the period. As it happened, the man and the moment found each other. He and the theatre grew up together and he was able to learn his craft as the Elizabethan playhouse found its form and purpose and then help shape that purpose. It was a happy happenstance.

Shakespeare the man and the mystique that surrounds him surely permeates the whole idea of building his theatre. There's also the fascination that lies in the popular experience the theatre provided for the Elizabethan and Jacobean theatregoer – the sense of being one of a crowd yet still being a participant in the event. It's an immediacy that we've long since lost, except in the twilight zone activities of the rock concert or the football fracas. But even they bear witness to the need of an audience to be part of the show and share whatever pity, terror, laughter is on offer.

The Shakespearean theatre experience was, by all accounts, something quite remarkable and it started well before the performance. If you could transport yourself back to a summer day in, say, 1600... you might find yourself strolling over London Bridge. Not the London Bridge of recent memory but a wooden construction filled with houses and shops, a thoroughfare over the bustling Thames, "the main artery" of Elizabethan London. You could just as easily have crossed by wherry (or flat bottomed boat) – as most of the spectators do – and be set ashore a few paces from either the Globe or its great competitor, the Rose. But the view from this particular bridge gives you the panorama of Bankside. Warrens of narrow streets teeming with people going about a variety of businesses, for this is a fiercely independent part of London – or of Surrey to be precise – across the river and outside the jurisdiction of the City Fathers. This freedom – some call it licence – is why Bankside is fast becoming the home of all the entertainments the City frowns on and will have none of – bear and bull-baiting, gambling, prostitution and the lewd excesses of the playhouses!

A flutter of movement catches the eye. It's the breeze rippling the pennant on the top of a three-storied round building that stands taller than its neighbours. The new Globe is flying its white flag to announce a play is to be performed today. As you draw closer, you'll see it has the design of Hercules bearing the world on his shoulders. Shakespeare was to write of the world being a stage and on this stage

3

depict so many of the aspects of that world. The Globe's ambitions were great indeed, as befitted its motto – *Totus mundus agit histrionem* (generally translated as 'All the World's a Stage').

Notice the crowd around the playhouse. A bunch of noisy apprentices stealing time from work and feeding the conviction of the City Fathers that these plays are proving to be a subversive force in society and no good will come of them. As for the rest... tinkers, tailors, soldiers, sailors, old men, young men, ladies of the street, Ladies with their chaperones (to make sure no one mistakes them for the other kind!), lords and lawyers, town clerks and beggars, country gentlemen and cutpurses... and most of them will see themselves up on that stage, personified as one character or another before Mr. Shakespeare is very much older. The noise of their chatter fills your ears.

To the playhouse itself now. Three galleries high to give all the spectators a good view. Not truly circular at all, when you get closer to it, but twenty sides, so plastered as to give the impression of an enormous 'O', at least thirty feet high.

The buzz grows louder. Time to push your way through one of the two narrow doors, handing your penny to the 'gatherer'. This one's a woman – the nearest she'll get to the stage, where all the parts of women will be played by boys.

Into the bright sunshine of the courtyard and another world... people mingling and greeting, pushing through to find friends, stopping to buy something to eat or drink – a market place for gossip and the exchange of news, all contained within the embrace of the circle of wooden galleries that rise up all around you, reaching for the open sky.

Another penny to another gatherer and you're climbing to the top gallery. Below you the stage thrusting out into the centre of the yard, right into the middle of the crowd of 'groundlings' who will stand throughout the performance and leave the actors in no doubt as to their views. Supporting the 'heavens' above the stage the two massive pillars – wooden, too, but acting the part of marble and gold to perfection. And around the galleries the decorations... fantastic and ornate, transforming the plain timbers into a casket of jewels.

Suddenly the trumpeter in the stage tower blows his third and final note. The actors are ready. The play is about to begin...

For *as we see at all the play house dores,*
When ended is the play, the dance, and song,
A thousand townsmen, gentlemen and whores,
Porters and serving men together throng

John Davies (1593)

There were nine amphitheatres that we know of and – since several of them will play recurring parts – it is as well to list them now. In order of construction they were: the Red Lion (1567), the Theatre (1576), the Curtain (1577), the Rose (1587) the Swan (1595), the Globe (1599), the Fortune (1600), the Boar's Head (1601) and the

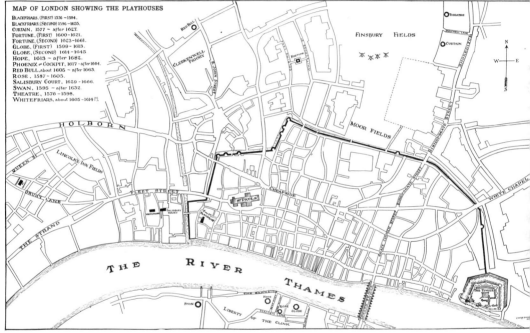

MAP OF LONDON SHOWING THE PLAYHOUSES

BLACKFRIARS, (FIRST) 1576 –1584.
BLACKFRIARS,(SECOND) 1596 –1655.
CURTAIN , 1577 – after 1627.
FORTUNE, (FIRST) 1600–1621.
FORTUNE, (SECOND) 1623–1661.
GLOBE, (FIRST) 1599 – 1613.
GLOBE, (SECOND) 1614 –1645.
HOPE, 1613 – after 1682.
PHOENIX or COCKPIT, 1617 – after 1664.
RED BULL, about 1605 – after 1663.
ROSE , 1587– 1605.
SALISBURY COURT, 1629 –1666.
SWAN , 1595 – after 1632.
THEATRE , 1576 –1598.
WHITEFRIARS, about 1605 –1614 (?).

Turn of the century map showing the supposed location of the Elizabethan/Jacobean playhouses. It would take until 1989 to resolve some of the arguments.

Red Bull (1604). A tenth – the Hope – was built in 1614 and doubled up as both playhouse and bear-baiting house. The second function rapidly overtook the first and its interest today lies mainly in the fact that the new Globe project had as its first permanent premises the buildings that occupied the site of the Hope.

Nor were the plays dry literary concoctions. Since a high proportion of the playgoing population was illiterate, the plays were their newspapers and contemporary playwrights used them as such – throwing in asides on political events or satirical observations, rendered immune from official retribution or, indeed, preventive censorship by the fact of being manifest fiction.

The disguise was transparent enough for those with the wit to see and hear and sometimes rebounded on its authors. Ben Jonson was put in prison for things he wrote. And when Essex decided it was time to make his move to unseat the ageing Queen Elizabeth, he tried to persuade the Lord Chamberlain's Men – the Globe's resident troupe of players – to put on a performance of Shakespeare's *Richard II*, a play about a monarch who is deposed, in the hope that the populace would take the point and act upon it. The Queen did get the point and did act. Essex was arrested and eventually executed.

The theatre did much to deflect popular attention from the problems of the day and the last decade of the 16th century was not an easy one in Elizabeth's England. There were sustained wars in Spain and Holland and the Plague – Europe's first involuntary collaboration – was an intermittent but regular visitor.

The Play was the very thing to put all the things you couldn't affect into some kind of popular perspective – very much as television was to become three centuries later. By the turn of the century the population of London was probably no more than 150,000, most of them living north of the Thames, yet it's reckoned that in a typical week 10% of them saw a play. If that isn't popular art, what is? But the flowering of the playhouses hadn't happened overnight...

> *...a poor player*
> *That struts and frets his hour upon the stage,*
> *And then is heard no more*
>
> Macbeth, Act V Sc. v

Until the middle years of Elizabeth's reign the actors had been nomads, literally 'strolling players,' putting on a play wherever they found an hospitable setting. When all else failed, they would erect a platform stage on the back of one of their carts – presumably the origin of 'treading the boards.' A top booking would be in an inn yard. The intimacy of the setting, the close proximity between players and spectators was something deliberately copied in the eventual design of the later amphitheatres – the only difference being the change to a circular shape in emulation of the classical Greek and Roman theatres.

There were other factors that kept the show 'on the road.' The regular recurrence of the Plague would result in the periodic banning of public gatherings in the cities, forcing the troupes to find their audiences in the villages and hamlets or – if they were lucky – in the house of some nobleman. The more   fortunate ones – or perhaps simply the better actors – were those who found a noble patron and were able to use his name. There was little long term future without one. The Earl of Leicester's Men, The Lord Admiral's Men, The Lord Chamberlain's Men... names like these could be advertised in advance and guarantee a degree of professionalism in the performance. It was just such a troupe that Hamlet welcomed to the court of Claudius and Gertrude. In Act II Hamlet bids Polonius -

> Good my lord, will you see the players well bestowed? Do you hear,
> let them be well used; for they are the abstracts and brief chronicles of
> the time: after your death you were better have a bad epitaph than
> their ill report while you live.

And Polonius' reply underlines the low reputation actors really enjoyed in polite society -

> My Lord, I will use them according to their desert.

But the main reason for their regular absence from London was the marked disapproval of the City Fathers and the established Church. As Andrew Gurr puts it: "The spokesmen for Puritan London described the audiences as riotous and immoral; the poets described them as ignorant and wilful; the City Fathers regarded them as 'rioters and seditious'." By 1598 they had formally banned all public playhouses within the gates of the city – which meant that a keen playgoer was in for an unpleasant walk through sewerage-infested streets and then muddy fields. Or he could seek his pleasures south of the river, which was part of the county of Surrey with Bankside being within the diocese of the somewhat liberal Bishop of Winchester. Without the public support of the Queen and certain of her Court, there's no doubt that the players would have been banned outright. As it was, the City Fathers could do no more than banish them. The ordinance read:

> ...all fencers, bearwards, common players of interludes other than those
> belonging to any baron of this realm shall be taken adjudged and
> deemed rogues, vagabonds and sturdy beggars and shall be stripped
> naked from the middle upwards and shall be openly whipped until his
> or her body be bloody.

Actors have traditionally complained of being flayed by the critics but never with such real cause!

Cynicism, it must be said, went hand in hand with concern about public morality. The ten per cent of London's population who called themselves playgoers was by no means confined to the idle rich with nothing better to do with their time. The City Fathers were rather more concerned with what happened to productivity when their apprentices took time off to see a play, as they regularly did. And while the Church's more conservative element was concerned, no doubt, with whatever heretical nonsense was filling people's heads in the playhouses, they were rather more concerned with a very real loss of authority. For a largely illiterate population, the spoken word was traditionally the Church's domain and The Word was intended by God to be spoken on approved topics and only by those ordained by Him in His Theatre and at a playing time of His Choosing. And, after all, hadn't earlier popular theatre quite properly been the 'mystery plays', which dealt exclusively with religious themes?

But as things now stood, both Church and local state had to bide their time. It would come, but before then some things would have happened that would change history and survive the destruction of any amount of bricks and mortar – or, rather, lath and plaster...

> Sit in a full theatre and you will think you see so
> many lines drawn from the circumference of so many
> ears, while the actor is the centre
>
> John Webster

The man who turned street theatre into a commercial proposition was James Burbage, a businessman who just happened to find himself in the theatrical business – something most of the later great impresarios seem to have in common. Tired of touring, he decided to put down some roots.

The Red Lion playhouse had been built in Stepney as far back as 1567 – possibly with Burbage's involvement – but so little is known about it that he is generally given the sole credit for London's first permanent theatre. He built it just outside the Bishopsgate entrance to the City of London in 1576, giving it the name that has since become generic – the Theatre – which he derived from the Greek *teatron* and the Latin *theatrum* (seeing or viewing place). To that extent, Burbage has been claimed by some scholars to have replaced the

Richard Burbage, actor.
For the Lord
Chamberlain's men he
created the roles of
Hamlet, Macbeth,
Othello and King Lear.
Dulwich Picture Gallery

concept of the 'audience' (those who merely listen) with that of the 'spectator' (or one who *watches*), thanks to the design he adopted with the audience seated in a series of galleries not unlike the old Roman amphitheatres. (The Greek theatre, of course, had experienced the same sort of evolution from oratory and poetical declamation to action).

The Theatre suffered from the same limitations as its classical predecessors. There was no roof over the yard, which restricted performances to the daylight hours and, one would have thought, mostly to the summer months – although the Rose does refer to winter performances. It now seems that, once they were restricted to the amphitheatres (from 1594) the companies played all year round.

There was one other drawback that Burbage underestimated in the excitement of the enterprise – he only had a 21 year lease on the site.

Happily the confidence he showed by building a permanent theatre at all suddenly broke the ice for others who were equally frustrated. The Theatre opened its doors in 1576 – the year Drake started out on his own great adventure, to sail the world from West to East. A year later in 1577 the Curtain theatre put on its first performance in nearby Shoreditch and ten years later a rival impresario, Philip Henslowe, opened the Rose on Bankside with the proceeds of his bear-baiting interests. The professional rivalry that began there between Henslowe and the Burbages was to provide a thread that ran through the next decade – and surfaced three centuries later in a somewhat unpredictable form.

What set the Rose apart at the time – and the Swan, when it opened in 1595 – was that they were built *south* of the Thames, far beyond the reach of the City ordinances. The fact that their location made them literally neighbours with the bear pits, cutpurses and courtesans ('the Bishop of Winchester's geese' as they were popularly known) simply confirmed the worst view critics cared to take of the 'theatricals' – and one that has never been entirely erased! 'Satan's Synagogue!' trumpeted the Church – 'Nest of the Devil!' How could any red blooded man not make his way there?

Burbage, meanwhile, felt that he was making progress with the Theatre, but even he could soon see that the new theatre south of the river would prove formidable competition.

He decided to take on the Blackfriars, a 'hall' theatre he built in the converted upper frater of an old 'dissolved' monastery near St. Paul's. Although it was inside the City walls, it had never fallen under the jurisdiction of the City. This would be his replacement for the Theatre.

'Hall' or 'private' theatres had always been in competition with the open air playhouses. Smaller, enclosed, artificially lit, they offered music and masques as well as plays and were generally considered to be more 'up market'. Until 1608 they were used almost exclusively by the favoured troupes of 'boy actors'.

Burbage soon found himself beset with a new set of problems. The Blackfriars was smaller and would be more expensive to run. Two theatres would be a heavy burden indeed. The problem was solved for him when the local residents began to petition against the disturbance performances at the Blackfriars would undoubtedly create. 'The noise of drums and trumpets', they claimed piously, would interfere with church services. Burbage and his troupe were never able to play in the Blackfriars. Two years later, it had to be leased to a company of boy actors, who would presumably make less noise! He had spent £600 for nothing.

In 1597 James Burbage had died leaving his two theatres – only one of them open – to his two sons, Richard and Cuthbert, who soon faced one more dilemma. The Theatre had been built on a site leased from Giles Allen and the Burbages had always assumed the lease would be renewed. But, seeing the success enjoyed by the Bankside theatres, Allen had other ideas. Or perhaps he simply saw the obvious value in the timbers of which the Theatre was built. Only a decade ago the oak forests had been ravished to provide the timber for the ships that would take on the Spanish Armada. In due course, Allen foreclosed on the Burbages' lease. Two theatres would soon be *no* theatre.

Legend has it that on a night soon after Christmas 1598 – one hopes by moonlight – a carefully orchestrated 'flit' took place. The Chamberlain's Men – helped by master builder, Peter Street – dismantled the Theatre and transported the precious timbers across the Thames to a site the Burbages had discreetly leased on Bankside. The 'one night' smacks of the biblical creation of the world in six days but it makes a romantic story. What's certain is that on Bankside, Street used the old timbers to build the basis of a new circular playhouse. The Wooden 'O' they christened the Globe, a topical name in view of the enlightenment explorers like Drake and others were bringing to understanding precisely what sort of new world people were living in – a word that had only been in the language since 1550.

It was to be nothing less than a stage for the world (*theatrum mundi*) or – as Will Shakespeare, the company's resident playwright and sometime actor – wrote in one of his first plays created for the new stage, *As You Like It*:

> All the world's a stage;
> And all the men and women merely players;
> They have their exits and their entrances;
> And one man in his time plays many parts...

Thomas Platter, a Swiss visitor from Basle in 1599 attended an early performance. He notes in his journal:

> ...after lunch, at about two o'clock, I and my party crossed the water, and there in the house with the thatched roof we saw an excellent performance of the tragedy of the first Emperor Julius Caesar with a cast of some fifteen people.

By this time the Burbage family knew a thing or two about running theatres and took this 'stolen' opportunity to set up their new venture in the light of that hard won experience. It was fine to have a working playhouse and not have to worry interminably about petty rules and regulations. Instead, they could concentrate on the things that really mattered – the plays and the players.

In the time since the Theatre had been running, they had suffered the loss of key actors and, clearly, some defections of that kind were inevitable. The theatrical firmament has never been able to hold too many stars in close proximity for long – unless they have a strong financial incentive.

The Burbages provided that incentive at the Globe by making their key colleagues 50% 'sharers' in the new company. In addition to the Burbage brothers – Cuthbert being a partner though not an actor – the other 'sharers' were John Heminges, William Kempe, Augustine Phillips, Thomas Pope and William Shakespeare, the company's leading playwright. The sharers invested their own money for the running of the theatre, commissioning the plays, paying the actors and so on and took their 'share' of the profits – assuming there were any! Presumably the theatrical 'properties' he brought to the partnership were a large part of Shakespeare's 'collateral.' Looking at the numbers alone, the proceeds don't seem impressive. Details of the Globe's finances haven't survived but the Rose's affairs are well documented and reveal that the 27 performances in May 1596 took a total of £44.19.00, (which represented half the gallery money) indicating some 20,000 customers.

Throughout the 1590's theatrical competition grew fierce – particularly when the theatres began to concentrate south of the river. For the next forty years there were never less than five active playhouses and from 1603 on an average weekday – the Church was allowed its Sundays – there were never less than four companies performing. You could have your choice for one penny of seeing a bear being baited or the latest effort of Shakespeare or one of his contemporaries. The parameters of popular taste were set even then – as they had been since Roman times!

Once the Globe was established, the game was soon over for the competitors. Henslowe had revamped his Rose once some years ago but finally yielded to the new competition and moved north of the river to his new Fortune. He closed the Rose in 1602. The other playhouses were never really in the hunt. The Globe was simply too impressive in every way. It was better run, it had better actors and better plays – thanks to its in-house genius and other writing talents Burbage was able to attract.

The early years of the new century were the golden age of the emerging theatre. Elizabeth's successor, James I, proved an even more active patron of the arts and the Chamberlain's Men were rapidly promoted to being the King's Men. Back in the City their opponents simmered but were powerless to interfere.

Wenceslas Hollar's view of the Globe in 1647; wrongly described Beere Bayting. *detail*

Something electric was in the air. Play after play flew from Shakespeare's inventive mind. Some of them were translated from page to stage in a matter of days. But then, these were devised as entertainments – not plays for posterity.

> So bewitching a thing is lively and spirited action that
> it has power to new mould the ears of the spectators
> and fashion them to the shape of any noble and
> notable attempt
>
> Thomas Heywood

The system worked with impressive efficiency, despite the many problems the companies faced. There was no question of the long runs we have become accustomed to in the modern theatre. No putting on a play, finding it pleased the audience and then continuing to perform it until its appeal was naturally exhausted. No matter how well it was received, a play took its place in the company's repertory and was repeated in due course. The Globe, for instance, performed some fifteen different plays every month! The actors could expect to be required to appear in several different plays each and every week, rehearsing one while playing another. And even considering that the parts they would play had often been written – by Shakespeare and others – to fit their particular talents and specialities, the modern English-speaking theatre has seen nothing to compare to these disciplines of performance – with the possible exception of provincial 'rep'. And no one is seriously going to argue the consistency of professional standards in that arena!

Nor would the Shakespearean actor have had much sympathy with the modern actor in his search for 'depth' and motivation. He simply wouldn't have had the *time*. Many Shakespearean experts – such as producer, Patrick Tucker – believe that, before he trod the stage with his colleagues for that first performance, it was highly unlikely that the actor would have been either able or allowed to read the complete play before that first performance. He would have been given only his own lines and the merest indication in terms of cues of who said what before and after. To be on the boards meant being on your toes. It also meant that a disaffected actor could not walk off with a play script and sell it to a rival playhouse, which would have been all too anxious to purchase it. A play was a valuable property – particularly if you were a 'sharer' like Shakespeare. In the first ten years of its commercial life the Globe probably staged around 150 new plays.

By the time the Globe was ten years old the King's Men were feeling confident enough to try and attempt James Burbage's dream once more. They moved back to the old Blackfriars theatre in 1609 and used it predominantly as their winter home. Their experiment succeeded and the two theatres were run in parallel until the end of the period.

Certainly, there would have been significant adaptation to be done when a 'Globe' play was transferred to the radically different enclosed space but then, they were used to that from their frequent appearances at Court and in noblemens' houses.

> *Audience is like a great beast which the actor must*
> *tame into silence*
>
> Thomas Dekker

It's tempting to think of the two playhouses being used alternately by season but some scholars, like John Orrell, are beginning to believe that *both* theatres were kept more or less permanently open year round, although there is no hard evidence for this. It would make sense in that the different playhouses would attract different audiences, both geographically and financially. And since the Blackfriars had a capacity of only around 600, it seems very likely that the Burbages would not have wished to deprive their 'popular' Globe audience of performances – or 'citizen fare' – for such a large part of the year. In any case, the two kinds of theatre provided two quite different experiences. The outdoor experience of the Globe was a melting pot of society with the masses actually closer to the action and actively influencing the way the play was performed. It was a genuine people's theatre of a kind we have never consistently seen since. What must have been interesting would have been to see the way a play written for the Globe was adapted for the Blackfriars and how the actors had to scale down their performance for the smaller environment.

Transfer the performance to the more expensive hall theatre – where the cheapest seat was sixpence – and something quite different occurred, as far as the audience were concerned. The best seats – those nearest to the stage – were occupied by the richer patrons. The less rich were put in their place further back. The groundlings – the close up confidants to the outdoor actors – were effectively banished. It was a paradigm of the social structure with which we've become all too familiar. The spectators became a more controlled and controllable audience. The 'great beast' was tamed. Realising they were dealing with what was virtually a new medium, the better playwrights like Shakespeare adapted their style. Just as the middle period plays can be read in the knowledge of the physical setting for which they were written, so the later plays seem to suggest a more sophisticated stage environment.

That there was room for both kinds of theatre was proved beyond doubt in 1613, when the Globe was burned down. During a performance of *Henry VIII* a prop cannon discharged its wadding on to the thatched roof, causing it to catch fire. It says much for the security system, whatever it was, that all three thousand members of the audience were able to leave in safety through 'two small dores', while the Wooden 'O' burned to the ground within two hours. The only recorded casualty was a man whose breeches caught fire and had to be put out by the unorthodox application of a bottle of beer!

Instead of using the natural drama to write an end to the history of the Globe, the popularity of the place prevailed and the Second Globe was rapidly built on the foundations of the old. This time Burbage took the precaution of replacing the thatch with tiles and did what he could to improve the drainage, should the weather prove unkind... By 1614 the Globe was back in business.

After all the ups and downs of its early history, the second Globe was to enjoy another thirty years of reasonably untroubled and profitable life as London's leading theatre – and this despite the growing competition of hall theatres that could now operate with impunity within the City bounds. Their reputation was now such that they had first refusal of the new host of dramatists like Beaumont, Fletcher, Middleton and Webster.

The turning point came as the militant Puritans took a firmer grip. Before long there was no Crown or nobility to offer the players protection. The 'dens of thieves and theatres of all lewdness' were doomed. In 1644, the second Globe was pulled down like the rest. Over time the site was home to a non-conformist meeting house, a workhouse and brewery but initially it housed a profitable row of tenements – an ironic decision in the light of some of the arguments that were to come centuries later over what should be public priorities. The most vocal local opponents to the building of the new Globe throughout the 1970's and 1980's wanted to use the land for – council houses!

By the time of the restoration of the monarchy with Charles II in 1660 and the reopening of the hall theatres, it was as if the Globe had never existed, except in the minds of a dwindling group that could not hear the clarion call of a trumpet without recalling the days when it meant hurrying along Bankside to hear a play. From now on the theatre would belong to the elite, the players kept at a safe distance behind the formality of the proscenium arch and the reduced stage.

With his unimpaired sense of theatre, Shakespeare missed this dying fall. He wrote no new plays for the second Globe and retired to his native Stratford-on-Avon, where he died in 1616, having written some thirty-eight plays we know of, a substantial body of verse and almost certainly collaborated with other playwrights in his early years. He was 52.

❖

By 1660 the Globe and all the old theatres on both sides of the Thames were gone. In its 43 year 'run' the Globe itself probably played to something like 15 million people – roughly three times the population of England at that time. As if by some malign intent, almost all written records vanished too. The Globe became a theatrical Atlantis, a dream in many different minds.

The cloud-capp'd towers, the gorgeous palaces
The solemn temples, the great globe itself,
Yea, all which it inherit, shall dissolve
And, like this insubstantial pageant faded,
Leave not a wrack behind

The Tempest, Act IV, sc. i

Shakespeare's own reputation might easily have proved just as insubstantial. During his lifetime there were few published texts of any of his work and none of most of it – for the very good reason that plagiarism was rife among the rival theatrical companies and a printed play would only encourage open season. Word of mouth was, in every sense, the only means of record. But in 1623 two of Shakespeare's former colleagues – John Heminges and Henry Condell – produced the First Folio edition of what they took to be his collected plays, half of them from the prompt copies, and from that modest beginning the 'Shakespeare Industry' took off. The theatrical craftsman dedicated to nothing more than producing 'product' for his factory gradually took on the status – and the inaccessibility – of an academic 'classic'. The man whose work had been expressly designed to bring the theatre to the people and the people to the theatre would have been surprised and probably amused to find himself an elitist icon... his work taught by tedious rote in the schoolroom and played with increasing stylisation and affectation on the mannered stage.

As in all the best drama, there was a *deus* in the *machina*. In the late 1890's William Poel gave tangible expression to the frustration many genuine Shakespearean enthusiasts were feeling, faced with an endless series of productions put on by actor-managers of the old school like Henry Irving and Beerbohm Tree, producers who took refuge behind the security of the proscenium arch, often cutting and transposing the text to give space and time for the theatrical effects in which they delighted. None of which, by the way, had Shakespeare himself required to conjure up his effects on the imagination! In contemporary productions his plays were performed at a much faster pace and without the need for intervals.

Poel and others of like mind believed that the essential meaning of the plays lay in the way they had been originally performed – and *written* to be performed. Shakespeare's physical stage – or a facsimile of it – would unlock the secret. Why not placate the theatrical gods

17

and recreate it as near as God and guesswork would allow on Bankside, within reach of whatever vibrations still lingered?

In 1900 Poel asked the then London County Council for a site. He was following in a tradition that dated back to at least the 17th century. In their time such diverse personalities as George IV, Coleridge, Thackeray, Nash and David Garrick had supported the cause of rebuilding the Globe. Unfortunately for him and his project, his application became enmeshed in a more political and ongoing debate about the shape of a future National Theatre. Surely *that* should be based in some way on Shakespeare? That particular debate had been going on for at least fifty years even then, since industrialist, Effingham Wilson proposed something similar in 1848.

As we now know, the question of a National Theatre was not to be resolved for *another* fifty years. Poel's project finally fell victim to a rather more immediate distraction – the Boer War. But even without that dramatic intervention, he would have faced the fundamental problem that was to frustrate so many of his successors – precisely *where* on Bankside was the original site and precisely what had been the *shape* and *size* of the legendary structure?

Denied a permanent venue, Poel stuck to the other part of his plan. He would attempt to replicate the way the plays had been staged by producing them in the kind of settings the travelling players had used before they had permanent playhouses. He went to the Inns of Court and – among other experiments – staged *Twelfth Night* in Middle Temple, where Shakespeare had played in 1602.

The freedom the sheer nature of the space provided, the intimacy of contact between actor and audience vindicated the convictions of Poel and his followers. This was the kind of theatre Shakespeare had written for and it *was* a significantly different emotional experience.

In 1912 Edward Lutyens, an architect with a leaning towards the experimental – some said the bizarre – built a half-size replica for the 'Shakespeare's England' exhibition at Earl's Court of what contemporary scholars thought the Globe probably looked like. More a novelty than a genuine theatre, it was really only suitable for the playing of excerpts and isolated speeches – but even that was better than nothing. The experiment was sufficiently interesting to inspire talk of this being the matrix for a 'real' Globe. But it was not to be.

Shakespeare wrote much of war – and war did much to frustrate the Globe enthusiasts. The Boer War stopped Poel and World War 1 prevented the Earl's Court experiment from going further. The war to end wars left people with more on their minds than building a 300 year old theatre of uncertain shape and size all over again. It was only in 1924 that one W. W. Braines fixed the location of the original Globe with a degree of certainty that effectively ended further debate and four years after that before the next chapter of its story came to be written.

The Tokyo Globe, one of many replicas around the world of varying degrees of authenticity.

At the Chicago World's Fair of 1933/34 a large model Globe was one of the most prominent attractions. Designed by John Cranford Adams, it caught the eye of many visitors, including the young Sam Wanamaker. The Dream, it could reasonably be supposed, started right there and then in his own back yard.

After Chicago, Globe fever spread and over the next few years replicas of varying degrees of accuracy were built in San Diego (California), Odessa (Texas), Ashland (Oregon), Cleveland (Ohio), Cedar City (Utah), and the Folger Shakespeare Library in Washington – with even more planned. All of which spurred Globeophiles in the UK into new life.

In 1935 the Globe-Mermaid Association of England and America was formed with a mission very similar to today's International Shakespeare Globe Centre. The plan was to build a complex which would include the theatre, a library and a pub. It was to be on Bankside and the site chosen was the one now occupied by the power station. The theory was that theatregoers visiting the Globe could refresh themselves at a replica of the old Mermaid tavern and mingle with the ghosts of Ben Jonson and his contemporaries. This particular project was well advanced and strongly supported by the great and good in politics and academia, when the familiar story of frustration came full circle with World War II.

One big missing piece of the puzzle had long been – what did the Globe really *look* like? With the American home town replicas it didn't really matter too much. They were aiming to recreate a feeling more than an historical fact. But more and more academics were coming to the reluctant conclusion that most of their earlier theories were seriously flawed and that it was probably just as well that nothing had so far been built.

When the possibility was next aired in 1951 at the time of that austerity-conditioned celebration of national survival – the Festival of Britain – this lack of academic confidence had as much to do with the decision to defer yet again as with any lack of funds. The proposal to include a replica Globe among the other buildings on the South Bank was quietly dropped.

Adams's elegant octagon based on Claes Visscher's 1616 rendering, had long been a 'given' in any discussion of building a new Globe. By 1948 that theory was generally discredited and the question became – if not that, then what? The question became like grit in the academic oyster. But the greater problem was how to harness the combined brainpower that might just unravel a conundrum that was now over three hundred years old and receding further into the mist by the minute.

I doubt if we have had any popular art in England
since the Shakespearean Theatre.
Graham Greene (1936)

What is it about this particular structure that continues to haunt the imagination of certain individuals in every generation beyond the point of a nostalgic desire to re-create one of the world's great 'lost buildings?' Nobody, after all, seems to have a similar obsession about resurrecting the missing Wonders of the classical world. There's no record of the existence of a Society of Friends of the Colossus of

Rhodes or the Hanging Gardens of Babylon. But then the Globe had a ghost called Will Shakespeare...

There are those who feel there's something mystical about its shape – the theatrical equivalent of the Great Pyramid or Stonehenge. Elizabethan scholars, anxiously straddling the divide between medieval thought and the new teachings of Renaissance thinking – which Frances Yates termed the 'mystico-magico – scientific movement' – sought meaning in everything from grains of earth thrown on the ground to dots on a page. They believed with Hamlet that there was 'a special providence in the fall of a sparrow'. Science and mysticism were by no means considered incompatible as subjects for study. A man like Isaac Newton, working just one generation after the Globe, happily mixed research into the fundamental laws of physics with speculation about geomancy and black magic in general. To people with this mixed mind set, such as the Elizabethan builders, for instance, the proportions of the Globe we have so recently determined might well have seemed enchanted, since they appear to correspond to music harmonies. To modern sensibilities it may seem a strange notion but, then, the Elizabethan Renaissance was a strange time with European thinking steadily infiltrating and often running counter to a late medieval and isolated Protestant culture, 'an age in which science was emerging from magic'.

Part of the attraction is undoubtedly the oddity of the actual shape with its amateurish air of being an overgrown toy theatre. Historically, from what little we actually know of it, it stands firmly on the crossroads of design between the classical open theatre (like the massive Roman amphitheatres) and the modern enclosed theatre with its proscenium stage. And, of course, it had more than a nodding acquaintance with its inn yard forebears, not to mention Spanish 'corral' courtyard theatres. To the modern eye its outward appearance of wood frame and thatch immediately suggests Tourist Quaint but its size and symmetry add *gravitas* and a sense of awe that take it far beyond a complex feat of woodwork.

❖

The Globe's Artistic Director, Mark Rylance sees it as a symbol of something particularly meaningful in Elizabethan culture, where the lines between the 'scientific' and the spiritual had yet to be drawn.

"Divine proportions", many scholars believed, ran through man and the universe, uniting such apparently diverse subjects as music and mathematics.

"Geometry was at the heart of this building", says Rylance. "The round shape was considered the heart of a human being – the marriage of what you can imagine and what you can do... the body and the spirit coming together in the soul. They took a lot for granted that seems strange to us... They were conscious of the marriage of male and female within society and within each of us. With that in mind, I can see the Globe as the female womb containing the square (male) tiring house out of which pour a stream of men, some of them playing women... That sounds fanciful to us but it wouldn't to them".

Standing inside the new structure is to feel the 'tingle factor' – what contemporary audiences must have felt and what brought them back again and again to the exciting security of this theatrical womb in which anything was possible. All the world was on this stage, conjured up into the mind by the verbal wizardry of Shakespeare and his contemporaries. It was totally appropriate to call it the Globe and due recognition of the classical tradition – on which it's reasonable to assume, its creators knowingly drew – of the circular shape to symbolise theatre-as-universe with the actor as Man, the microcosm, playing his parts within the Macrocosm.

It's tempting – but uninformed – to think of the long period between classical times and our own as some sort of barbaric artistic wasteland, enlivened with the occasional happy accident and here the Globe's 'amateurish' design appears to prove the point – until it is analysed more closely with expert eyes. Then it can be seen that the design is inspired as much by the sophisticated requirements of sight lines, the geography of the specific location and the prevailing light and weather conditions during the limited summer season as it is by the limitations of what 16th century carpenters could actually construct in wood. The high – for then – retaining walls embrace the audience, creating a feeling of being part of something. No one is far from the stage and the thrust platform adds to the intimacy. The Globe – infinitely more than its ancient models – brought theatre to the people and, therefore, continued to bring people to the theatre. The enclosed theatre that followed put the audience back where new generations of managers and actors, unversed in the old ways, felt more comfortable with them – the other side of the footlights, where they could be seen and, hopefully, controlled. But the individual spectator's experience of magically being three thousand people strong for a few hours was lost once the 'O' was torn down and taken away to be turned into so much domestic lumber. The magic of the myth that surrounds the Globe, then, is to recreate the experience of which we were cheated.

> *I would applaud thee to the very echo,*
> *That should applaud again*
>
> *Macbeth*, Act V Sc. iii

In 1971 at the 1st World Shakespeare Congress in Vancouver something very unexpected happened. Four hundred Shakespeare scholars from 29 countries arrived at a consensus as to what the Globe must have looked like and what the design of any new version should be:

> ...the Congress wishes to encourage the hope that a studied effort will soon be made to build a full-scale reconstruction of Shakespeare's Globe Theatre. The Congress considers that such a reconstruction would be of the greatest value to Shakespeare Scholarship and to the history of the Theatre, as well as of widespread interest to people and to education everywhere in the world. Because it is believed that a site very close to the original location of the Globe Theatre on Bankside in London may soon become available for development, this Congress wishes further to express its opinion that this site might be eminently suitable for such a reconstruction.

Sitting in the audience was the grit that had produced this very cultured pearl. His name was Sam Wanamaker...

Will Kempe, comedian, was used to dancing the traditional 'jig' to end a performance. British Library

CHAPTER TWO

THE QUEST BEGINS...
(1969 – 1971)

We are such stuff
As dreams are made on, and our little life
Is rounded with a sleep

Prospero, *The Tempest*, Act IV Sc. i

It began – as important things so often do – as something of an accident. If you believe in accidents, that is...

In 1949 Sam Wanamaker was a young and successful American actor who should have been scaling the upper slopes of post-war Broadway, instead of trudging the cold, bomb-blasted streets of post-war south London. But for Sam, all the wars were by no means over. His work in various movements concerned with civil liberties had caught up with him and now threatened to affect his own liberties – particularly the freedom to find work in his own country.

The late 1940's in America had turned into a hothouse for prejudice. There was a growing neurosis – fanned by the media – about the way Communist infiltration was insidiously undermining the American Dream. The emotional ground was fertile for such happenings as Senator Joseph McCarthy's witch hunts of suspected Reds in the performing arts. Such people, after all, would only brainwash us with their subversive propaganda and must be eradicated with as much media visibility as possible, no matter how long it took! Wanamaker, S. was one of the names firmly ticked on the Senator's list.

With the political clouds visibly darkening, he signed a contract to star in a film that could only aggravate the situation. *Christ in Concrete* – released in Britain as *Give Us This Day* – could almost have been autobiographical, given Sam's lifelong commitment to union causes. It was a grim story of an immigrant worker who, during the

Depression, can only find work on a non-union building site. The hero ends up drowning in a pool of setting concrete – hence the title.

This was hardly the kind of film fare America was in the mood for. Since almost everyone on the project – from director, Edward Dmytryk, down – was also on the Senate black list, apart from being commercially unlikely, the concept was decidedly perverse. But Sam even then being Sam – the opposition only deepened the commitment. It was decided to shoot this all-American subject in liberal England – which is how our hero came to be wandering around the seamier side of south London. On his first day off from concrete-dipping, he'd decided to try and find the end of a personal rainbow.

The Chicago Globe at the Century of Progress Exhibition 1934 where Sam had his first taste of a Wooden 'O'. *Special Collections Dept. University of Arizona Libraries.*

Fifteen years earlier, the scale 'model' of the Globe had caught his youthful imagination at the 1933/34 Chicago World's Fair, right in his own back yard. By a series of similar 'happenstances' over the succeeding years, its image had grown in his mind. Now was his chance to find the spot where the real thing had stood...

Clink Street, Rose Alley, Bear Gardens, Skin Market Alley, Cardinal Cap Alley, Swan Alley... the very names he sees all around him are redolent of history, even though the more pervasive smell today is one of urban neglect and decay. And where in this warren of forgotten streets is the Maid or Maiden Lane he's seeking?

Tired of folding and refolding a map that clearly refers to a totally different place and time, he hails a cab and asks to be taken to the site of Shakespeare's Globe. As in all the best Hollywood movies, the cabbie undoubtedly scratched his head and said something to the effect of – "That's a new one on me, guv", before dropping Sam at the Anchor Pub, advising him to ask there. It appeared that nobody in Southwark had the faintest idea what he was talking about. *Shakespeare?* Stratford-on Avon, wasn't he? Funny people, these Yanks! Eventually, someone did seem to remember seeing some engraved thing on a wall nearby.

A couple of warm British pints and an hour or so later, Sam found himself staring at a small and blackened bronze plaque on the wall of the Courage Brewery in Park Street, which at one time had been Maiden Lane. He later learned that it had been put there as

The 'blackened plaque' that triggered the quest to rebuild the Globe. Erected in 1908 by The Shakespeare Reading Society of England and India. *Dominik Klimowski*

recently as 1908 by The Shakespeare Reading Society of England. It read simply: "Here stood Shakespeare's Globe" and something about its very understatement moved him deeply. How could this be the only memento, not just to a particular theatre, but to the whole area that in its early 17th century day had been every bit the equivalent of Shaftesbury Avenue or Broadway? How could the Brits *do* this – or rather, not do this – he wondered? The greatest playhouse in the history of the theatre... and that's all there is? It was not the first and it would certainly not be the last time that the actions and attitudes of these sharers of the common language would puzzle him.

If any passers-by were surprised to hear a solitary figure declaiming: " 'O'! for a muse of fire that would ascend the brightest heavens of invention" – *with an American accent* – the incident was never reported to the authorities.

Strolling bemusedly back along the river, he passes another site a hundred yards or so further on that has something familiar about it, yet – to the best of his knowledge – he's never set foot here before. The sign reads: "SOLD for Redevelopment". Then he realises what had jogged his memory. The concrete mixers! Time to get back to his fictionalised version of ugly modernity bulldozing the past. It would be a few more years before all the pieces fell into place and the site he'd just seen became the home of the new Globe...

❖

Most of the next two decades – the 1950's and 1960's – would be taken up with the normal activities of an actor in the process of transferring his talent and reputation from one country and culture to another and bringing a wife, Charlotte, and two daughters, Abby and Zoë, along for what turned out to be a lifetime ride. A third daughter, Jessica, was born in 1954.

Predictably, *Christ in Concrete* sank with little critical and no commercial trace but it did bring with it the invitation to make a return visit to appear in a John Mills' vehicle, *Mr. Denning Drives North*. After which it was Sam's *theatrical* experience that clinched the permanent move.

Laurence Olivier had taken the St. James's Theatre for the 1952 season, which he intended to stage in true actor/manager style. In addition to the 'classic' productions in which he would star with his then wife, Vivien Leigh, he added – as a contemporary counter-balance to the repertory – a recent Broadway hit, Clifford Odets' *Winter Journey* – and asked the young Wanamaker to both star opposite Michael Redgrave and direct the play.

The impact on a conventional West End theatre-going public was immediate and almost physical. Audiences and critics were unprepared for the shock of contrasting acting styles but they decided they liked what they saw. Sam was welcome to stay and be the modern American in their theatrical midst – and stay he did.

The family Wanamaker took up residence in Regent's Park in accommodation lent to them by artist, Felix Topolski, and for the next few years, acting and directing took up all of Sam's time and most of his mind. But at the back of it, nagging like the rumour of an impending headache, lingered that blackened plaque. It was unfinished business – but whose?

As Sam's professional and social circle of acquaintances grew, people comparing impressions after meeting him for the first time would invariably come round to asking: "Did he go on to you about Shakespeare's bloody Globe?" To which the invariable answer was likely to be: "Yes, and he seemed to think I should be doing something about it!"

Divided by that common language as he was, Sam never chose to learn – although later he perfectly well understood – the English art of circumlocutory non-confrontation. It was to underlie many of the later problems with the theatrical establishment, many of whom felt he had a point. On the other hand, who was *he* to have it? He was an *American*, for heaven's sake!

The unsuspecting were dragged off for walks along Bankside and treated to a re-run of his own experience. If there were no likely candidates, the walks would be solitary. It's doubtful if even the longest-lived local knew those mean streets as well as he did. Nor did they grow more lovely with familiarity.

But Sam, by this time, had fallen in love with Southwark, warts and all, and he saw none of this. His eyes and ears were filled with the echoes of the Elizabethan theatre-going crowds, the noise from the bear-baiting pits, the stench from the sewers, the sheer sense of *life* these streets enshrined. Now he began transmuting it into a vision of what it could be, should be... In his mind, the whole stretch of the river between London Bridge and Southwark Bridge was already teeming with new life. An 'Elizabethan Shaftesbury Avenue?' Of course, but why stop here? Why not Shakespeare's London?

> Thy brother was a furtherer in the act
>
> *The Tempest*, Act V Sc. i

In early 1969, Sam was visited by his elder brother, Bill, a Chicago doctor in London for a medical conference. Sam accompanied him to register at the Royal Festival Hall, where the conference was being held. Finding themselves on the South Bank –

although who's to say that Sam didn't make the trip *because* it took him to his favourite shore? – the brothers took a stroll along Bankside, finishing up at the plaque.

All the way along Sam had been talking non-stop about his hopes and fears but when they reached the familiar spot, he fell silent. There was something different since his last visit. Then he realised what it was. They were pulling down some of the derelict river warehouses, the rotting teeth that had become the distinguishing feature of post-war Bankside... But now, standing with his brother by the piece of metal that had started him on what he was to describe as his "epic journey through an ocean of icebergs", he found himself looking at a view of London no one had seen in years.

A few paces away Old Father Thames was rolling along, imperturbably watching kingdoms coming and going. On the far north bank, almost opposite where they stood, the dome of St. Paul's caught the afternoon light. Whoever was handling the production certainly knew his stuff.

Excited by the prospect all over again, Sam went into his instinctive pitch for a reconstructed Globe as near as possible to its original site... a working memorial... a stage for the world... the educational value of such a focus... the social benefits all of this would bring to this derelict area... Suddenly brother Bill pulled him up short, as only a brother can. "If you're *that* keen", he said, "why don't *you* do something about it?"

When the two men returned to the Wanamaker home for tea, Charlotte could tell immediately that something significant had happened. Time and again she'd seen Sam return from one of his walks but this time was different. There was a light in his eye. "I'm going to do it myself", he said. She didn't need to be told what 'it' was...

> Your tale, sir, would cure deafness
> *The Tempest*, Act 1 Sc. ii

Once he started, there was no stopping him. All the ideas and fancies that had been bouncing around in his head now had permission to emerge and take their chances. All that nervous energy need no longer be channelled into bracing Bankside walks but could instead be devoted to The Dream.

Letters and phone calls went forth – east and west and south and north to summon an array of the Great and Good – or anyone else, for that matter, who might prove helpful. With the wisdom hindsight so irritatingly brings, it was easy for him to see later that his blunderbuss approach might well have undermined subsequent credibility with some of those he confronted with such unfocused enthusiasm. It is, after all, a fairly fundamental rule of salesmanship that, when you make your pitch, it's preferable to have something to sell. But Sam's had never been a soul to be possessed in patience...

The response was mostly qualified. The idea – insofar as they *understood* the idea – certainly had merit and was to be encouraged.

Sir Hugh Casson replied on behalf of himself and his wife, Margaret:

> We were excited and impressed by the splendid project. This is an opportunity which might never occur again and it must not be missed...

He went on to warn prophetically:

> My faint reservation is that it might be better to concentrate on the downstream section rather than spread your glory so wide.

But a more typical reaction was – Count on us for any help short of actual assistance. As for money – well, why don't we see how you get on? It was to be a repetitive refrain he would hear over the next twenty years or so.

He would need to associate himself right away with leading figures in the performing arts. In early 1970 he jotted his list of Possible Trustees on a scrap of paper: "Michael Redgrave, Alec Guiness [who would probably have preferred his name to be spelt correctly!], Peter O'Toole, Robert Shaw, Michael York, Alan Bates, Sean Connery, Richard Attenborough, Nicol Williamson, Vanessa Redgrave, Maggie Smith, Glenda Jackson, Sarah Miles, Dorothy Tutin".

The project clearly had to be 'merchandised'. Sam cast around for a catchy quotation that would encapsulate what he was attempting. His scribbles reflect the range of attitudes he considered.

The simply descriptive:

> *The Globe, the glorie of the Bank*
> Ben Jonson

The patriotic:

> Love they land with love far brought
> From out the storied Past, and used
> Within the Present, but transfused
> Through Future time by powers of thought

Tennyson

The pessimistically philosophical?...

> If you can look into the seeds of time,
> And say which grains will grow and which will not

Banquo in *Macbeth*

And finally, in frustration, the ironic:

> To be... or not to be

William Shakespeare

> To be!

Sam Wanamaker

To which he couldn't resist adding:

> Ask the LCC — Ha!

> ...every minute now
> Should be the father of some stratagem

Henry IV (Pt.2), Act 1 Sc. i

Along with the letters and phone calls came the *plans*. If you were thinking the unthinkable, why not think big? An early draft document indicates just how big. Headed "The Bankside Globe Development Plan", it lists among other items 600 flats, 1400 hotel rooms and thousands of square feet of office space. The whole of Bankside was to be re-developed between Southwark Bridge and Cannon Street railway bridge in a London equivalent of Paris's Left Bank with all the same artistic associations. It would include:

- The Paris Gardens Hotel
- Conference and trade centre over railway
- The Swan – mixed media entertainment building
- Historic houses 49, 50, 51, 52 retained as residences: 47/48 The Stews' a period restaurant

- Adventure playgrounds
- The Clink Liberty Inn – with balconies overlooking a square for public entertainment
- The Bear Garden Playhouse (later stage – tentative only) for the performance of plays by Shakespeare's contemporaries: Marlowe, Jonson, Dekker, etc.
- The Globe Hotel
- Authentic reconstructed Tudor and Elizabethan buildings. Used as shops, public houses, restaurants, library, exhibition rooms and service flats.
- The Globe Playhouse
- The Anchor Public House retained in the scheme
- The Southwark Bankside Hotel
- Clink Street Museum and studios in reconditioned warehouses and railway arches.
- Winchester Hall reconstructed for joint use by the Worshipful Guild of Glaziers, the World Centre for Shakespeare Studies (WCSS), the Globe Playhouse Trust and a new musical organization for the performance of early English music and opera. (Purcell, etc.)
- Travelator over London Bridge
- Concert platform and band shell

Careful readers would be relieved to note that Southwark Cathedral, Southwark Bridge and Cannon Street railway bridge would find themselves incorporated untouched in Sam's New Jerusalem!

Interestingly, there's some indication from some of his early conversations that the Globe he first envisioned was not the detailed reconstruction it later became. His first thought was a modern building which simply reflected the *form* of Shakespeare's Globe. It was to have been a brick drum with galleries, a roof and stage lighting. It was a 'draft' dream and didn't survive long in the heady air...

By the end of 1970 he was describing to *The Daily Telegraph* "as close a replica as can be built, open to the skies" – a vision rendered more than a little questionable when he went on to mention "a plastic roof that will close over the pit in bad weather". Around the site itself he and his then architect, Ove Arup, hoped to rebuild 15th and 16th century houses that had to be demolished in other parts of the country. They had discovered that there were plenty available.

The sheer size of the undertaking wasn't altogether surprising to those who knew something of Sam's approach to the performing arts. From his early years he had always seen theatre not in isolation but as part of a broader community experience. Theatre belonged to the people.

It's easy to say, in the light of what happened subsequently, that vaulting ambition o'er leaping itself was to be the fundamental flaw in the project from the beginning. But in 1970 – at the tail end of that deceptive post-war renaissance called the 60's – things looked very different.

The LCC (London County Council) – forerunner to the GLC (Greater London Council) had ambitious plans of its own for re-building a Brave New London. Sam was well aware that they were conducting a public enquiry called the Greater London Development Plan with special emphasis on the development of the South Bank. Nor was this an isolated show of interest. As early as 1943 the government's Abercrombie Report had singled out the South Bank riverside ("extending on the front as far as London Bridge and inland to York Road, Stamford Street and Southwark Street") as "a major potential amenity for all of London" and had even made a passing reference to the possibility of a reconstructed Globe, together with a museum and library on "its original Bankside location". In the end the most visible result of Abercrombie was the 1951 Festival of Britain of which the architect in charge was – Hugh Casson.

Once again the legend had surfaced but this time it didn't require a war to prevent its realisation. Until the war, the area had been a thriving industrial concern and the question of redevelopment had been irrelevant. But time and Hitler's bombs had changed all that. The warehouses that lined Bankside were for the most part ugly and empty, looming like gravestones marking the demise of an industrial revolution that had promised so much. The question now was not whether the area should be developed but for what purpose? And there would be conflicting views on that, too...

If you intend to improve the lot of a particular community, it's as well to find out how that community feels about having its lot improved. One of Sam's first actions was to consult the burghers of Southwark in the shape of Southwark Council. It was to be the first of many conversations and perhaps that first contact with a generally benevolent Planning and Development Committee lured him into a sense of false optimism. A statement of intent is, after all, just that –

an indication of intent for now. Nonetheless, those first soundings were positive. If Mr. Wanamaker was prepared to organise such a project, the Council did not see why they would not support it. Which, when you consider the wording more carefully, is not the same as saying they definitely would support it.

In the light of what happened later, (see *The Councillor's Tale*) Sam's reputation for intransigence was somewhat unfair. He'd consulted. He thought he had a deal. The ground rules changed – but he didn't. In the first year or so of his "epic journey through a sea of icebergs" all the subsequent themes were stated. There would be times when one element would dominate but all of them were always present. In those early days the struggle was a solitary one. Sam was literally working from home and where's the credibility for a global organisation in that? There had to be something more formal. There had to be an address – and it had better be on Bankside... In the wheeler-dealer atmosphere of 70's London you needed a piece of property to be taken seriously as a player.

By this time Sam knew the Southwark back streets rather better than the average London taxi driver. He remembered that Ready Mixed Concrete had a site on the corner of Bankside and Emerson Street and that the tiny site office was now unused. He approached them to see if he could negotiate a licence to use the premises on a purely temporary basis.

Ready Mixed were sympathetic but were on the point of selling the property to another company, Town and Metropolitan. From this point on the incestuous complexities of the property market sound like one of those Old Testament litanies in which everyone is busy 'begat'-ing everyone else. It would take a separate volume – and a very boring one – to trace their genealogy but it didn't take long for Sam to realise what Prime Minister Edward Heath meant by 'the unacceptable face of capitalism'.

The face that faced Sam and nodded grudging agreement to the deal was that of the representative of Town and Metropolitan, a subsidiary of the Freshwater property group, which was even then busily snapping up bargains in the vicinity, such as Bear Gardens and Rose Alley. Their game plan was to piece together their corner of the Monopoly board until they had three contiguous plots of land – the block to the east defined by Bankside, Park Street, Emerson Street and Rose Alley and the block bounded by Park Street, Emerson Street, Sumner Street and Southwark Bridge Road. The third parcel of land would be what is now the Globe site.

They were in a hurry. Other property developers were abroad with identical intentions. This was not made too clear at that first meeting but it did explain why the welcome Sam received was at best tepid. Not that it worried him unduly. He was glad to leave with what he came for plus a vague promise that Town and Metropolitan would consider the possibility of incorporating a reconstructed Globe on the eventual development of the site. Sam was under no illusion that this was to be done out of deference to the Bard or to enrich the cultural life of the community. He knew perfectly well that it would be a valuable card for a developer in subsequent negotiation with the Council. Throw in a community benefit with a cultural gloss to it and your conventional office development plans may be regarded with a less jaundiced eye.

Ay, marry, sir, now it begins to work
The Taming of the Shrew, Act III, Sc. ii

In mid-1970 Sam had a toe-hold. It may not have been much but it was infinitely better than nothing. In a movie it would have been more than enough to bring out hordes of colorful locals thrusting their hard-earned pennies into the pocket of a tearful Sam, while the property tycoon, converted on the Road to Damascus, would hand over the deeds, as the Globe magically built itself. But real life isn't wonderful and Sam was no Jimmy Stewart...

He was a street fighter through and through and the back streets of Southwark held no threat after the Chicago ghetto. Once established, he set off to do a little property speculation of his own. The fact that he had nothing to speculate *with* seemed to him purely incidental. The money would always come from somewhere. It remained his firm belief. After all, in America projects like this were commonplace. There was always a convenient benefactor, a Ford Foundation or the like. *Stratford* had been built with American money in its time, for heaven's sake.

He must have looked like some sort of latterday Don Quixote as he prowled the streets on his quest. His notes would annotate his findings. This building had "interesting original windows but largely obscured by later additions"; that one was "a mock Gothic building of excellent design". He would instruct one of his team of unpaid Sancho Panzas to "write *innocently*, asking if the Globe Playhouse Trust can rent this property". He gained a reputation as a character in the area. Workers in the remaining warehouses would call out to him: "Hello, Sam – come to chuck us out yet?" To which Sam would flash his wolfish smile and resume the scent...

> *When we mean to build,*
> *We first survey the plot, then draw the model*
> Henry IV (Pt. 2), Act 1 Sc. iii

One of the unwritten rules of Monopoly is that if you own a piece of land, you'd better put a house on it as soon as possible. In Sam's case he legitimised his tenancy of the Emerson Street site by setting up the Globe Playhouse Trust Ltd. The principal objective of the Trust was stated as being:

> to encourage and stimulate the public appreciation and understanding
> of the dramatic art in all its forms and generally to cultivate and
> improve public taste in such art as a memorial to William Shakespeare

...a slightly florid dedication, one might feel, that owed rather more to Polonius than to the people... But then, it was probably written more to be read into the Southwark Council minutes than to be *read*.

Since the Trust had a charitable tax status, he tied the commercial knot tighter by creating, in parallel, Bankside Globe Development Ltd with the sole purpose of acquiring and developing a site for the Globe and, hopefully, some adjoining land to give the project room to breathe. It was a modest little corporation with only two directors – Sam and Charlotte.

It was high time to put down some freehold roots in Southwark, if only to have something to bargain with when the Great Whites among the property sharks came cruising by in their feeding frenzy. Sam could see perfectly well that, when that happened, money would speak louder than any amount of understandings and gentlemen's agreements.

In October he announced his plans...

The *Evening Standard* described it as "the most spectacular attempt ever to open up an old wharf-lined stretch of Thames bank... for nearly three-quarters of a mile between London and Blackfriars Bridges". While acknowledging that a reconstructed Globe would be part of the plan, the *Standard* reporter felt that "Far more important for the commercial success of the venture is the proposal to build a massive trade centre on the lines of those planned in Chicago and New York... Mr. Wanamaker, I understand, has strong financial backing from groups in this country and America. A consortium of large companies is believed to be considering the scheme". Most of them, it must be said, were doing so in Sam's fertile imagination rather than in their own board rooms but the fact remained that Sam *had* put the proposition to them. And with all this publicity, how could they possibly refuse?

Given time they all turned out to be as adept at disposing as Sam was at proposing...

Let my presumption not provoke thy wrath
Henry VI (Pt. 1), Act II Sc. iii

One of Sam's undeniable qualities was the ability to provoke. When he took up a cause or expressed a deeply-held point of view – and few of them were shallow! – previously apathetic people would realise they *did* have an opinion after all. Quite often a contrary opinion. The man was a magnet for dissent, a polariser who dispersed disinterest by his presence.

The Globe was the supreme example of the Wanamaker Effect at work. As soon as he announced his plans, it appeared there were others who'd been working on something similar for years, presumably in blessed oblivion and often in total secrecy.

In 1970, once the initial publicity for the project began to circulate, he began to take notice of the activities of a group called the St. George's Elizabethan Theatre Ltd. The artistic director was one George Murcell and its Advisory Board boasted such names as Sir Tyrone Guthrie, John Neville, Michael Benthall, Christopher Plummer and Tanya Moiseiwitsch. The letterhead alone must have made Sam salivate.

What happened next makes a typical case history of Sam's tactics. If it had been a sport with a set of rules, the sequence of moves would have been codified as – *The Flirtation*... during which both sides talk amicably... *The Presumption*... in which Sam hears what he wants to hear and rushes to – *The Pre-Emption*... in which he announces the consummation to the world... leading to – *The Rejection*... in which the object of his affection publicly denies any amorous intent... and ending in *The Recrimination*... which has been known to last indefinitely.

After a meeting with Murcell, Sam's rush to judgement caused him to dash off a letter informing Equity of "an extremely satisfactory meeting" in which they had "discussed the possibility of affiliation of our two organisations". He concluded: "I have no doubt that such a close association will be effected, I hope in the near future, and that we will thereby strengthen the possibility of the successful reconstruction of Shakespeare's Globe Playhouse on Bankside".

The St. George's group, however, didn't see it in quite the same light...

Murcell was quick to respond: In his letter he reminded Sam that he didn't see any advantage in collaboration. They were already well advanced with their own Globe restoration project. He also professed himself to be "further amazed" at the similarity of the objectives of Sam's group to their own. "It would, I think, be true to say that, except in scale and dimension, they are almost identical".

If they had reckoned on this being a bucket of cold water, they clearly didn't realise they were dealing with a man who had a back like a duck. Sam simply shrugged it off – at least publicly – and a few days later was in animated correspondence with Sir Tyrone Guthrie, trying to correct the negative impression the St. George's group had obviously given their Chairman of the intentions of this American upstart.

"I felt", Sam said hopefully, "whatever the problems involved, you would take an Olympian position and examine the situation objectively". He went on to ask Guthrie to direct a Shakespeare play that summer (1971) on Bankside as a way of demonstrating four points:

> That talk of a theatre on Bankside could be translated into a tangible reality;

> That by our offering you the first production we demonstrated that we cared more for getting the Bankside scheme going than for maintaining any possessiveness about the project;

> That by John Neville agreeing to act we could effectively join the forces of our two groups;

> And lastly, we could prove there was a large and important audience for such a theatre on Bankside.

Having defined the dignity of his intentions, he indulges briefly in self-pity – or is this the actor fleshing out the part?

> It grieves me deeply to think that the whole of my career and personal integrity, the genuine and exhausting effort I have made to bring about the reconstruction of the Globe and some of the glory of Bankside is of so little worth as to be denigrated by a man of your sincerity and stature...

Having got that off his chest, he picks himself up and re-enters the fray:

> As to a tent on Bankside, I fear you have not visited the area recently. Should you do so... you will find a quietude which no doubt will surprise you... better than the roar of traffic past the Old Vic, or the street and traffic noises of most London theatres. As for aeroplanes, if they are not banned over Central London, there must be some other reason why they do not fly over Bankside.

The letter ends with a bravura flourish, as Sam offers Guthrie the role of Executive Head and Artistic Director of the entire enterprise.

It was, unfortunately, an offer Guthrie could and did refuse and I go into the letter in detail only because it sets a pattern that was to be endlessly repeated. Sam's passion led him to express himself in extreme and often conflicting ways that some people interpreted as lack of sincerity – and in a tone that frequently grated on British recipients. One didn't approach these things in this way, did one? It was a lesson he never fully learned or perhaps chose to accept. Nonetheless, it was the one quality that would turn inertia into action and get things *done*.

> *...Lead these testy rivals so astray,*
> *As one come not within another's way*
> A Midsummer Night's Dream, Act III. Sc. ii

A couple of weeks later (February 12th) he's writing to *The Daily Telegraph* to put the record straight about these St. George's people.

They were claiming they had started their odyssey earlier than his – which was true. The group was formed in 1967 – at least two years before Sam had formally declared himself. But, as he pointed out to the Editor, their stated intention at that time was "primarily... to establish an authentic Elizabethan Playhouse in London". A year later they announced that they had "been fortunate in discovering the redundant parish church of St. George's in Tufnell Park" and launched an appeal for £140,000. Neither announcement made any mention of a Globe or Bankside.

In 1970 – after Sam's project *was* under way – they talked about trying to raise £500,000 (such is inflation) "to refurbish a 19th century Byzantine church in the Islington area". Again, no mention. It was only after the abortive merger discussions in January 1971 – said Sam in self-righteous wrath – that the St. George's group launched a new appeal, "this time for the staggering sum of £750,000 for the reconstruction and operation of the St. George's church in Islington *and* revealed their 'phase two' ambition to *also* build a Globe on Bankside!" The underlining and outraged emphasis were in Sam's own hand...

From the pattern of his behaviour through the whole of the project, it's clear that he *believed* what he said when he said it. By now he had developed the knack of filtering out unwelcome information. Certainly the records suggest that in this particular letter he was, emotionally speaking, "being somewhat economical with the truth".

In a previous letter (November 19th) Murcell had gone to pains to point out what "We have always been aware of the possibility of the old site of the 'Globe' theatre becoming available one day and in this respect we have been in contact with the owners of the site, their representatives, agents and architects *for nearly two years*. We have an agreement from them in writing that we should be involved in their plans for the Bankside site..." Allowing for the heat of the moment, it's unlikely he would have been so specific if the paperwork didn't exist.

He went on to reveal his sources: "Both Laing Development Co. Ltd. and Legal and General Assurance Society Ltd. are keen to take advantage of the valuable work we are doing here which will later bear fruit on the Bankside. Although they do not wish for publicity now, the issue of further statements by your group implying involvement on their site will provoke them to publicise their association with us". And then he made a fatal psychological error in dealing with Sam – he showed weakness. "I am telling you this in the strictest confidence as we intend to make no publicity value of this at present for obvious reasons, nor do the developers wish for any public announcement at this stage since the scheme is some years away yet". You don't do that to a Chicago street fighter, if you hope to walk away intact.

Sam told everyone that he was being upstaged and went on doing so even after his continued provocation had flushed Laing out into the open. In December – as Sam well knew before he wrote to the *Telegraph* – Laing managed to compress 'some years' and announce a comprehensive scheme for redeveloping Bankside. Apart from incorporating the historic Anchor Inn – which no self-respecting plan could afford to ignore – Laing envisaged a 250 foot office tower which would be the bread and butter of the project. Oh, and there would be a replica of the Globe Theatre...

A clearly irritated spokesman for the group was forced to acknowledge The Wanamaker Factor: "(He) came out of the blue but he certainly stirred up public interest in Bankside". Their own scheme, he said – confirming Murcell's claims – "was first discussed with Southwark Council in November 1968 and with the GLC last summer (1969)". He added petulantly: "Wanamaker gave everybody the impression that he owned the site". At that point in the game, in fact, Sam didn't own a square yard but what did that have to do with anything? You had to dream to have a hope of getting it done. Laing's commitment to an Elizabethan theatre was soon seen to be superficial. By the end of 1973 it had been replaced in their revised planning application by a nurses' hostel!

Murcell remains bitter about the media's treatment of the episode. He feels he lost funding and support because the Globe was seen to be a "rival thing – when it's not". "My motive", he still insists, "was not to build a replica but to build a playhouse in order to put the plays on in the style which they were intended to be performed without putting up a great barnstorming Disney place".

In many ways a mirror image of Sam, he has never given up his dream either and to a great extent has achieved it. Twenty-five years later he still visits the Islington site most days to arrange the occasional letting or to put on a talk for the many schools that remain consistent supporters. He claims that "30,000 school kids come through here every year". Those who knew both men comment on the similarities between them – the intensity of manner, the determination to pursue their vision with or without a little help from their friends. Couldn't they have joined forces – or would the sum have been less than the parts? Does even the biggest dream have room for more than one Begetter?

What the St. George's episode does illustrate is Sam's emerging *modus operandi*, his determination to wrench events to his way of thinking – if they wouldn't come of their own accord. From this early point on he heard not only the sound of Time's wingèd chariot but the stealthy footsteps of competitors intent on stealing his dream.

The Battle for the soul of the Rose theatre was foreshadowed eighteen years in advance. Sam was not to be caught the same way twice...

> And for this cause a while we must neglect
> Our holy purpose to Jerusalem.
>
> *Henry IV (Pt. 1)*, Act 1 Sc. i

The Laing development disappeared, as did several others that ventured to plan beyond a specific building. Attention on the South Bank was focused on the long planned National Theatre and its surrounding complex and that was quite enough to worry about for now, thank you. After which came the oil crisis and the days of the developer were numbered...

As he sat down to assess the year, Sam could list one or two pros to balance the cons... The Globe Playhouse Trust was now in existence to act as a formal focus for the task of building the actual theatre. It would also organise a series of events to show the doubters – local and elsewhere – that the proposition was a viable one. Already the sounds from Southwark seemed vaguely encouraging.

They were on-site squatters, to be sure, but late in the year there had been an opportunity to snap up some local property and put a genuine card in his hand. A disused Georgian warehouse, No. 1 Bear Gardens came on the market and with it Nos. 1 & 2 Rose Alley. Financing the £48,000 purchase had been difficult and ended up with Bankside Globe Developments (i.e., Sam and Charlotte) taking out a bridging loan and bringing in a friendly property company (Chestergrove) as joint owners. But it would all work out, once the money started pouring in. And this wasn't just *any* piece of property. On or near that very site had stood another Elizabethan playhouse – or, more accurately, a playhouse-cum-bear baiting pit. Philip Henslowe had taken it over in 1613. It was called the Hope. Now, if a name like *that* wasn't an omen...

CHAPTER THREE

THE RAINMAKER'S TALE: SAM WANAMAKER

He was a man, take him for all in all,
I shall not look upon his like again

Hamlet, Act 1 Sc. ii

Before I even met him I had two images of Sam Wanamaker, Actor. They both turned out to be true.

The first was of a coiled spring. A man of no more than middle height the stage could scarcely contain. Finger jabbing, jaw jutting, spitting out his words as if expectorating his soul. The English actors he was sharing the stage with – the play was Clifford Odets' *Winter Journey* (1952) – looked vaguely apprehensive, as indeed they might. The West End, still cocooned in pre-war gentility, was getting its first

Maurice and Molly Watenmaker c.1923 with the four year old
Sam and his six year old brother Bill. *Bill Wanamaker*

Sam as Bill Starbuck, the Rainmaker, the man who makes the impossible happen in
J. Richard Nash's play of that name. *Mander Mitchenson*

taste of 'The Method' and wasn't sure if it could take so much undiluted passion.

The second was gentler, almost romantic. As Bill Starbuck in Richard Nash's *The Rainmaker* (1956), Sam arrives in a small American town stricken with drought – a symbol of its lack of confidence in itself. No self-respecting American play in the fifties would be seen dead without a psychological 'message'. The Rainmaker talks them out of their doubts, makes the plain girl feel beautiful and, as he leaves town – mythical heroes always leave town in American plays of any pretension – the rain starts to fall. Did Sam *make* the rain fall – or would it have fallen anyway? Who cares? All that matters is – it fell and brought the town back to life.

Passion and belief were the threads that ran through his life... on stage or off.

That what you cannot as you would achieve,
You must perforce accomplish as you may

Titus Andronicus, Act II Sc. i

The beginning was pure show business – though it's doubtful if that thought occurred to Maurice and Molly Watenmaker, Russian Jews from families fleeing the 1905 pogrom and finding work in the Chicago rag trade, where they met and married. The families that gave birth to movie moguls like Sam Goldwyn, Louis B. Mayer, Jack Warner and many others, had undertaken similar odysseys in their time.

It was there in the Windy City that Sam and his elder brother Bill, were born – Bill in 1917 and Sam on June 14th 1919 – and there that the iron entered his soul. It was the era of Al Capone and Prohibition. Gangster John Dillinger was shot outside the cinema Sam and Bill used to frequent. You couldn't live in the ghetto and not be able to look after yourself. It was a lesson Jewish *emigres* learned wherever they set up their new home. Sam never forgot having to fight his way out of school past Jew-baiters, protecting his older but frailer brother at the same time. After that it becomes second nature to put up your fists. He even considered becoming a boxer for a short while.

"All my problems... and I have a great *many*, I think (and even some of my *assets* as a person)", he once said in a radio interview, "come from my awareness of this kind of problem. Constant aggression and fighting for survival shapes you".

As in so many Jewish families, a boy had to grow up to *be* something. One son would be a doctor (which Bill became). Sam would be the lawyer – but it didn't work out that way, except on film. Certainly, the young Sam Wanamaker – a smoothed down version of Watenmaker – went off to Drake University in Iowa. But the damage had already been done by the drama teacher who'd offered him a part in the school play. The experience wouldn't go away and back home in Chicago during his vacations he talked his way into the city's prestigious Goodman Theatre School at the Civic Repertory and made a precocious debut at seventeen. Prophetically, he joined the Globe Shakespearean Theatre Group and a photograph of him taken only a year later shows him heroically posed in front of a sign board next to a plywood replica of the Globe in which the company was to perform. It was half size and a pretty slapdash job, by all accounts – a gift from the British government to the 1936 'Great Lakes Festival' in Cleveland, Ohio. In view of their profound lack of interest when it came to the domestic equivalent, the wonder is that they bothered at all. In some bureaucratic mind it probably ranked with Anne Hathaway's Cottage as a curiosity for the tourist mentality. It might just as easily have been a commemorative teapot.

The young Sam at the 1937 Great Lakes festival in Cleveland, Ohio in front of a replica Globe donated by the British Government. He was to play Shakespeare here for the first time... and the dream was born. *Charlotte Wanamaker*

Probably estimating audience interest all too accurately, each of the plays performed was cut down to 30 minutes. It was 'fast food Shakespeare' – but so what? It gave Sam a chance to play a variety of servants and minor clowns and earn the princely sum of $25 a week for doing so. The plays might be short and the stage small in reality but for him it stretched to infinity as he stood on it acting in an abbreviated *As You Like It* and *A Midsummer Night's Dream*.

The arm of coincidence was actually longer than any stage drama would readily permit. Cleveland was his *second* Globe! He'd seen an even smaller version three years earlier even closer to home – at the 1933/34 Chicago Centenary Exposition, featuring performances by a company led by Ben Iden Payne, soon to be director of the Stratford Memorial Theatre. No wonder that Wooden 'O' was imprinted in his mind for life.

Whatever its shortcomings, the pseudo-Globe caught his imagination. So what if the structure *was* somebody's best guess and the plays being performed severely truncated – the words were the real thing and he was there to hear them. When he returned to the Goodman in his Fall vacation, not only was he the only 'professional' actor in the school by somehow acquiring an Equity card, he was now considered to be an authority on Shakespeare. Ironic since, to the end of his life, he never claimed Shakespearean expertise – simply enthusiasm.

> But pardon, gentles all,
> The flat unraised spirits that hath dar'd
> On this unworthy scaffold to bring forth
> So great an object
>
> Chorus, *Henry V*

If lightning struck, it was that day in Cleveland, Ohio. "It must have been about then", he was to reflect later, "that I began to think to 'bring forth so great an object' ..." But first there was a career to make and Shakespeare was not considered a necessary qualification by those who called the shots in Hollywood or on Broadway in those days. In fact, during the next twelve years Broadway audiences had the opportunity to see only two professional productions – one of them local, the other the touring Olivier/Richardson Old Vic company with Richardson as Falstaff. Those years, of course, did have their distractions – not least World War II.

Before he became involved in that particular distraction, Sam had laid some solid foundations for that career. In the city that had given him his start, he did some directing for the Jewish Peoples' Institute but it was never his intention to specialise in Jewish theatre. Throughout his life, he was proud to be a Jew but was never interested in the emotionally parochial approach that many Jewish actors of his generation chose to take. He wanted the broadest possible canvas on which to describe his art.

1940 found him moonlighting from his studies to act on radio – his first professional money. Radio was then the dominant medium after straight theatre for a serious actor. Hollywood was the ultimate sell-out – always supposing someone was asking you to sell. He'd started in Chicago, which in the 1930's was a centre for radio 'soaps'. When the show he was in (*Against the Storm*) transferred its production team to the network's New York studio, Sam was asked if he'd like to make the move and continue to play the character. He most certainly *would!* New York... Broadway... anything was possible. His only regret was leaving behind a fellow actor, Charlotte Holland, who decided not to follow the show.

At the time Charlotte was at least as well regarded as an actor as Sam himself. She had already turned down an offer to work with Bertolt Brecht's Berliner Ensemble and was considering an offer from Orson Welles's Mercury Theater Company.

> *Why, there's a wench! Come on, and kiss me, Kate*
>
> Petruchio, *The Taming of the Shrew*, Act V Sc. ii

Sam soon had an answer to the problem of separation. One weekend he returned to Chicago and invited Charlotte on a rather special date. It involved a marriage licence and a change of name. She took the booking and a few days later Mr. and Mrs. Samuel Wanamaker piled their worldly goods into a small Pontiac 'blue bird' and drove down to New York to start their new life together. The 'run' lasted for 53 years...

It was the kind of impetuous act Charlotte would grow used to. On an earlier date she remembers Sam deciding she should be taken home in style. The only trouble was that, while she lived on the socially acceptable lake side of Chicago, he was still on the wrong side of town. He decided he'd steal a car and drive her. Only when he'd tried all the cars in the street and come up empty handed did he remember that he couldn't drive anyway!

Back in New York, he made enough of an impact for Broadway to beckon. At 23 he opened at the Cort Theatre in *Café Crown*. After which – good notices notwithstanding – his next assignment was one he couldn't debate. For the next three years Sam found himself in a supporting role for *Uncle* Sam's theatre in the Pacific playing a Marine... and Iwo Jima was distinctly off off-Broadway, though marginally less dangerous, Sam once said.

> *We go to gain a little patch of ground*
> *That hath in it no profit but the name.*
>
> Captain, *Hamlet*, Act IV Sc. iv

Sam had a 'Sam' kind of war. Despite his energy and intelligence, he never rose above the rank of private. There were always inequities that called for comment and it was not in his nature to take other people's direction in life. "I'll have you busted!" an irate officer once shouted at him after some insubordinate remark. "Busted to *what?*" Sam snapped back. "You're going to take away my *privacy?*"

1945 – and the Yanks are no longer coming but going home. For Sam it would mean starting over. With all the big names once again available, who was going to remember a young Chicago actor with only a couple of Broadway credits to his name? On his way home he stopped off briefly in Hawaii to join a theatre company put together by Maurice Evans, a real Broadway name. The project was to direct and act in the try-out production of a writer called Tennessee Williams who – Evans thought – looked like he might have promise. The play was *The Glass Menagerie* and Evans was quite right.

Sam needn't have worried. Broadway hadn't forgotten and within a year he found himself playing headstrong juvenile leads in plays like *This Too Shall Pass, Joan of Lorraine* (with Ingrid Bergman) and in 1948 he both directed and acted with Madeleine Carroll in *Goodbye My Fancy*. It would not be the last time coincidence cropped up in the titles of his material. The Big Goodbye – in fact not fiction – was just around the corner.

His fighting instincts and his intuitive sympathy for the underdog had always encouraged him to lead with his Left. Working class Chicago with a father as union organiser had been the ideal breeding ground and the only difference a war made was that the enemy was trying to kill you, not exploit you. You fought your corner – and other people's, too, if the need arose. But what was perfectly acceptable in Chicago of the 1930's took on a very different complexion in the hysteria of a post-war America that saw enemies everywhere. Names were being taken, dossiers compiled for the House Un-American Activities Committee – unpopularly known as the McCarthy witch hunt. Those famous in the performing arts were of especial interest to Senator Joe McCarthy. They were as good a guarantee of visibility in the media as you could expect to get in those fledgling days. Sam wasn't named in the 1947 'list' as one of the 'Hollywood Ten' but he had reason to suppose it was only a question of time. He had, after all, made the trip from New York to Washington to show solidarity for the 'Ten' at the original hearings. By then, the pattern was becoming depressingly familiar. You either refused to appear before the Committee and were found guilty of some unspecific charges *in absentio* – or you appeared and pleaded the Fifth Amendment, the right to remain silent. Either way, you were now effectively unemployable. By the late 1940's Sam had seen it happen to enough of his friends to be under no illusion as to what was coming down the pike to meet him.

Although he was and would remain primarily a stage actor, it was movies that would provide the answer. In 1948, Hollywood had thought enough of his stage performances to offer him a lead in a small budget film – *My Girl Tisa*, the story of an immigrant girl in America who is saved from deportation by the President himself. Within a very short time the plot must have seemed highly ironic to Sam, since he was soon to deport himself.

> I rather would entreat thy company
> To see the wonders of the world abroad
> Than, living dully sluggardiz'd at home,
> Wear out thy youth with shapeless idleness.
>
> Valentine, *The Two Gentlemen of Verona*, Act 1 Sc. i.

A year later it was the offer to film abroad described earlier that found him in England making another 'liberal' subject that was only likely to provoke the Committee further. In fact, Sam also missed the 1951 revised list but by now it was time to shed the 'Red' reputation – even though he'd never been a member of the Communist Party, even in his most militant days – in favour of England's green and pleasant land.

Laurence Olivier's invitation to join his 1952 St. James's season and direct and act in *Winter Journey* (*The Country Girl* in the US) opposite Michael Redgrave decided him to stay and – just in case he might still be in two minds – he finally received the subpoena. He filed it in the waste basket. With Charlotte and daughters, Abby and Zoë he made England their home.

Exile – however arrived at – is not an unmixed curse. It gives the exile the chance to start again, perhaps to be what they now know they'd *like* to be without the embarrassment of having someone say: "Well, that's not the Sam Wanamaker *I* knew".

In point of fact, there wasn't much making over to be done. What had been building up nicely on Broadway would do very well in a post-war London that still retained a healthy respect for most things American. Sam, by the frequency of his appearances, as well as the sheer power of his stage presence, became the West End's favourite American actor. And, because he was available at a time when the theatrical mood was changing, theatre managements now felt able to put on productions of some of the stronger meat that was sustaining Broadway audiences.

Clifford Odets was a revolutionary voice in the 1930's with *Waiting For Lefty, Golden Boy*, and other plays of social discontent and, if his post-war tone was a little querulous and repetitive, it still held the attention over an insipid drawing room piece which opens with the maid arranging the flowers. After *Winter Journey* came another Odets, *The Big Knife* (1954) and after that what one critic called "other highly-flavoured slices of raw New York theatre" like *A Hatful of Rain* (the first play to deal overtly with drugs) and Tennessee Williams's *The Rose Tattoo*. The only obvious part calling for a brash and virile young American Sam missed was Stanley Kowalski in Williams's *A Streetcar Named Desire*. He turned the part down. He'd seen Brando on Broadway and felt he couldn't match the performance.

His style was physical and confrontational. Critic Kenneth Tynan described him as "downright dangerous". "He enjoys smouldering and when smouldering is not enough, he throws things – among them a medicine bottle, several articles of clothing, and a hail of half-smoked cigarettes. If there is nothing portable to hand, Mr. Wanamaker, profoundly stirred, hits himself on the forehead with a painful and audible smack... (He) pads ferally through the debris, wearing that neurotic, almost poetic look which goes, in America, with acute sinus trouble".

Although the West End clearly needed him, many of its elder statesmen in the establishment began to find him a thorn in their collective flesh. The man was just too – *aggressive*. Michael Redgrave, his first acting colleague/opponent, had a typical response to their collaboration in that first production, *Winter Journey*. Redgrave played an alcoholic actor, busily drinking his way down the ladder but doing it with restrained English style until he came into collision with Sam and his version of 'Method'. Redgrave had always professed to be a disciple of Stanislavski but he wasn't ready for the improvisation Sam – as director as well as actor – insisted on. In the opening scene – a rehearsal – he agreed that they should throw each other different lines every night. Although he was never comfortable with it and had a battle with Sam that lasted throughout the run, it was considered by one critic "among the peaks of post-war acting". In his autobiography, *The Face Behind the Mask*, Redgrave recollected in tranquillity that: "Not the least of personal influences on my work has been Sam Wanamaker. A great quarrel, like a great love affair, sharpens the intelligence".

Over the next forty years many people – not always on stage – were to experience the same feelings. Few of them were able to express them with the same elegant eloquence.

> *Those that come to see*
> *Only a show or two, and so agree*
> *The play may pass, if they be still and willing,*
> *I'll undertake may see away their shilling*
> *Richly in two short hours.*
>
> Prologue, *Henry VIII*

In 1957 Sam received an offer no theatrical populist could possibly refuse – the chance to run his own theatre just the way he wanted to.

A group of Liverpool businessmen approached him to discuss the future – if any – of a local theatre. The Shakespeare – or the 'Old Shakey', as the locals called it – was a neglected Victorian (c. 1888) pleasure dome having been a theatre and music hall in its time. In recent years it had shared the fate of so much 'provincial' British theatre as TV drained away the audience for 'live' performance. The few theatres that remained subsisted on a diet of occasional touring productions that filled in some of the gaps until the next Christmas pantomime – which necessarily featured a couple of TV stars.

Liverpool's 'Old Shakey' theatre became the New Shakespeare Theatre Club under Sam's direction and for a brief time redefined the theatregoing experience for that gritty city. (1957)

The Old Shakey's glory days were long since gone and now its lease was up. Did Sam have any ideas? Put that way, he had plenty. What neither side had was the money to implement any of them.

Then came a transformation scene worthy of any panto, performed – according to the best tradition – by a Fairy Godmother. In this case the part was played by Anna Deere Wiman in her own family tradition. A wealthy American socialite, her father had been a big investor on Broadway in his time. Now Miss Wiman had taken to lavishing her own and her husband's money on various theatrical projects on both sides of the Atlantic. Since the backers of shows are traditionally known as 'angels', she came well qualified to perform miracles when she approached Sam. She wanted to invest in some worthwhile theatrical project. Did he know of one? Well, as it just so happened... And would he be interested in a joint venture – her money, his talent?

The New Shakespeare Cultural Centre – when it opened in October 1957 – was more than just a theatre. In many ways it was a dress rehearsal for the project that was to haunt him for most of the rest of his life. As well as a conventional theatre, there was a special children's theatre, a film society and a restaurant-cum-social centre. There were lectures, art exhibitions and jazz concerts. It was to be a virtually round-the-clock people's recreation complex. "One of the most enterprising out-of-town playhouses in provincial theatre history", said *The Daily Telegraph*. "Not since Donizetti", reported Kenneth Tynan, "have the arts wooed Liverpool so fervently". He could just as easily have said "the Provinces". After just six months the theatre had over 19,000 members and Sam was talking enthusiastically of it becoming "the Glyndebourne of the North" – minus the picnic hampers.

The inspiration, Sam said, had been taking a New York theatre for a summer season. It had taught him a fundamental lesson in theatrical economics: "Why were the rents so high? Because the building functioned only three hours a day compared with eight or ten hours for an office block or store. I got the idea for an arts centre which would have some full-time identity like the places of culture in the Soviet Union or the old *Haus Vaterland* in Berlin..." As a concept it was unique for the UK or America – ten years or more before its time. It was also highly impractical as a commercial enterprise.

Sam made sure it was no provincial rep, by this time confined to revivals of hoary old perennials. While not ignoring conventional tastes, he put on some of the more challenging and disturbing plays that Londoners were only recently able to see, since the Lord Chamberlain's censorship function had been amended a year or so earlier to allow 'club' theatre to operate outside his jurisdiction. The sexual permissiveness – for those times – of Arthur Miller's *A View from the Bridge* and Robert Anderson's *Tea and Sympathy* was a little more than the good citizens of Liverpool were expecting. Nonetheless, they turned out to give it a try. Why should all the pioneering be done down South?

Sam's plans for the New Shakespeare took root and began to grow apace. All of them required money and few of them were negotiable. He was not an easy colleague and the differences between him and Ms. Wiman proliferated. Voices were raised and tempers lost. The lady regarded the theatre as a toy – *her* toy. One day she stamped her angelic foot and threatened to take her money away. Anyone who knew Sam at all could have predicted his reaction – "Go ahead!" There were those who muttered something about six of one and half a dozen of the other but the result was the same. The New Shakespeare went dark.

Those who took pleasure in being wise after events claimed that the lady had a notoriously short attention span and that this was par for the course. Others blamed Sam's mercurial temperament and said that his 'vision' bore no relationship to the realities of what a gritty northern city could and would support in the name of culture.

Whatever the reasons, less than two years after it was rescued, the New Shakespeare project was old hat. Its two patrons had moved on to new projects and the theatre was left to fend for itself. A new management took over and continued to run the New Shakespeare Club, despite a fire which necessitated some rebuilding. The theatre continued to operate, although its glamour days were behind it by the time a second fire closed it for good in 1976.

Years later, Sam fondly remembered the good bits. The work they had all done, he felt, "had immense ramifications. We created a number of experiments there – ways of operating a theatre at maximum capacity throughout the year, day in and day out – which have been taken up by most of the major theatres throughout the country". A little wishful thinking there, even for the boom days of the mid-1970's, when he gave the interview. Nonetheless, there was a ripple effect around the provincial theatre world post-Liverpool. New constructions like the Nottingham Playhouse and the Belgrade at Coventry were certainly designed to be more than bricks and mortar. But his 'vision' still shone brightly: "We wanted the theatre to appeal to a whole strata of society who were, traditionally, non-theatregoers. We took our cue from the Philharmonic Industrial Concerts".

Still, the lesson of what actually *happened* in Liverpool was one that might have saved Sam and his subsequent followers a deal of anguish in tackling the Globe project. Had he started with the theatre and *then* added the other elements as he secured his base camp, he might have had a chance. But with Sam, it was all or nothing – and *now*! In this case, it was to be nothing. Perhaps worse than nothing, because there would be people who – a few years later – would remember a northern castle built on sand. And now he wants to build a theatre... an *Elizabethan* theatre?

> Reputation is an idle and most false imposition;
> oft got without merit, and lost without deserving.
>
> Iago, *Othello*, Act II Sc. iii

On his return to the theatrical mainstream Sam found himself playing Shakespeare for the first time in a major production. Despite his life-long fascination with the Bard, he never laid claim to any special skill in interpreting Shakespeare as an actor. He felt his contemporary emotional 'Method' approach was unlikely to suit traditional productions of the plays – particularly in his adopted homeland.

Consequently, it came as something of a surprise when director, Tony Richardson – given the task of opening Stratford-upon-Avon's 80th anniversary season in 1959 – invited him to play Iago to Paul Robeson's Othello. But there was a play within a play here, which Sam probably didn't appreciate until later.

An American Iago was unlikely, but an American Iago *and* an American Othello – at *Stratford!* But there was a logic to Richardson's casting that made a strange kind of sense. Robeson, a significant pre-war actor as well as a legendary singer, had hardly worked in years in the States. Like Sam, he was the victim of the fanatical anti-Communist forces busily purging the arts of all fellow travellers. Unlike many others on the 'list', Robeson refused to purge his Communist sympathies, opting to pay the inevitable price. No retraction – no work. And no passport to go and work elsewhere.

It was only in 1958 that the ban was lifted but the Paul Robeson who turned up in Stratford via Moscow, tired and sick, was a husk of the man his loyal fans flocked to see. Still physically impressive, he was understandably nervous. As Richardson observed later: "Paul was Othello but, alas, the years and his persecutions had left their mark and he no longer had the energy and the technique he once had". (Robeson had played the part memorably opposite Peggy Ashcroft at the Savoy Theatre in 1930).

Realising the danger of entrusting such an important production to someone who might be unable to bear the dramatic weight on those once mighty shoulders, he packed the cast with young talent. Mary Ure was Desdemona, Albert Finney played Cassio; Zoë Caldwell, Ian Holm and Angela Baddeley were a powerful supporting cast, and towards the bottom, for those with 20-20 foresight, the name of Vanessa Redgrave, understudying Desdemona in the production, and soon to play the leading role of Richardson's wife.

Richardson hired Sam *because* he was an American! Certainly, his West End credentials more than qualified him for any stage but on this occasion he was cast specifically to act as a foil to Othello in more ways than one. "By choosing an American", Richardson reasoned, "I thought Paul's accent would blend more easily into the ensemble".

The production turned out to be a success with the paying public – Robeson was still a box office draw – but many critics reacted much as Richardson had feared. He confided to his journal that the "anti-Americanism, always latent with so many so-called Europeans, boiled up and, as Paul was sacrosanct, it was directed mainly at Sam..." Words like 'Hollywood' and 'cowboy' were used freely. In retrospect, it's easy to see that the whole project presented an easy target to those professional protectors of our theatrical heritage.

Richardson provided a few obvious hostages. In his late 20's at the time, he was heady with the success of directing the early Osborne plays and breaking new theatrical ground. Faced with the combined challenge of Robeson, *Othello* and Stratford, he tried to have his theatrical cake and eat it. He allowed Robeson to give a classical reading of the part and indulged himself with peripheral production flourishes, like rock & roll sound tracks. Many people also felt he encouraged Sam to overplay his natural stage persona. One critic wrote of Iago coming across as "a mid-Western confidence man", another of "a slick gangster devoid of any plausible air of honesty". Ian Holm recalls an intense performance, "rather like a gunslinger". This Othello would surely have had no dealing with such a man? The director himself felt that Sam gave "a fine and striking performance" and indeed, the sheer theatricality has stuck in my own mind to this day. But when I got to know him years later I began to understand a certain dissonance I'd felt. Coriolanus, perhaps. Tamburlaine, certainly. Towards the end Prospero and even Lear. But he was no Iago – for the simple reason that you were never in any doubt about Sam's agenda. He wore it on his face. As so often, Kenneth Tynan coined the memorable epithet. "Above all", he wrote, "Iago should be disarming. Mr. Wanamaker... is profoundly arming".

Certainly, the relationship between the two men was perfectly amicable as the run ended – so much so that when he was planning the major production of his 1973 outdoor season for the Globe, Sam had no hesitation in asking Richardson to direct it and – while he was about it – why not have his by now ex-wife, Vanessa Redgrave, play the lead?

...then to the elements
Be free, and fare thou well!
Prospero, *The Tempest*, Act V Sc. i

Whether he was playing in Shakespeare at Stratford or trying to revive a theatre bearing the name in Liverpool, some quirk of destiny seemed to be linking WS and SW. Readers of tea leaves or tarot cards, however, might have divined that, so far, their stars were not in perfect alignment.

Liverpool was a brave and perhaps over-ambitious failure; Stratford, a curate's egg – good in parts. Certainly, Sam never appeared at Stratford again nor did he play another leading role in the West End. Perhaps London theatregoers – and producers – had simply seen enough of the Method style that had appeared so fresh a decade earlier. Whatever the reason, Sam's moment in the sun as a leading stage actor had passed.

Not that it concerned him unduly. His bow had many strings – directing, film acting, directing opera. His calendar remained full and, besides, another door was reluctantly creaking open. Paul Robeson's 'release' – though jealously monitored by J. Edgar Hoover's FBI – was simply the most visible evidence of the end of the anti-Communist black list.

Sam discovered his personal door had been left on the latch almost by accident. Invited to appear in the 1961 film, *Taras Bulba*, a Hollywood production to be made off-shore in Argentina, he tentatively approached the American Embassy in London. Was there a possibility? No problem, Mr. Wanamaker. Have a nice day...

When the movie was finished, Sam finally went 'home' and spent the rest of the decade – and, to some extent, the rest of his life – commuting between his two homelands. One of his early bookings – and one which gave him special pleasure – was with his *alma mater*, Chicago's Goodman Theatre, where he directed and played *Macbeth* (1961).

He was busy at a variety of tasks and, if his name had disappeared from 'above the title' in terms of billing status, he found satisfaction in broadening his range as producer or director. To those who knew him best, he was a gentleman-in-waiting, though not even he was sure for what. By the end of the decade, however, it had become abundantly clear.

Sam as Iago in the 1959 Stratford production of *Othello*.
Mander Mitchenson

CHAPTER FOUR

BRINGING THE HOUSE DOWN
(1972 – 1973)

A plague o' both your houses!
Romeo and Juliet, Act III Sc. i

With the purchase of the Bear Gardens/Rose Alley site Sam consolidated his place on the Bankside Monopoly board. Not only could he now keep the developers at a respectful distance; if there was to be any further conversation, they would have to come to him: "Any development that included this site would have to meet with our agreement", he used to point out gleefully. He was now within touching distance of the original Globe and what made the theatrical vibrations even stronger was the fact that literally next door on a spot he could see from his window had stood the Globe's great rival theatre – the Rose.

Ideally, the Globe Playhouse Trust should have purchased the property but, when they couldn't raise the relatively modest asking price of £50,000, Sam bought it himself through Bankside Globe Developments Ltd., by mortgaging his Highgate home and taking out a 90 day bridging loan from Barclays Bank.

Over the years some of his detractors claimed that Sam's interest in the Globe project was financial. The money was what mattered. They were right – but for the wrong reasons. Sam never took a penny out of the Globe project. At critical moments he was prepared to put his own money into the scheme, quite apart from acting in a totally unpaid capacity throughout. By the time of his death the Trust *owed* him a substantial sum. The sacrifice of the Highgate house was particularly upsetting for the family. It was their first real home since their arrival in the UK; it had been lovingly designed and built to their own specification and they'd lived there happily for the past fourteen years. For Charlotte especially it was quite a wrench. "But Sam said we were going, so we went. What he wanted to do, we did..."

Where they went was into deepest, darkest Southwark. Sam was determined to strengthen his case with the community by visibly becoming a local. He wanted to live 'over the store'. He bought the remaining lease of an old building in Trinity Street known as 'The Surrey Dispensary' from actress, Mai Zetterling, who had only managed to modernise one room. The rest was virtually derelict. To make matters worse, they had to stay derelict until Sam could negotiate a new lease. Charlotte remembers having to cook for the whole family on a solitary Belling gas ring at the top of the house. Quaint it may have been. Comfortable it was not.

As far as the Bear Gardens property was concerned, Sam leased it to the Trust with an option for them to buy at a later date under favourable conditions. Meanwhile, part of it (No. 2) was to be turned into a Globe Theatre Museum. He made one major proviso – should the Trust come to own the property and then decide to sell it subsequently, they could only do so if the purchaser guaranteed to provide – on what would presumably be a larger overall site – an area for the Globe and a replacement Museum.

It all sounded impressively tycoonish but reality wasn't long arriving. The Trust simply had no means to exercise the option and Sam had no means to repay the bridging loan. In fact, he needed every penny he could lay his hands on to buy The Dispensary – so he entered into an agreement with Chestergrove Properties Ltd. (a subsidiary of Chesterfield) to become joint owners. It was to prove a happy arrangement, since Chestergrove had no property ambitions on Bankside and the option terms could stay in place.

Not surprisingly, he hadn't heard the last of Town and Metropolitan. Having tried unsuccessfully to beat Sam to the sale they now approached him with a 'financial incentive' to *re*sell. Sam – who now found himself sitting pat right in the middle of a parcel of sites all owned by the 'opposition' – not surprisingly refused. Piggy-in-the-Middle was a game he could quite enjoy because it was, in truth, the only game in which he had any real power.

I mention this in detail not in an attempt to chart the minefields of 1970s property speculation but to make the point that the rebuilding of an Elizabethan theatre in a down-at-heel London borough was perhaps the least of the problems facing Sam and his small but growing band of loyal followers. More and more they would find themselves enmeshed in the complexities of late 20th century city life that seemed peculiarly designed to tax both time and temper.

But at least – as the witching hour of Shakespeare's 1972 birthday approached – there were real blessings to be counted.

The Shakespearean academics – all 500 of them from 26 countries – had agreed at their 1971 Vancouver conference that the project had merit.

The local Council – after a frosty start – seemed to be warming towards it, too.

And they did have their place to stand – right in the heart of Shakespeare's Bankside

Not too bad a record after their first full year.

On the debit side the shoulder presented by the theatrical establishment was cool, to say the least, while the Arts Council – supporters of many an activity that would have been dignified by the description 'peripheral' – cast a stony eye on the proceedings.

MP Hugh Jenkins wrote to Sam from his House of Commons office early in January to say that: "I think the truth is that Arnold Goodman, who is in many ways by no means a bad man and has done much for the arts in general and the theatre in particular, thinks you are on to a big flop and does not want to associate the Arts Council with something he believes will collapse at some stage".

> – I will do such things, –
> What they are, yet I know not, – but they shall be
> The terrors of the earth.
>
> Lear, *King Lear*, Act II Sc. iv

While possession is popularly reckoned to be a large part of the law, Sam knew perfectly well that being a Bankside squatter, however legal and well-intentioned, wouldn't suffice. An ill-assorted community of interest was gathering just below the horizon, anxious to develop the area for profitable housing and office space. Councillor and Developer would overlook their differences just this once and unite against the common enemy, this elitist alien interloper. The Trust had to be seen to be doing things to justify its existence and its occupancy... Luckily, it already was.

In September of the previous year the World Centre for Shakespeare Studies (WCSS) had been registered to authenticate the project's educational credentials and in December permission had been granted to change the newly-acquired 42-44 Bankside site into an arts centre.

This year April 23rd was the obvious day to launch a programme of events. Shakespeare's birthday.

Sam's ambitions were great as he faced 1972. A six week Summer School series of lectures involved forty ranking academic names like Neville Coghill and Jan Kott. For the birthday week itself a Shakespeare Birthday Festival attended by Prime Minister, Edward Heath and with an oration read by Sir John Gielgud. Poet Laureate, C. Day Lewis, composed a special hymn:

Hymn for Shakespeare's Birthday

The Word was the beginning,
Spirit's and Reason's sire -
Sent the chartered planets spinning
Down the tracks of fire.
After that fiery birth
What endless aeons throng
Before this green and troubled earth
Can grow to her full song!
The all-creative Word
Surveying earth's huge span
From every maker these preferred
One man to speak for Man -
Gifted with art beyond
The best who'd worn the bays,
Sure pilot still on the profound
Heart's uncharted ways.
This man whose vision ranged
Life's whole from bliss to woe,
Perceived how love, warped or estranged,
Will bring the highest low.
Today his birthday fell:
But he is born once more
Each time we come beneath his spell
And to his genius soar.

Other events included a gala concert by the Royal Philharmonic Orchestra in Southwark Cathedral, and the publication of a specially commissioned, limited edition book of poems, *Poems for Shakespeare*, which included new work by Ted Hughes, Robert Graves and W. H. Auden among others.

No. 84 was presented to Prince Philip. While other 'establishments' were making a public point of holding back, Prince Philip let it be known that he personally was in favour of the project. Once it could demonstrate its public credibility, he indicated that he might well be prepared to accept a more public role.

Welcome to Stratford-on-Thames!

Evening Standard

But the plays were undoubtedly to be the thing to catch the conscience of the doubters and the nay-sayers. Performances would take place, somehow or other, on and around the site itself. The Trust had a toehold, it was true, in the shape of their rented hut but the rest of the site was now sub-leased as a car park, which the current owners (The Central Electricity Generation Board) were persuaded to give up for the duration after a little prodding from Southwark Council.

Perhaps they felt the good neighbour brownie points would come in handy at a later date. John Player & Sons provided a subsidy of £25,000, the GLC found £5,000 and the London Electricity Board gave free electricity. A large canopy was thrown over the entire space under which a temporary theatre was erected. For the first time in over three hundred years a Bankside audience heard the voice of the Bard as a variety of performances were staged, including Keith Michell's modern dress *Hamlet* and a Malaysian version of *Macbeth*, to underscore the international nature of the venture.

Director Tony Richardson and actor Nicol Williamson discussed their current filmed version of *Hamlet*. Strolling players strolled purposefully. Down the road on another piece of 'borrowed' land a prefabricated structure served as a temporary cinema in which Classic Cinemas sponsored the showing of no less than 63 films relating to Shakespeare. There was an outdoor sculpture exhibition and – most encouraging of all, it seemed – a joint exhibition with Southwark Council called "In the Clink", a somewhat ironic title in the light of the role the law would play in the project's later history.

Keith Michell's modern dress *Hamlet*, a highlight of the 1972 season.

The *Evening Standard* – sceptical up to this point about the project as a whole – admitted that what Sam had wrought had "to be seen to be believed... an architect-designed terraced theatre of 700 seats beneath a suspended plastic awning, complete with lights, gallery and box office; a fully-equipped cinema; a luxuriously-appointed temporary pub – the Bull Ring – in five linked caravans; a barbecue cafe with outdoor patio; a set of theatrical offices; an exhibition centre in a converted warehouse; and a rudimentary sculpture gallery on the river walls". They dubbed the whole thing "Stratford-on-Thames".

It was an ambitious and auspicious start. Spirits were understandably high. Even the project's apparent opponents seemed to have called a truce. The Arts Council – perhaps out of embarrassment over the 'big flop' remark – even came through with £3,000, as well as helping with individual events such as recitals and a jazz concert.

The Summer of 1972 was a happy time – until the reviews and the box office receipts came in. The former were mixed but the critical – what would now be called 'politically correct' line – was expressed by *Time Out*, which claimed the whole project "exists to propagate fashionable, even gimmicky, art". Bad weather at the start didn't help and by the end of the season in September they were about £10,000 out of pocket – hardly the object of the exercise. Sam made a note at the time that he had "personally made loans to the Trust totalling £5,942... in order to ensure the continued operation". The loans were interest free and for an indefinite period. Once again, he had put his money where Shakespeare's mouth was...

It was a pattern that would be repeated with minor variations many times over. An ambitious event performed on rather less than a shoe string, involving a certain amount of smoke and mirrors. Like King Lear, Sam was determined to 'do such things' and his inspiration was never less than prolific. He would continue to embellish and improvise in his search for perfection, oblivious to the taxi meter that kept on ticking, confident that some God bearing gold would descend from the Machine. He never did.

Cry God for Bankside, Southwark and Sam
Wanamaker!
Good luck telegram 1972

Two souvenirs of the 1972 season that Sam particularly treasured were two good luck telegrams. One from Dame Sybil Thorndike commended him on his 'splendid enterprise' but the one that must have dragged forth a wry smile in the dankest days of that wet summer came from a member of the public and read: "Cry God for Bankside, Southwark and Sam Wanamaker!"

A month or so later Southwark did do something to earn the accolade in Sam's eyes. The Council gave planning permission to convert the warehouse at No.1 Bear Gardens into a permanent Elizabethan museum – The Museum of the Shakespearean Stage. Sam and his team wasted no time acting on that and the Mayor of Southwark was on the doorstep to formally open and dedicate the new premises on December 13th. In his 'remarks' he was pleased to point out that the attractive shrubbery and plantings in the Museum's tiny forecourt were a gift from the Borough!

It wasn't much of a museum – a few theatre models and a series of temporary exhibitions ranging from Life on the River Thames to trade unionism and bear-baiting (*quid pro quo?*). Sam's intention was always to set his project in the context of the local area and its history. He and Charlotte ran the place almost single handed and

The Globe project's first permanent home, the Museum of the Shakespearean Stage at
No.1 Bear Gardens which opened on December 13th 1972. *June Everett*

took great pride in changing their 'exhibitions' every month.
Attendance was small but at least it was a start... at least changing an
exhibition was doing something.

> Though it be honest, it is never good
> To bring bad news; give to the gracious message
> An host of tongues, but let ill tidings tell
> Themselves when they be felt.
>
> Cleopatra, *Antony and Cleopatra*, Act II Sc. v

Although there were only a couple of weeks left on the calendar,
1972 wasn't quite over yet...

Sam's mind was already rehearsing their 1973 season and – as
would often happen – his tongue acted as pre-emptive prologue to
his swelling theme. A letter from Vanessa Redgrave gave him
momentary pause...

Yes, she *did* want to play Cleopatra with Tony Richardson
directing but she wanted him to know that she agreed with her
ex-husband that, if they couldn't between them come up with a
'superb Antony', then *Antony and Cleopatra* was not a realistic possibility
for either of them.

She goes on to speculate about the likelihood of securing the calibre of actor in time and then summarises her position: "So, to bang the nail on the head, if we have a smashing Antony then I am on, if not, I am not". She then comes to what P. G. Wodehouse would have called the *res*...

What had really irritated her was that she felt Sam's premature publicity had compromised her – and Tony Richardson, come to that. If they now didn't do *Antony and Cleopatra*, for whatever reason, it would look as though they had reneged on a commitment, when no formal commitment had, in fact, been made.

She made the pill palatable by assuming that the mistake had been made by "someone in your office". She trusted that it would all work out satisfactorily but he must understand that, until the conditions were met, there was no commitment.

What everyone who worked with Sam knew was that there was no such person as "someone in your office"; there was only Sam, tossing the stones in the pond and hoping for helpful ripples. Who had time for all these niceties when shows had to be got on the road and amphitheatres built. Vanessa was Vanessa letting off steam. He'd worked perfectly well with Tony at Stratford. It would all come out in the wash.

❖

Not that there was universal agreement that amphitheatres should be *built* at all. The academics might have reached intellectual consensus but, then, they didn't have to find the money and build it, did they? In the architectural community there was a deeply sceptical core with views that were summed up by one Peter Moro, a key advisor to the Arts Council on new theatre proposals, who wrote to Sam re: "A New Globe on Bankside:"

"Even if it were possible to establish what exactly the Globe was like, we know enough to suggest that such a theatre would be totally unacceptable to actor, audience and the local authority. An audience standing closely packed in their thousands, under an open sky, surrounded by a wooden structure with no exits, no lavatories, no bars, to say nothing of actors without proper dressing room facilities, surely is not a working proposition... Apart from a stunt, and a possible tourist attraction, I can see no future in faking the past".

Around the same time – early 1973 – Hugh Casson was much more encouraging and had clearly given the matter considerable thought. He urged Sam not to worry about archaeologists or historians: "They'll never be satisfied and detailed accuracy is totally unimportant – particularly as the GLC will any way mess it up with their regulations on escape, fire, etc. What is wanted is character, atmosphere and illusion".

There were, he felt, three options:

1 As accurate as possible a 'Replica Theatre.'
2 Ditto, but perhaps demountable and erected for seasons within a general all-purpose excitingly-packaged 'hangar.'
3 A Globe Theatre Mark 3, predominantly designed for Shakespearean production, but capable of other types.

He came to the conclusion that "All three solutions are technically possible. Each is capable of a visually exciting treatment. The difficulty lies in balancing tourist/school attraction versus flexibility (including local social contribution)". He declared himself quite happy to support any of the options.

Sam's abiding fear throughout the whole enterprise was to be seen to be taking even a single inadvertent step in the direction that could be castigated as Shakespeare-in-Disneyland. It had to be the Bard, the whole Bard and – to begin with, at least – nothing but the Bard...

If he re-read the Moro letter carefully, it might have brought forth a small smile. How could that closely-packed audience of thousands have got *into* "a wooden structure with no exits" – and, therefore, presumably, no *entrances*?

❖

In April 1973 Sam could be forgiven for thinking that the highest hurdle was now behind him as Southwark Council gave approval in principle to the idea of a reconstructed Globe playhouse on Bankside. In fact, in their 1973 strategy it stated that the Thames-side heritage was to be more strongly emphasised in future and that "theatres and museums linked to the history of the area would be actively encouraged". Where he came from a governing body was a governing body, bound by the decisions of its predecessors. This was a decision on which he could literally pin his hopes. What he didn't appreciate was the serpentine subtlety of English equivalents, where a decision is inclined to be a relative matter – depending on who took it. The Voice of Southwark had been heard in the land – well, sort of... for now...

Let's have one other gaudy night
Antony, *Antony and Cleopatra*, Act III Sc. xi

In any case there was the next Summer Season to plan and – for the first time in a long time – Sam had a conflict of professional interest to worry about. Since the project had cast its spell in the late 1960s, he'd steadily allowed it to take precedence over other commitments – taking acting jobs whenever his self-created timetable allowed to keep the wolf from the Wanamaker door. But a year or so earlier he'd received an invitation he really couldn't turn down – the opportunity to direct the opening production at the newly-built and controversial Sydney Opera House. The only trouble was that opening night was to be right in the middle of the Summer Season.

This year they could benefit from last year's mistakes. Why, this year, properly organised, the season would just about run itself and already the signs looked promising. John Player renewed their sponsorship and even found a little more money. So that was encouraging. Once again there was to be a theatre season, a cinema festival, the summer school, a gala concert and – this year, of course – exhibitions at the new Museum.

It was irritating that the local authorities, so helpful in some things, chose to impose much more stringent conditions on the temporary structures Sam intended to use. Such was bureaucracy. But was it really so surprising, considering the improvisatory, let's-do-the-show-right-here approach of the previous season? Nonetheless, the extra safety requirements made a nasty dent in the budget.

With one eye down under, the other was distracted by the ongoing saga of Vanessa, Antony and Cleopatra. The casting dilemma had by now been resolved. Julian Glover was available and more than acceptable to the two principal actors in the off stage drama – Ms. Redgrave and Mr. Richardson. Bob Hoskins had been signed for Pompeius, there was a strong supporting cast and prospects for a major production finally looked set fair. 1973 was the year when Bankside would certainly make headlines.

My tongue will tell the anger of my heart,
Or else my heart, concealing it, will break:
And rather than it shall, I will be free
Even to the uttermost, as I please, in words.

Kate, *The Taming of the Shrew*, Act IV Sc. iii

Behind the scenes, however, there was a distinct shortage of oil to pour on troubled egos – of which three loomed large. Although she had finally agreed to take part, Vanessa Redgrave had neither forgotten nor forgiven Sam for his press 'leak'. Nor was Tony Richardson to prove an easy colleague. Perhaps he thought he was theatrically slumming it. Years later in his memoirs he refers to it as a "sketch production" staged in "Sam's small festival in a tent on the site of the original Globe" and goes on to elaborate his recollected lack of enthusiasm for the project: "I've always had a dread of reconstructed Shakespearean theatres – however much the features of the contemporary stage may have influenced the play's construction, there are better ways of staging them now".

While his argument was perfectly valid, it was still a strange thing to say – or at that stage, think – when the whole purpose of the exercise was to create a faithful Shakespearean replica. If he felt such 'dread', why bother? By this stage of his career a man who had built his theatrical reputation on plays of words – such as John Osborne's *Look Back in Anger* – seems to have lost confidence in his ability to hold his audience without displays of stage cleverness and was showing early symptoms of the soon-to-be-prevalent 'director's theatre'. Whatever the reason, he decided that production trickery was needed to enliven the bleakness of Bankside.

❖

And then, of course, there was Sam for whom something like this was a *fait accompli* from the moment he thought of it. The boring details were for someone else to take care of – preferably without charge. It would be surprising by this time if the strain of juggling so many balls in the air wasn't getting to him. That, at least, is the charitable explanation for the particularly harsh tone of the correspondence that ensued on the eve of his departure for Sydney.

The production was doomed from the beginning. The mistrust and resentment went deep and the real question was the one Sam posed in his letter to Vanessa: "Why, if you have so much contempt for me – for what we are doing – did you agree to work here at all?"

The touch paper was lit by Tony Richardson telling Sam that he had "never known such an unhappy cast (and) had never seen stage management treated so abominably by the Management". The key issue was a contractual error. In the standard contract issued to the cast the engagement period was stated as "four weeks" instead of eight weeks that included rehearsal and performance. It was such a gross error that it could only have been accidental but, in the atmosphere that prevailed, it appeared distinctly Machiavellian, inserted as a kind of fail safe in case the Trust went bust.

Whatever the cause, Sam hit the roof. In an open letter to "The Antony and Cleopatra Company" he dealt with the specific issue and gave vent to a number of others that had been on his mind, only incidentally to do with this particular production.

He referred to accusations of "the Wanamaker Enterprise being subsidised by the low pay of the actors, while huge profits were being creamed off the top and stashed away in a Swiss numbered bank account..." and suggestions that the Globe was "a West End operation and therefore should be operated on a West End contract".

The facts were quite the opposite. The losses of the 1972 season were £10,000 more than the John Player subsidy. This year the projected additional loss would be something like £17,000 over the subsidy. "I personally have spent almost all of my savings on this project and have last week, with others, guaranteed a further £2,000 against a bank overdraft for the Trust". The temporary theatre had cost £9,500. Burbage's original Globe had cost just £600.

But it wasn't the money that exercised him. It was the role in which people persisted in casting him – the Shylock American entrepreneur lining his pockets with the money he was coining from Britain's glorious cultural past. There was already a faction in Southwark that saw him as the creator of a "luxury play centre for the rich" and exhorted him in graffiti to "Go home, Yankee, get out of SE1". Couldn't they see it was only *him* – scrappy little Sam, perpetual crusader for any underdog that cared to be counted? How wrong could they be? It wouldn't be the first time he had to deal with the problem, although later he would manage to turn it aside and try to grow an extra layer of skin. But it hurt him to the very end to be so misunderstood. On this occasion, he couldn't help but let it pour out.

"If anyone is interested in my motives, I'd be happy to direct them to an investigation of my career. For those of you too young to remember, I was a victim of McCarthyism and blacklisted from pursuing my profession in the United States... No socialist Labour League member among you [*a reference to Vanessa's well-publicised sympathies*] should forget that there were other militants before them who fought for social justice against Fascism and for the organisation of Labour Unions, and I mean with bullets and bayonets and hand grenades. There were those of us who were also blacklisted by our own American Equity for our left wing 'Red' beliefs. Look up a book called *Red Channels* and read the record of crimes against The State which I and others like Joe Losey and Carl Foreman committed in the name of Social and political justice. It is sad to be labelled by some of you as "the 'Class Enemy', the 'Exploiter' of members of my own profession".

In a private letter to Vanessa he returns to the theme: "I sense a deep and powerful contempt emanating from you towards me. This astonishes and disturbs me. I know from your activity and public statements your commitment to causes against social injustice..." He then returns to the events that triggered the outburst – the actors' working conditions: "...no, they are not to the standards of the West End or Stratford that *you* are used to – but we are *truer* to the real spirit of theatre – than the phoney ambiance of, say, the Roundhouse which is the fashionable 'in' thing of blue jeans and health foods. Yes, our prices *are* too high – but can the actors be paid less?... We get no real subsidy from the pockets of the people through the Government, the Arts Council, the Local Authority unlike the Royal Court or Joan Littlewood... Where is the money to come from to pay for it? I have poured my life savings into this project – *and* I've mortgaged my house to do it. Oh yes, you say, how much is he getting out of it? Why don't you ask and find out instead of 'assuming, guessing, accepting' untruths – why can't you believe in my integrity as much as you would expect others to believe in yours? – Yes, the place is full of problems of *all* kinds – and as you well *know* – my reputation is horrific – if you *did* choose to come here in spite of all that – why make it difficult for all of us by your rudeness, incivility, hostility and unco-operation?" He went on to add: "I hope you personally and the production have a great success – we *need* it to survive". With that he left for Australia.

What would have happened if the production hadn't been imminent is anyone's guess. As it was – *sans* Sam – the show went on.

> Antony: *Would I had never seen her!*
> Enobarbus: *O, sir! you had then left unseen a*
> *wonderful piece of work*
>
> *Antony and Cleopatra*, Act I Sc. ii

Recollecting things in the relative tranquility of some fifteen years later, Richardson felt "...we served the play very well... We set it vaguely in the 1930's. Cleopatra was like a Hollywood star – Theda Bara, Tallulah Bankhead and Bette Davis all in one. Antony was a dashing Errol Flynn aviator..." Pompey was a buccaneer and the Romans wore Mao-Stalin jackets ("the style of the world to come"). "Vanessa", he recalled, "by her daring was able to explore sides of the character with a harshness and truthfulness unparalleled in any other Cleopatra I've ever seen". Everyone who saw it agreed it was – *different*.

Antony (Julian Glover) remembers the whole experience as being exciting with nothing of the 'work in progress' quality that Tony Richardson accords it. Glover was in no doubt then or now that "this was his production of the play, with all he had to give, and if he felt he had to make such apologetic gestures, he must have known that he'd basically failed". After the opening night director and cast hardly met. Glover was less than impressed, however, with the conduct of his co-star, who sent her current boyfriend (Timothy Dalton) to see him with a few tips on how to play the role!

The reviews were predictably mixed, one reviewer finding Vanessa's Cleopatra "a performance to be seen to be believed. It is off-beat, extravagant, shrill, theatrical – and magnificent". The production was "quite absorbing in its alignment with the present day world". *The Times* found her performance "physically and textually courageous". In the *Evening Standard* Milton Shulman didn't quite see it that way. In his view "the sublime verse is tossed away almost with contempt and the plot is reduced to something that might have been written by Noël Coward called *Public Lives*". Ms. Redgrave, far from appearing "magnificent" is "as unlikely a looking Egyptian dish as Golda Meir in a yashmak". Whatever else it was, this *Antony* did not go gentle into that dark Bankside night. Bookings were solid until – with one week of performance to go – on the Monday evening – the roof fell in!

Such sheets of fire, such bursts of horrid thunder,
Such groans of roaring wind and rain, I never
Remember to have heard

King Lear, Act III Sc. ii

After four weeks of glorious weather and capacity houses a sudden rainstorm struck. Heavy rain found the fatal flaw in the temporary theatre – a structure of canvas over a steel frame. As the performance proceeded, water began to collect in the canvas, which started to sag ominously. Fearful that the entire tent would collapse, the show was abruptly cancelled. Bob Hoskins – in the best traditions of the Blitz – told stories to keep the audience calm while the canvas was slashed to allow water to escape. For all the wrong reasons he lost his audience. End of show. End of story. Advance box office takings had to be refunded, the cast paid off on their contract and the rest of the run aborted. The Gods were determined to be angry and didn't much seem to care with whom. They even gave a few people temporary delusions. In her autobiography Vanessa Redgrave vividly recalls Sam baling out the flood water, crying – "The show must go on!" While the incident was dramatically correct, even Sam would have had trouble playing it, since he was some 12,000 miles away at the time. The Rainmaker was presumably reprising his role in absentio...

While the headlines went to the on stage drama, the less recorded story was the growing success of the summer seasons with the man, woman and child in the streets of Southwark. If the whole venture was 'elitist', nobody had told them. Encouraged with cut price rates for local citizens, they came in their thousands, strolling through the exhibitions, then popping into the pub – very much as their Elizabethan forebears must have done. Meanwhile, their kids poured into the cinema (25p for a cartoon and a feature film), tired themselves out at the 'loudly popular' junior discotheque or created their own outdoor art gallery. ICI and Berger supplied the paint and before long "the formerly Dickensian prospect of sooty brick and concrete had been transformed into an amusing, visually lively example of street art". Instead of standing around tugging their forelocks like the serfs in some Hollywood movie – as the project's critics depicted them – the people of Southwark had only one question – "Are you doing this again next year?"

74

Sam arrived back from Australia in October to find unqualified catastrophe. What should have been a triumphant second season with audiences overall up by 60% ended in a huge loss, a direct debit to the Trust. When all the figures were in and all the excuses made, it was clear that the project in its present form was out of its depth. In December the Globe Trust was wound up.

❖

If this were a movie, we'd now pan across Sam's desk to discover the discarded programme from his Sydney Opera House production. It was Prokofiev's *War and Peace*.

CHAPTER FIVE

THE SCHOLAR'S TALE

And thus do we of wisdom and of reach,
With windlasses, and with assays of bias,
By indirections find directions out

Polonius, *Hamlet*, Act II. Sc. i

It was July 1969. Since that fateful afternoon stroll with brother Bill, Sam hadn't wasted any time. Three hundred plus years, after all, was long enough to wait.

Cramped in the tiny 'office' of Sam's Highgate house sat the 'Gang of Three', as Glynne Wickham was to christen them. He was one of the three. Professor of Drama at Bristol University, he had been Sam's first choice once he'd determined to tackle his 'great object'. Wickham was well aware of the key role he and others like him would need to play if the Dream was to have any chance of being fulfilled.

"The idea, of course, was Sam's", Wickham recalls, "but he lacked the confidence to proceed with it single-handed. As an actor, he had lived long enough in the UK to be well aware that within his own profession (which had survived well enough *without* a replica of any Elizabethan-style playhouse!) he was unlikely to muster adequate support from that quarter. He thus turned to the world of academe..."

He knew perfectly well why he featured on Sam's academic hit list. In his department at Bristol was an Elizabethan style playhouse. "This had been designed by Dr. Richard Southern and had attracted considerable attention from the press since it opened in 1951 as an integral part of an open-plan, multi-faceted studio theatre".

The third man in the room was Professor Terrence Spencer, Director of the Shakespeare Institute at Stratford-upon-Avon, and right from the start of the conversation Spencer left Sam in no doubt as to his views on the practicalities involved. Based on his own experience at Stratford, he said, there was no way of funding a 3rd Globe, if it was only intended as a Shakespeare Memorial Theatre built in London for strictly professional use.

Sam was, for him, curiously silent. He'd already done his own homework.

Even those first tentative talks with the Arts Council had served to disabuse him of that notion, though that was originally part of his master plan. Throngs of modern day Elizabethans trooping across the metropolis to see a play once more! But if that was not to be, then the Bristol experiment might indicate another way to reach the goal – the "academic Shakespeare industry" (as Wickham dubbed it). It might well be that – or nothing.

There was enough accord at that first meeting for the three of them to agree to proceed with a view to finding "(a) a site; (b) an architect; and (c) academic back-up".

Sam took on the role of exploring Bankside – of which he already knew every inch – and the property developers specialising in the area.

Wickham went back to Bristol to try and interest Richard Southern in the project, since Southern was at that time a part-time member of staff and could be of immense help as an architectural advisor.

Spencer would start to tap into the well-established network to which the Institute had access and specifically canvas support from the biennial Shakespeare Conference at Stratford that included representatives from the UK, North America, Continental Europe and the then Commonwealth.

There has been much throwing around of brains
Hamlet, Act II Sc. ii

When they met again three months later, two of the Gang of Three had good news to report. Spencer produced a file of replies supporting the idea. Wickham was able to tell Sam that Richard Southern would be happy to hear from him personally, while Sam – with a degree of confidence that was still bright and unrusted – assured his co-conspirators that he was convinced a site could be found as part of a deal between one of the many developers who were sniffing around Southwark Council.

So great was Sam's enthusiasm at the progress they had made – why, the damn thing was as good as built! – that unwilling to waste another moment, he decided to drive to Bristol and prophetically burned his clutch out *en route!*

The object of the trip was to see Southern's mini-portable version of the Swan playhouse, the model commissioned by the British Council for exhibiting abroad to mark the Shakespeare Quatercentenary in 1964. When he saw it, said Sam, "the years rolled back and I was that kid again in Cleveland. It clinched it for me". Sam's enthusiasm clinched it for Southern, too, and at the next London meeting he was part of the new "Gang of Four".

Be great in act, as you have been in thought
Philip, *King John*, Act V Sc. i

Out of that next meeting came the first 'manifesto'. "We decided", Wickham remembers, "that the site must be large enough to house:

a) The Globe (i.e., the first Globe: the one Shakespeare actually wrote for)
b) A library and small museum
c) An international hostel
d) A pub
e) An administrative office and rehearsal room
f) Adequate car parking and storage spaces"

These were the six components then thought to be the essential ingredients of the package to be offered to interested property developers; to Southwark Council for planning permission; and to potential sponsors (academic and industrial).

This was the brief Southern was to work on and it was the basis of Sam's conversations with the people he had undertaken to charm. It was 1970 by now and, looking back, Wickham now feels that even then the first fatal flaw in the whole scheme was built into it, though none of them recognised it.

The flaw was in the original casting. By profession Southern was a stage designer and an amateur theatre historian. He was not an architect and the brief, properly analysed, cried out for one. (As it happened, there was already a *deus in machina* in the cherubic shape of Theo Crosby, whom Sam had recently met for the first time and whose interest in the project was flickering to life. But he was not a member of the Gang and it was not yet time for his entrance.)

Once they began to work together, Sam and Southern rarely saw eye to eye. Quarrels dragged on for several months until finally Southern had had enough and walked out – fortunately leaving enough behind for Sam to cobble together a reasonable facsimile of his dream – certainly enough to convey what he had in mind to whoever came next.

In August 1971 – almost exactly two years after their first meeting – Wickham and Spencer (with Sam as their guest) attended the first International Shakespeare Conference in Vancouver. One of the main topics on the agenda was "Shakespearean Playhouses" and two of the keynote speakers – Richard Hosley and C. Walter Hodges – were later to become involved with the Bankside project.

Introduced by Wickham, Sam unveiled his – by now their – plans for the reconstructed Globe on Bankside. A conference stunned by the audacity of the plan could think up no adequate objection and gave it their unanimous approval. Sam hardly needed the plane home. Academia had legitimised the dream and now they could take on all comers. They were on their way.

It could be argued that the Conference missed the opportunity to detect the second flaw in the scheme which – if not fatal – was to bedevil it in years to come. The whole idea was just too *big!* Rebuild the Globe? Why not? Add a facility for educational purposes? Of course. And from there a perfectly logical sequence of thought that said, "Build it and they will come..." And if they're coming, why not make sure it becomes a major *tourist* attraction? But not *Disney* – definitely not Disney! Which means we're going to need ... It all made emotional sense and, since it had never been attempted before, who could really argue the logistics? In any case, how long is a piece of string?

> Thou wilt be as valiant as the wrathful dove
> or most magnanimous mouse.
>
> Falstaff, *Henry IV (Pt. 2)*, Act III Sc. ii

And here is as good a place as any to say something about Disneyland and lay that particular criticism to rest. The tag was an integral part and parcel of the 'That American...' syndrome. Sam did initially have grandiose plans for developing huge stretches of Bankside, but there is no indication in any of them that he intended to create the World According to Walt or 'Falstaffland' as *The Times* dubbed it. Quite the reverse. As an 'outsider' he was pathetically anxious not to give offence and well aware that his aggressive personality – which he was neither willing to nor able to change – was a hostage to fortune. He wished to be totally faithful to his adopted culture and felt genuinely aggrieved that the colour of his passport provoked this particular charge.

Later, he could point ruefully to the analogy of Stratford-on-Avon and its theatre built – then subsequently *re*-built – almost entirely with American money and its Anne Hathaway's Cottage with its tourist bric-a-brac. If Stratford hadn't been turned into a theme park back in the 1930's, what else would one call it? And what about the more recent Heritage Theatre, written up as "a £1 million family entertainment" which offered in its promotion to give the visitor the opportunity to "Travel back in time to the World of Shakespeare... You are a bystander and actually experience the excitement of bear-baiting – the horrors of the Plague cellar – the spectacle of royal fireworks..." *This* wasn't Disneyland...?

The problem was that Sam now saw the complex and saw it whole; nothing less would do. And now that he'd been given the nod from the group that had concerned him most – and so easily, too – there was no need to recast the Dream. Until the last few years of his life he persistently argued that it must be all or nothing. It was only when he was persuaded that, in that case, nothing was the only possible option that he conceded to the 'modular' argument. Build the Globe and they will come – which will make it possible to raise the money to complete the rest of the project in stages. But on the way back from Vancouver such a scenario was impossible for him to contemplate. The academic euphoria saw him through several more of the ups and downs that were to become commonplace – many of them self-generated by his tendency to fire then take aim.

> *He thinks too much: such men are dangerous.*
> Caesar, *Julius Caesar*, Act I Sc. ii

Richard Hosley was invited to replace the departed Southern. Now *he* would design the Globe. There was only one problem – Hosley wasn't an architect, either. Nor was he even a stage designer. He was a highly respected theatre historian with views on how an Elizabethan playhouse should be designed. More rows and exit Hosley.

Enter Hodges... and with him one of the major philosophical arguments that was to haunt the early years of the project. *Which* Globe? Why rebuild the *first* Globe about which so little was known? Why not the second which, presumably, had been built, after fire had destroyed the original, with all the knowledge accumulated during the period? Surely, the second Globe was the definitive Globe – the Globe Shakespeare and his colleagues would have built, had they known in 1599 what had been learned by 1614?

One very good reason would have been that – whatever else could be argued in its favour – by no stretch of the imagination could you call the second Globe – *Shakespeare's* Globe. By the time it was built, Shakespeare had written his last play (*The Tempest*) for the Blackfriars in 1610 and retired to Stratford. None of his plays was written for the rebuilt Globe.

Although his enthusiasm for the whole subject of Tudor drama kept him interested in the Globe, Hodges and Sam were never truly theatrical soul mates and he, too, soon left centre stage.

> And thus the native hue of resolution
> Is sicklied o'er with the pale cast of thought,
> And enterprises of great pith and moment
> With this regard their currents turn awry,
> And lose the name of action.
>
> Hamlet, *Hamlet*, Act III Sc. i

By now, the fun had gone out of the project for Wickham and Spencer. They were '1st Globe-ers'. Why was Sam even bothering to discuss the matter when he knew where they had always stood? But then, something was happening to Sam... "At this point in the project's history", Wickham recalls, "Sam's behaviour began to become so erratic, secretive and unpredictable as to propel Spencer and myself into believing that we were being marginalised into occasionally consultable, but ultimately expendable commodities within an egocentric and wholly expedient scheme of things".

The likelihood is that by this time Sam was beginning to feel he was in over his head. It's all very well to woo and win the academic community but what do you do when they talk about things you don't truly understand – and then start to disagree? What Wickham observed as personal lack of loyalty and intellectual consistency was Sam performing his regular party trick of trying to keep a number of balls in the air, while he decided what to do next. And since there was no site, no money and only talk was cheap – then let's keep talking and juggling.

Neither Wickham nor Spencer felt strongly enough to actually resign from the project, which could easily have collapsed without their names on it at that stage. In any case, time and events made their own decisions. Spencer – a sick man for some time – died of cancer and with the formation of the ISGC (International Shakespeare Globe Centre) Trust in 1982 the curtain fell on Act I.

For some time Sam had been petitioning the authorities to have the project recognised as a legitimate charity. This would enhance its status and help considerably with raising funds – particularly in the U.S. where donations would be tax deductible. That was the theory. He was finally successful. The result was that, as a licensed charity, a Trust must be set up and the Shakespeare's Globe Centre Trust with the ISGC as its commercial entity. To the Trustees passed all future decisions on matters like fund-raising and Sam's free-ranging 'executive' authority was circumscribed for the first time. Although this was inevitable, it was not inevitably pleasing to him and the situation was to be a burr to him for the rest of his life.

To ease the pressure – and because the Trustees couldn't be expected to deal with too many detailed matters – a Board was set up in parallel with Sam as its chairman. By this means he hoped to keep matters of policy separate and simply report the Board's 'decisions' to the Trustees on a need-to-know basis. It was an arrangement that was never entirely a comfortable one.

Less than enchanted with the way the project seemed to be drifting and being frequently committed overseas, Wickham increasingly delegated his academic duties to the Deputy Chairman he had appointed – Professor Andrew Gurr, who was already running the Academic Committee. By the time Act II was really under way, Wickham was mostly watching from the wings.

> At last, though long, our jarring notes agree:
> And time it is, when raging war is done,
> To smile at 'scapes and perils overblown.
>
> Lucentio, *The Taming of the Shrew*, Act V Sc. ii

Andrew Gurr – the next, almost involuntary keeper of the academic flame – first took centre stage in 1981, when he was invited to give the first plenary lecture at the 3rd World Shakespeare Congress, held that year in Stratford. It turned out to be an event at which the whole project was almost sandbagged.

Sam had been lulled into a sense of dangerous security by the easy ride they'd all enjoyed in Vancouver and by the way that the second Congress – held in 1976 in Washington – had endorsed Vancouver's verdict. Whatever other problems he had – and they were by now legion – the academics were safely on side. But he had, as the saying goes, seen nothing yet.

The Groves of Academe are every bit as political as the Corridors of Westminster or Washington. These congresses were and are run jointly by the Shakespeare Association of America and the International Shakespeare Association, based in Stratford. Thus, this 3rd Congress was on home turf and there were certain 'local' issues on the alternative agenda. Having had ten years to think over that impetuous day of decision in Canada and with the suspicion that this thing might now actually *happen*, there were those not a million miles away from Stratford who had decided that a rival Shakespearean venue not much more than a hundred miles south was perhaps not so devoutly to be wished.

Whatever the currents of personal motivation, at the Congress' business meeting, Chairman Kenneth Muir refused to accept the repeat motion, which had been expected to be approved 'on the nod'. As Gurr remembers: "Sam erupted from the floor and there was an undignified uproar, platform against floor, and pros and cons flying all over... In the event... no motion of support was passed and the refusal to give Sam's project support got a lot of media attention". A group of Russian delegates were clearly puzzled by the democratic procedures followed in the West!

Looking back on the episode, Shakespearean scholar, Franklin Hildy believes that an underlying reason for this apparent inconsistency had a lot to do with the members deciding to give Sam a slap on the academic wrist for his treatment of one of their own.

Walter Hodges, having become frustrated with the lack of progress on Sam's project, had succumbed to an offer from a group in Detroit, who were also talking of building a reconstructed Globe along the Detroit River as part of *their* project and were prepared to pay him for his consultative contribution. The local university (Wayne State) was interested, the City was enthusiastic to the point of donating a prime riverside site and funding for the $5-8 million project was well under way. Off went Hodges, taking with him his concept of a "Third Globe!" "Hold on!", cried Sam, "that's our concept!". The fact that he must have known perfectly well that such a common phrase was impossible to copyright didn't prevent the outburst.

The Detroit Globe was never built, though Hodges did contribute to a book on it. So, come to that, did Glynne Wickham, a fact which can have pleased Sam not at all. In the early 1980s a change in the hierarchy caused the university to revise its priorities and the project languished, until a group from North Carolina asked if they could take it over. Right now preliminary work is well advanced on a 72 acre site. Once again the advisor is – C. Walter Hodges.

> Keep up your bright swords, for the dew will rust them.
> Othello, *Othello*, Act I Sc. ii

Gurr himself had had to leave the Stratford meeting before the fracas but it was reported to him in gory detail. Like all the Globe loyalists, he was dismayed by the setback and feeling powerless to do anything about it. Then, some two months later, he received a visit from John Orrell, a Canadian academic and theatre historian who felt just as strongly. This was the first time the two men had met but they were to become as critical to the eventual building of the Globe as any part of its architecture.

Orrell's arrival was one fortunate result of the Detroit episode. A couple of years earlier in 1979 he'd been invited to present his findings on the Hollar panorama drawing to the conference at Wayne State University Hodges and Wickham had addressed. It was there he met the project's director, Sam Schoenbaum, who was sufficiently impressed by Orrell's scholarship to contact Sam. Sam, in turn, contacted Orrell and set up a meeting in London with Theo Crosby and himself. In August, Orrell turned up at Crosby's office, to find only Sam there. The chemistry worked immediately, though Orrell always found himself working with Sam 'at arm's length'. He found it the best way to keep intellectual and emotional perspective. With Theo, whom he met a few days later, things were different – "it became a real friendship". The two men worked closely together until a few days before Theo's death.

Prompted by Sam and Theo (by now the project's official architect), Orrell's mission was simple. Would Gurr join the newly-established ISGC and become a member of the Architectural Committee he was proposing to set up and chair? In the wake of the Stratford debacle, Gurr was just the man the project needed to marshall academic support. Like so many others before and after – and with just as vague a brief – Gurr found himself signing on for both Wickham and Orrell. Soon he became the visible focus of academic support for the project.

"In fact, it wasn't such a difficult job at first", Gurr recalls. "Many people who had been at the Stratford meeting had been upset and a bit baffled by it. Kenneth Muir, chairing it, was an old and long-respected figure, and they had been thrown by his refusal to accept the motion. In fact, it was backstairs politics – I got his signature as a supporter of Sam's project almost before anyone else's. All I did was prepare a letter inviting people to sign a statement that they supported the rebuilding idea, and of the two hundred Shakespeare scholars that I sent it to, only one refused. That was John Russell Brown, academic advisor to the National Theatre (since 1973), who had his own programme (sic) to run. All the others gave it warm support and a lot of them expressed their concern that the Stratford decision might have put Sam off". They clearly didn't know their Sam.

Soon after sending the letter, Gurr met Sam for the first time: "I wanted some assurances myself, after all. The theme park and Disneyland image was in my mind, too. We met at Pentagram (Theo Crosby's design company), first Sam and I for a long talk, then a gathering of about twenty people – including Theo, Michael Blakemore, Muriel Bradbrook, John Orrell – in which we went through all the basic arguments. I put the doubters' case, about the dangers of compromising the actual design – even then we had half an hour on whether to have a plastic roof – and I can still hear Sam's tone when he finally held up a finger and said – "No compromise!"... I've never had reason to doubt that in principle he did believe in getting it as faithful to the original as humanly possible. He was talking to academics and designers, architects and theatre historians when he said that... But whenever any question of compromise came up, he would always uphold that basic principle. That was why I never wavered in my support for him even ahead of his actual project".

A remark which puts things in a necessary context. In 1981 the project was in precisely the same position it had been in a decade earlier. It had support. It now had intellectual credibility. What it still didn't have was either a site to build a Globe on or the financial wherewithal to build it.

Once more, new servant, welcome
The Two Gentlemen of Verona, Act II Sc. iv

After more than ten years of travelling hopefully the thing that sustained whatever momentum the project possessed – other than the eternal flame that consumed Sam – was the regular changing of the guard. Not that the changes were the result of carefully-devised policy. Most of them came from the 'creative friction' caused by working with Sam in the first place and the subsequent explosion. Nonetheless – after the fashion of a relay race – it brought in a series of new runners, full of energy and bright with purpose. Andrew Gurr was one of them. Professor of English at Reading University and a specialist in Elizabethan theatre practice, he was ideally qualified to run what would surely be the short final lap.

Having sent out his 'support' letter, he immediately set up an Academic Committee to "keep an eye on the academic input, to start running the educational side of things and to collate advice to the architects about the actual design of the Globe".

While the reconstruction of the theatre was the idea that attracted the media headlines, the educational side of the project was considered by many people to be at least as important. The essence of the dream was that the crowds that would stream to the new Bankside would not simply be new Elizabethan theatregoers but also students from all over the world come to study the unique man who had written those plays. And it could be argued that in the darkest night of the 1970s that search for knowledge – despite the most meagre resources – was the element that had given the project both credibility and continuity.

Of course, education must be given a life of its own and Gurr saw to it that it was. He set up a series of activities to raise the visibility and argued the case for having someone in charge full time. In 1984 he recommended the hiring of a young academic, Patrick Spottiswoode, initially as Curator of the Museum and later to head up Globe Education – a role he still holds.

...by this face,
This seeming brow of justice, did he win
The hearts of all that he did angle for

Hotspur, *Henry IV (Pt.1)*

He also realised the absolute need to focus discussion and not be the victim of random sniper's shots from all parts of the known academic world. To a large degree he achieved this by organising a series of seminars – hosted by Theo and Pentagram – which he ran on the old Quaker principle of allowing people to argue until everyone agreed. Over the next decade it proved exhaustingly effective.

When the 4th World Shakespeare Congress came round in 1986, the setting was Berlin. Gurr was determined not to be blind sided now that he was in charge. He put the motion of support to the business meeting himself and breathed a sigh of relief when it was passed without opposition. Presumably any potential dissenters, having put their names to his earlier letter of support, lacked the gall to open the issue yet again. They could also calm any twinges of conscience with the thought that there was little point in further argument fifteen years after the original vote when the Globe seemed in truth no nearer to being built. Further discussion seemed, in every sense, 'academic'.

The fact that contrary views weren't aired in public on this most public of academic occasions by no means indicated complete unanimity of scholarly view. Throughout the marathon that pursuit of the Grail turned into, there would continue to be those who took the hard Left view that the whole project smacked of 'Shakespeare-worship' and was, therefore, anti-Marxist in principle. Typical of this was the Southwark charge of 'elitism'. It was further proof to such opponents, says Gurr of "the privileging of the sacred 'canon' of high culture, of which Shakespeare is the exemplar". He felt that there were even those academics who considered the whole thing "a capitalist conspiracy to make Shakespeare the model for young black Brits". Would they, one wonders, have preferred Othello to be *white*? Probably.

More generally, its critics considered the project to be either capitalist, American, un-American, un-English, impure, Disney-worldish and generally a Bad Thing. By their arguments shall ye know them. Today Gurr finds a nice irony in the fact that, with

Prime Minister John Major's personal backing Shakespeare has been reinstated as compulsory study material for all 14 year-olds in British schools, academic hostility has appreciably lessened!

With all the financial and legal problems the project was now facing, Sam's feeling was that the academic side of the equation, at least, was on an even keel. The Word was going forth, building up credibility for the day when... The academic ducks were in a tidy row. When the day came to build, we'd know *what* to build without doubt – wouldn't we?

Well, yes. And, then again, not necessarily. The ducks would have their feathers badly ruffled at what was literally the last stage...

I can tell you strange news that you yet dreamt not of.
Much Ado About Nothing, Act I Sc. ii

And then in early 1989 – while Gurr and Sam were on the West Coast, converting the occasional academic Californian heathen in Gurr's case or pocket picking the odd millionaire in Sam's – they received the news. Just next door to the Globe's offices under an ugly building being demolished to make way for an even bigger, uglier building – the builders found the remains of the Rose Theatre.

Act III was about to begin...

Andrew Gurr (left) and John Orrell, the two scholars who did most to determine the design of the Globe

CHAPTER SIX

THE THEATRE HISTORIAN'S TALE: PART ONE

(1980-1989)

> *Shakespeare's Globe was his hardware and the*
> *play-scripts... the software he wrote for that particular*
> *machine. It is difficult not to keep on making radical*
> *mistakes about what the software was designed to do*
> *until we have a clearer idea of the hardware it was*
> *designed to play on.*
>
> Andrew Gurr

NOTE: The design of the re-built Globe is as 'authentic' as the state of current academic knowledge can make it and current legislation will permit. A great deal of scholarly debate has gone into it, focused through a series of seminars organised by Andrew Gurr and over the period of the project – some twenty-five years.

The design eventually adopted, however, could only be considered a collective 'best guess'. The only direct 'evidence' available is a small corner of the foundation, some five per cent of the original Globe and the likelihood of further archaeological excavation in the foreseeable future is remote. A decision had to be made and the new Globe is the result of that decision.

What follows is a distillation of a great deal of discussion over many years, drawing heavily on the thinking of John Orrell, Andrew Gurr and Theo Crosby and the contribution of many other opinions – some of them contrary – which helped them shape their conclusions.

When those conclusions took physical shape, there were to be other arguments, which are detailed in Chapter 19.

❖

To rebuild or not to rebuild? Which *Globe* to rebuild? Always supposing there was ever the money to rebuild. Those were the questions that were debated for so long – cosily in the study or noisily in the committee room – with the comfort of knowing that nobody had to make a decision. Or, at least, not a decision that couldn't be reversed at the next meeting. As debates went, it was good rousing stuff and had been for the several hundred years since the Globe vanished.

Ten years into Sam's project, when academic coyness was wearing thin, two pieces of reality intruded that suddenly made things uncomfortably real.

First, there was an actual site that seemed beyond recall and enough money to start building on it. What do you want to put where? Admittedly, it wasn't much to look at – a hole in the ground, lined with a concrete diaphragm to keep out Old Father Thames, that on a bad day looked like a stagnant swimming pool. Second was that the discovery of the actual foundations of the Rose – and subsequently a tiny segment of the original Globe – now provided enough tantalising clues about the real thing to bring some of the higher flying theorists down to earth. Did their theories fit what few facts there now were?

From 1644, when the theatres were torn down by the Puritans, and 1989, when the twin discoveries were made, the would-be designer of a new Globe was as much a gambler as an historian. No plans of the original structure existed, no contemporary illustrations that could be considered hard evidence. Some of the sketches that did survive had been drawn second hand by people who had never even visited London. Even with the archaeological findings to date, the theatre historian was still in the business of deduction and interpretation, relying more on the probabilities suggested by previous documentary scholarship. And, like all scholarship, it depended on verifying, qualifying, and occasionally rejecting the tentative conclusions drawn by previous scholars.

There had been visions of the Globe in the past – plenty of them. There could hardly be a theatre historian worth the name who didn't carry in his head his own private image of the Wooden 'O'. Once it was given form in the shape of an actual model, the danger was that form became seductively persuasive. In the late 1960s and 70s the appeal became almost irresistible in the work of designers like Richard Southern (whose model had triggered Sam's passion), C. Walter Hodges and Richard Hosley.

A kingdom for a stage, princes to act
And monarchs to behold the swelling scene.

Prologue, *Henry V*

As the 70s ended the Globe team was joined by a man who was to prove to be one of its most influential members. John Orrell began corresponding informally with project architect, Theo Crosby in 1979 on his theories concerning the orientation of the Globe stage. In 1981, at Sam's invitation, he became the Honorary Architectural Consultant to the project. His views would be given due weight in the debates that would follow. Orrell was on the faculty of the University of Alberta in Canada as Professor of English. Distance alone made it a part time occupation but a full time commitment from that point on. He was also to work closely with Andrew Gurr and the continuity of their debate raised and resolved most of the subsequent issues where historical precedent was the guide.

❖

The problem of the Globe's design over the last three hundred years inevitably breaks down into several related elements – the first being size. How big was it? And was the Wooden 'O' really *round*?

One of the few pieces of 'evidence' seems to suggest that it should be 80ft in diameter. The Fortune playhouse, came a year after the Globe in 1600. Built and paid for by Alleyn, it was *de facto* part of the Henslowe empire, the new home for the Lord Admiral's men replacing the outdated Rose. Henslowe stipulated in its contract (which does remain) that it should be like the Globe. The Fortune was clearly 80ft. The only trouble was – it was *square*.

Claes Visscher's engraving of London 1616 showing the Bear Gardens
and the Globe. British Museum

Dimensions mattered a great deal. A larger playhouse would have a very different 'feel'. The relationship between stage and galleries would change; so would that of the audience and the players – not to mention the capacity. And some 3,000 spectators were housed in the original Globe. 80ft seemed awfully small. There wasn't much doubt about the height, however, The Fortune had been 33ft high, according to the specifications. Assuming that measurement, then the next piece of 'evidence' came into play. The second Globe was reported to have been erected on the ruined foundations of the original – a legal planning requirement – and to have had precisely the same shape and plan. And references of the second Globe *did* exist.

Wenceslaus Hollar in preparation for his *Long View of London* (1644) – had made a detailed drawing which included the second Globe. As with the models derived from it, though, seeing is not precisely believing. The Globe was 33ft high and Hollar had drawn it well over three times as wide as it was high, which made it something like 110 ft across – unlikely to say the least. At this point Orrell's scrutiny of the drawing convinced him that in most respects the detail was far too accurate to be the recollection of the unaided eye. It must have been done with the aid of a device called a topographical glass, a sort of drawing frame frequently used by Renaissance artists. The view was an exact linear perspective as seen from the top of the tower of St. Saviour's church (now Southwark Cathedral). Unlike other maps of early 17th century London, this was not interpretative but scientific. It could be analysed scientifically, including the distortions common to all linear perspectives. For instance, calculating the exaggeration to the width of 'round' objects distant from the centre – the 'anamorphosis' factor – gave the Globe a width of about 99 ft. Orrell wasn't about to die in the ditch for a foot either way – Hollar's drawing wasn't that accurate – but in his view the 80 ft and 110 ft. calculations were now certainly discredited.

When the fragment of the original Globe foundations was unearthed, his findings, though not conclusive, seemed to agree precisely with the conclusion based on Hollar.

By 1982, having determined the overall dimensions, the next question was: how was the design of the Globe arrived at? How did an Elizabethan master carpenter with the limited technology at his disposal put such a structure together? What was the art of the then possible? The concept of an 'architect' as we know it was not familiar to the Elizabethans. Street would have been a designer-cum-structural engineer-cum-quantity surveyor-cum-builder!

However persuasive the theories that had inspired previous reconstructions of contemporary playhouses, Orrell found it difficult to detect in them genuine insights into practical building methods. They seemed to assume on site construction, when in reality buildings of this kind were prefabricated in sections off site in the builder's workshop, dismantled and then taken to the site for re-assembly. The original Globe happened to be an exception that proved this rule, since it had not been constructed from scratch but reconstructed from the transported timbers of the old Shoreditch Theatre. Orrell firmly believed that the only way to gain a true insight into the Globe was to first understand the methods of the craftsman who had made such buildings. There was more to learn from men like Peter Street than any number of his fellow academics.

> Flavius: Speak, what trade art thou?
> Carpenter: Why, sir, a carpenter.
> Marullus: Where is thy leather apron, and thy rule?
>
> *Julius Caesar*, Act I Sc. i

One of the problems of dealing with earlier eras is to forget what we have learned since that period. But only by doing so can you hope to get inside the head of the original designer. The modern architect, for instance, instinctively thinks metrically and has the advantage of highly accurate measuring devices. Peter Street had none of these. Instead, he would have had his surveyor's 'line' calibrated in 'rods' – a rod measuring 16ft 6ins. The sections of a round building 99ft in diameter would have been exactly 49ft 6ins (or three rods). For Orrell, the internal evidence was piecing itself together.

Like his medieval predecessors, it's highly likely that Street, lacking sophisticated tools, would have a highly-developed sense of geometry. To this day there are still craftsmen who pride themselves on their ability to make precise calculations with nothing but a classic carpenter's square. It would be surprising if Street had not been in that tradition. The structure of the Globe would be in his *mind*. After all, this was the man who'd supervised the dismantling of the original Shoreditch Theatre and the re-assembling of its framing timbers into the new Globe. Why would he – indeed, how *could* he – have changed the basic design?

The Theatre was built in the traditional manner with marked timbers prepared off-site, transported there and fitted together in a frame. When he took it apart, Street undoubtedly would have ensured that the timbers were carefully arranged with the original carpenters' marks showing. Meanwhile, over on Bankside, new and identical foundations were dug ready to house the frame. Naturally, there were significant modifications to the detail of the interior, entailing *new* timbers, but essentially the Theatre begat *both* Globes.

As Orrell notes: "A large polygonal timber frame of galleries calls for some nicely calculated and very complex joints, as well as great exactness in the preparation of the timbers". Anyone disposed to think of the Globe as nothing more complex than an overgrown child's building set had this fact brought home when the first two bays of the new Globe were put in place in the Spring of 1992. The mismeasurement of a quarter of an inch took eight men, a large crane (which Street *certainly* didn't have!) and five hours to correct!

Everything points to an original Globe being a geometric construction in the mind of its builder. Orrell was convinced that he understood Street's psychology enough to predict that the most likely geometric model for him to adopt was the classic *ad quadratum* method, much favoured by medieval builders. Orrell describes how the 'sacred geometry' works:

> Medieval builders worked most of all from the geometry of circles, squares and triangles. Their commonest trick was that of *ad quadratum* design: one part of a building would be the length of a square whose diagonal provided the dimension of another, related part. As, for example, the length and the width of a room. A variation, useful for setting out round buildings (or for the woodwork at the roof level of a building like the Globe), was to make a circle equal to the whole diameter of the building. Inside it the carpenter drew a square, its corners touching the circle; inside that square he drew a smaller circle, whose perimeter just touched the sides of the square. Now the smaller circle was proportioned *ad quadratum* to the larger one (in fact its diameter was equal to the larger one, divided by 2) . It wasn't always necessary to work all this out in a drawing, because certain numerical series were well known as approximations of the proportions. 7:10, for example, or 17:24, or – the one used at the roof level of the Globe – 70:99. The diameter of the Globe was 99ft. Overall, while its top part, measured between the angles of the gallery fronts across the top storey, was 70ft. A perfectly traditional *ad quadratum* design.

This basic geometric methodology is at the heart of the design of many medieval buildings. It was decidedly likely, Orrell felt, to be the basis of this one. But there were other influences to be considered.

Orrell believed, along with many other scholars, that the Elizabethan playhouse was less an accidental evolution of the inn yard or bear baiting arena than a considered adaptation of the classical Roman amphitheatre. It owed its design to the architectural teachings of Pollio Vitruvius, a Roman writing in the time of the Emperor Augustus (400 BC), whose work had been rediscovered during the Renaissance. They argued that, although Henry VIII's attitude to Catholicism had largely isolated England from the cultural changes taking place in Europe, enough of the current thinking had crossed the channel, including the teachings of Vitruvius. One of the distinguishing design features of Vitruvian theory evident in what is known of the Swan, the Fortune and, almost certainly, the Globe is a stage that extends to the diameter of the house. The Inigo Jones drawings (which we'll come to later) followed the same formula. The measurements were too close for coincidence.

Orrell set about proving his case empirically. Hollar's drawing, as now determined, seemed to fit. The popularity of the *ad quadratum* theory at the time the original Theatre as built in 1576 made it extremely likely that Street had transported the design, lock, stock and timbers when the Theatre was turned into the 1st Globe in 1598-99. And since it was reported that the 2nd Globe was built on the foundations of the original... *ergo*, the 2nd Globe retained the original approach of the Theatre and was, therefore, *ad quadratum*.

Positive proof may never now emerge, due to the archaeological complications involved, but we have a very good best guess. As Orrell himself writes: "As yet we were a long way from understanding the full complexity of the Elizabethan design process, but we had succeeded in discovering some of its medieval methods: I had managed to introduce both the ad quadratum method and the rod as a fundamental unit of measurement to Elizabethan theatre studies, where they had been unknown. Through Theo Crosby's determined agency, both lie at the heart of the design now realised on Bankside".

> Look, as the fair and fiery-pointed sun,
> Rushing from forth a cloud, bereaves our sight;
> Even so, the curtain drawn, his eyes begun
> To wink, being blinded with a greater light
>
> The Rape of Lucrece

Then there was the question of *sunlight*. In the theatre of our minds we always see the stage bathed in sunlight. But the design being considered in 1981 – when Gurr and Orrell formed their decisive partnership – had the Globe facing 7.5 degrees east of north. The reasons were more pragmatic than academic. Given the shape of the site, it would provide more convenient back stage access and present the theatre's best face to the river view. The artist's impression of this projection showed the stage typically sunlit, an effect only feasible if the afternoon sun shone high in the north-east.

Now, back to the invaluable Hollar, who showed the stage roof to be in the south-west quarter of the structure. Yet, in reality, *south-west* was the quarter of the afternoon sun. In which case, the stage itself would have been *shaded* from the sun by the 3-storey tiring house and its roof.

Once again, Orrell found himself questioning assumptions based on modern theatre practice, all of it derived from the enclosed hall theatre in which we illuminate the stage and leave the audience in

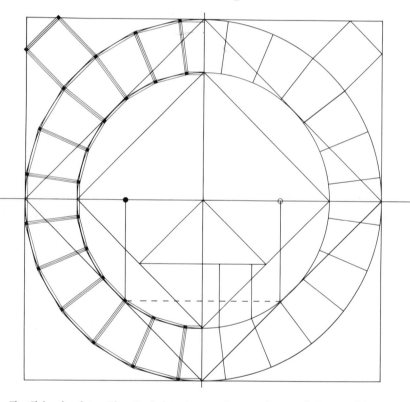

The Globe *ad quadratum*. Theo Crosby's setting out diagram, showing the layout of the stage with the circle of galleries, including the external stair turrets. *Pentagram*

darkness. Yet, logically the Elizabethan designers would have commonsense on their side, if they'd done precisely the opposite, leaving the actors to perform in a protected and consistent light.

From Hollar, Orrell deduced that "the Globe's central axis lay on a line 48 degrees east of true north". On the same drawing the Hope also appeared to follow that line. Searching for supporting Elizabethan precedent, he recalled the Boar's Head at Whitechapel, an inn-yard theatre, where the line of the final structure also matched within a couple of degrees. The only three known bearings an historian could call upon all put the stage in the shade.

(There was to be an unforeseen stumbling block. When the Rose was found in 1989, it became clear that both the original building of 1587 and its enlarged version of 1592 had located the stage in the *north*, thus exposing it to the afternoon sun. But then, the Rose was significantly smaller than either the Globe or the Hope. The height of its galleries shaded both the stage and most of the yard anyway, no matter how high the sun. Having considered the evidence of the Rose, Orrell believed he could safely set it aside.)

> ...my mistaking eyes,
> That have been so bedazzled with the sun.
>
> *The Taming of the Shrew*, Act IV Sc. v

By the beginning of 1982 he had managed to persuade Theo to turn the theatre around. Theo was strongly opposed to the idea on purely logistical grounds. Admittedly, everything was still on paper but where the stage went, so must follow all the services that fed it. It would mean, for instance, that the exits would now be through the museum. "The result", he wrote, "is disastrous!" It was a major task of redesigning and, before they undertook it, they decided to try an ingenious experiment in replication.

In June 1982 with the help of two friends – Martin Wilkinson of Bath University and Ian Liddell, a consulting engineer – they set up a model of the Globe on a draughtsman's table that could both tilt and rotate. On it they shone a theatrical spotlight to represent the parallel rays of the sun. By adjusting the table they could reproduce the Globe's relationship to the sun during that afternoon's performance at different times of the year with the calculations adjusted to the period and the location around 1600. There was no doubt about it. Even in mid-summer with the sun at its highest, the stage was always fully shaded, the actors always performing in even light.

There were several possible explanations for this orientation. To protect expensive costumes? To save the actors from unnecessary distractions? A squinting soliloquy would, of course, lose a certain dramatic impact. Whatever the reason, in the search for authenticity this new fact couldn't be ignored. In Theo's subsequent design the building was realigned in the original 48 degree axis. Which just happened – or did it? – to be the same orientation as Stonehenge...

> Methinks the truth should live from age to age.
> As 'twere retail'd to all posterity
>
> Prince Edward, *Richard III*, Act III Sc. i

At every stage of the project the clarion call was – *Authenticity*! But such a concept could only be relative. Even if a complete set of Peter Street's original plans had suddenly come to light, the authorities would never have let you build such a structure in today's London with its myriad safety regulations. Illuminated EXIT signs are the minimum requirement and there is a limit to how discreet they can be. The first Globe famously had 'two small dores', each three feet wide; the *third* Globe is required to have four six foot entrances. The authorities insisted that the structure must be capable of complete evacuation in 2½ minutes, so two staircases had to be added with slightly greater stair widths. Other decisions are more discretionary. For instance, if the Globe team should decide to do without artificial light and sound amplification, that was between them and the Bard. After long debate, they did so decide, though later, that decision was slightly modified to experiment with non-directional floods in the eaves to make evening performances possible.

If they decided to stick to the seating space typical of Elizabethan playhouses – some 18ins fore and aft – that was also their call. And that, indeed, raised a tricky issue in terms of what was and was not authentic. The playhouses had been built for the people, yet there was evidence that Shakespeare's contemporaries were a good deal smaller in physique than their late twentieth century equivalents – and town people had been particularly diminutive. Judging from the burial plots for Plague victims, the average Elizabethan stood just 5ft 5ins high. One *could* insist on retaining the original Elizabethan dimensions, but it was doubtful if many modern playgoers would pay to repeat the 18ins experience! (A seat at the National's Olivier Theatre, for example, is 35ins x 23ins) It was decided to increase it to what the architects call 'a pitch of 27ins of which 10½ ins actual seating". While this did nothing to affect the design dimensions of the galleries, it did have a significant effect on the overall seating capacity. The original Globe was thought to have held some 3,000 people in all; it would now hold about 1,500.

But the most controversial question was the roof. The firm decision had been made to build the replica of the 1st Globe (which was thatched) and not the 2nd (which was tiled). And yet no thatched building had been permitted in London since the Great Fire of 1666. What possible chance was there of being allowed to use thatch? Even Sam had reluctantly yielded on that issue. It would be the 1st Globe – but with tiles. A curious hybrid that definitely undermined the claim to authenticity.

At this point a strange coincidence came into play to solve the problem. In November 1989 a letter from the Thatching Advisory Service landed on Theo's desk, yet he had no recollection of writing to them. Apparently, a Mrs. Vivien Lawrence of Southwark had started the process. A Globe supporter, she'd been visiting the Ideal Home Exhibition in search of some thatch to decorate her mirrors. In her wanderings she'd come across the TAS booth and got into a conversation, which came around to the problems of thatching the Globe. With the recent developments in fireproofing technology, the Service thought it was a distinct possibility and wrote to tell Theo so. It was all he needed to take the matter up formally.

He'd had positive reactions from the local fire inspectors at an earlier stage to the question of the timbers. Both sides had agreed that sizeable timbers – such as the Globe's would be – were not the fire hazard many people thought, especially in a construction open to the sky. Smoke is the most lethal aspect of a fire and that could easily escape. Oak burns slowly and, as it does so, creates an insulating charcoal layer that slows the process even more. There would also be boards buried in the walls that could withstand 1,000°C heat for three hours.

But *thatch*? It had been the subject of London's first building regulation, which banned it as far back as 1212. Clearly, the rule was never enforced but it was hard to forget that it was the thatched roof that had been the undoing of the original Globe, not to mention housing the colonies of rats that helped spread the Plague!

Theo and his associate, Jon Greenfield, set up another experiment. He replaced the straw used by Peter Street with treated Norfolk reeds and set up a one inch 'high tech plastic barrier', made of Rockwool mineral fibre, between the reeds and the ceiling joists. The inspectors gave this new, improved 'thatch' the nod. Once again, 'authenticity' triumphed.

> By the discovery
> *We shall be shorten'd in our aim...*
> *Coriolanus*, Act I Sc. ii

Flashback to 1980, when a footnote resurfaced to become part of the main story.

It was general knowledge that Shakespeare in his creative prime had had *two* factories. When the summer season at the Globe had finished in September, the King's Men would take themselves off to the Blackfriars theatre for the winter. At least, they were able to do that after 1609 when they regained access to their enclosed theatre. The Burbage family owned the Blackfriars, a hall theatre built in the 'upper frater' of an old monastery since 1596 and constructed at great expense. Then the Lord Mayor had banned performances at City inns. When influential neighbours objected, the Burbages found their own playhouse out of bounds and most of their capital tied up in it. By then they had left the Shoreditch Theatre, where their lease had expired, and were playing at the nearby Curtain. It's safe to say that, had the Blackfriars been available, the Globe would never have been built.

Shakespeare's last, elegiac plays, then, were written not for the Globe but for that enclosed space of which we also have no records. Nonetheless, there must be some way to compare the physical playing properties of both kinds of structure. That, at least, was Sam's hope, if Shakespeare's London was to be properly presented. Though even he couldn't see a way to reproduce part of an old priory, its walls several feet thick, with any degree of credibility or authenticity.

Still, the idea, although not front of mind, wouldn't quite go away. There were too many coincidences involved. 1969 – the year Sam committed himself to his quest – was the very same year that Canadian academic, Professor Don Rowan of the University of New Brunswick, had made a significant discovery. He was later to refer to it as "a theatrical missing link".

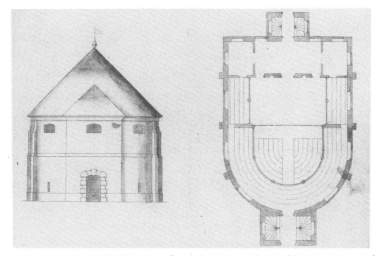

"The academic missing link". The plans of an indoor theatre designed by Inigo Jones and his pupil John Webb (c. 1616) but never built. The Inigo Jones theatre in the Globe complex will bring them to life for future generations. *Worcester College, Oxford University*

Rowan had made a study of the Cockpit-in-Court and during a working trip to London decided to check a few points that had been puzzling him by examining the original drawings in the library of Worcester College, Oxford. Having completed his task and with a couple of hours to fill until his train back to London, he started going through the college's collection of Inigo Jones's drawings – two sturdy volumes that had sat there for over three hundred years. There he found a complete set of plans for what he first took to be an anatomy theatre, before realising he had stumbled on something much more relevant to his own field.

He immediately had photographs taken and sent off copies to Glynne Wickham and Richard Hosley. Both men responded with alacrity, Hosley cabling back: "Ye Gods, man, you've done it – the most important piece of evidence since the Swan drawing! Glynne has written that he thinks the theatre is the Salisbury Court and John Orrell argues for the Phoenix or the Cockpit in Drury Lane. I think they are both wrong... and I believe they were for a theatre never built, but one which nevertheless closely reflected the private theatres of the time".

Jones had become an important theatrical figure from about 1605. A widely travelled student of classical architecture, which was enjoying a new vogue in Renaissance Europe, he began to adapt it to the enclosed theatre and with it to devise a totally different kind of entertainment from the fluid performances of the open public stage, such as the Globe. He was a firm believer in the precepts of

Vitruvius, who taught that the architect should be not merely a designer but also the conductor of the entire artistic orchestra. The entertainments or 'masques' Jones ("the Vitruvius Britannicus") designed depended more on theatrical effects of perspective, involving a great deal of scenery and taking place behind a proscenium arch. The masques were lavish and extremely popular with the patrons who willingly paid large sums of money to stage them in semi-private. One significant thing they did was to move the emphasis from the music of the spoken word to the ravishment of the eye. This created a good deal of artistic friction with the post-Shakespearean generation of writers like Ben Jonson, who saw a great verbal tradition mutating in front of them. It was another way of doing things.

The problem, as the writers and players saw it, was that Jones was not a man of the theatre, able to design structures to suit actors. He was a classical architect who was turning his hand to building theatrical temples as an expression of an aesthetic theory. Appointed Royal Surveyor to Queen Anne, he was commissioned in 1616 to do theatre work for her Court. In that year, too, a rival to the Blackfriars was built out of an old cockpit in Drury Lane.

From the time of Rowan's discovery of the Oxford drawings the debate continues as to the identity of the theatre he had discovered. What is generally agreed is that this is undoubtedly the most complete picture of a theatre of that period that anyone has seen.

Ten years later the Globe project has run aground. One of the new positive developments is the arrangement Sam has been able to make with the Inner London Education Authority (ILEA) and the Curtain Theatre company to bring their working 'model' theatre and re-erect it in his Bear Gardens premises. It's already called – the Cockpit and bears at least some resemblance to the Inigo Jones design. Now, if that wasn't an omen...

At around the same time – and quite coincidentally – John Orrell is discussing seating sizes for the Globe with Theo. To illustrate a point he produces an article arguing the case for the Jones design being the Cockpit in Drury Lane. Accompanying the article is a diagram linking auditorium to stage through an *ad quadratum* construction. Wouldn't it be wonderful (Orrell suggests) if they could include the Cockpit in the complex as an example of an enclosed theatre of the period, since a reconstruction of the Blackfriars was clearly out of the question?

Early in 1981 Theo produced a plan of the whole scheme, "and there was the Cockpit nestled into the corner, complete with my *ad quadratum* diagram, which he had adopted as the foundation of his grid system for the whole project!"

There was one academic/political hurdle still to negotiate. Glynne Wickham didn't believe the Jones drawings represented the Drury Lane Cockpit. He preferred to see the construction of the Cockpit-in-Court at Whitehall, using the drawings of another designer (John Webb, Jones' pupil). At the meeting of the Advisory Council in May 1982 the matter was put to the vote. Drury Lane and Jones were decisively preferred to Whitehall but out of deference to Wickham, it was eventually decided to adopt Orrell's tactful suggestion to call it – the Inigo Jones.

Adapting the drawings for their present purpose immediately raised practical problems. Jones's plan showed it to be an enclosed hall with a raised stage at one end and boxes on each side of it. The *frons scenae* had three entrances, the centre one being large enough for a grand entrance. With an external width of 40ft and a length of 55ft, this was significantly smaller than the Blackfriars. In some respects it would have been intimate to the point of being cramped – one more indication of the smaller stature of its intended audiences. The two smaller entrances, for instance, had a clearing height of only 5ft 6ins! It would seat about 700 people in that 18ins x 18ins comfort they had come to expect.

In 1988 Iain Mackintosh of Theatre Projects – the first person to go on record to suggest Jones's drawings were the basis for the refurbished Cockpit – found himself appointed by Sam as Honorary Adviser (with Orrell) for the Inigo Jones reconstruction and serious discussions began to take place.

The auditorium, as drawn by Jones, was just too small for modern use. To reconstruct it to the given dimensions would certainly result in a 'museum' theatre – a prospect totally alien to the concept of the whole project. Mackintosh, starting from the premise that the stage doors were too small, recommended enlarging the entire structure by up to 10% on all measurements. Orrell disagreed. That would only lose the intimacy Jones had intended. In any case, as Theo pointed out, current theatre regulations made it impractical. Once again, he found an elegant solution. Build the interior to the *original* specification – allowing, of course, for fewer but larger seats and cutting the seating capacity to 300 – then replace what had been the outer wall with a partition. Beyond the partition would be the main corridors and *then* the outer shell – 19% bigger than the original but built to the same proportions. While the outside would essentially be an invention, the interior would be reasonably authentic. It was a compromise but it would have to do.

A stage where every man must play a part
The Merchant of Venice, Act I Sc. i

The design of the Globe's interior posed its own set of problems. The size of the stage itself was deduced from that of the Fortune, which was 43ft wide and thrust to the middle of the yard. There was speculation that, since the Fortune was smaller overall, the Globe's stage might have been slightly wider but this approximate measurement has remained one of the few constants in the designs being debated.

The *height* of the stage was a different matter. Such contemporary drawings as still exist tend to suggest it was literally above the heads of the groundlings but then the performances depicted were frequently on temporary outdoor platforms. A permanent enclosed theatre would impose different constraints in terms of the platform's relationship with both the galleries and the tiring (or dressing) house. Put the stage balcony on the same level as the first floor galleries, for instance, and it would be 13ft above the yard. Give the stage a height of 6ft and you're only left with 7ft for the main storey on which the action must be played, the entrance doors located and so on. Not enough. Many an impressive entrance would have been spoiled as "Enter the actors – crouching!"

Although such a plan gave an aesthetic symmetry to the theatrical design – and there remains a strong body of opinion in favour of it – it was decided to bring the stage height down to 5ft, thus providing another foot of playing height. Such documentary evidence as existed could be used to justify anything from 18ins to 7ft but Orrell and Crosby were relieved to discover – shortly after incorporating the 5ft decision into their design – that the Red Lion, London's first public playhouse (1567) had a stage of precisely that height. And since the elder Burbage had been involved there, too, their calculations seemed to make sense.

Next, should the stage taper towards the front or be rectangular? The most influential of the previous reconstruction designs – John

Cranford Adams' 1942 version – had been tapered but the current version had never veered from the rectangular. The Swan had clearly been rectangular and the Fortune contract didn't specify. The design team was given pause when it was discovered that the stage of the Rose had been tapered in both of its incarnations but even that was not considered sufficient evidence to change the earlier decision. Tapering would create more audience space in that small auditorium but the Globe had room enough. Untapered, the Globe stage remained as Theo's designs progressed.

> And underneath that consecrated roof,
> Plight me the full assurance of your faith
>
> *Twelfth Night*, Act IV Sc. iii

The enigmatic drawing of the Swan by Aernout van Buchell from a sketch by Johannes de Witt which yields several different interpretations of Elizabethan stage layout and practice. (1596) *Bibliotheck der Rijksuniversiteit Netherlands*

The stage *roof* caused even more controversy. According to the evidence of the Fortune contract, the Swan drawing and Hollar's view of the 2nd Globe, an amphitheatre was equipped with a "Heavens" or roof over the stage. It was reasonable to suppose the lst Globe did, too.

By the early 1980's the working model – incorporating the latest thinking of experts like Southern, Hodges and Hosely – had the front of the tiring house (or *frons scenae*) forming a line across the bay of the polygon. At the top of the structure thus formed was a roof the width of the platform stage below but which didn't extend far enough forward to cover all of it. It also incorporated a 'hut' (in Orrell's view) "rather crazily perched between the main gallery frame and the stage roof". The hut was intended to house the descent machinery and other theatrical miscellanea, such as the trumpeter's station and flag pole. Its existence was mainly justified by its proponents as being visible in the ubiquitous Swan drawing.

The trouble with the drawing is that it is just that – a rough sketch and one quite capable of being interpreted in a variety of ways. Orrell and Wickham both read it quite differently as being an independent tower standing within the theatre yard, rising above the roof of the auditorium which 'leaned' against it. The top part of the tower was the "hut". It was known that the Red Lion had such a tower. The contracts for the Fortune and Hope also stipulated a separate structure.

But there was contrary 'evidence'. Hollar's view of the 2nd Globe – which had proved so accurate as to size – showed neither tower nor hut but, instead, an integrated stage roof that seemed to stretch much further forward, ending with a gable facing the audience. And while it could be argued that Hollar depicted a London scene forty years later than the heyday of the lst Globe, another detailed view – John Norden's 1600 panorama – showed a similar integrated view of both the Globe and the Rose.

In the spirit of this Elizabethan detective story Norden went on to plant a classic red herring by including with the same drawing an inset map which showed a *towered* Globe.

Orrell now went back over the known sources of the earlier theatres like the Red Lion (1567). Yes, many of them certainly had towers separate from the galleries. The Red Lion, in fact, had contracted the two buildings to separate carpenters. But wasn't it at least possible that this early practice had led Norden to accept this

Norden's Civitas Londini *Kungl Bibliotekt Sweden*

design as an icon for 'theatre'. If we were creating modern visual shorthand for purposes of public signage, wouldn't the simple image of a tower inside a cylinder stand for 'public theatre?' And wasn't it likely that by the time of the Globe construction – or even the Rose reconstruction (1592) the evolution of theatre design had reached the point of incorporating the integration that both Norden and Hollar seemed to suggest?

By the end of 1982, Orrell was convinced that this was the answer and produced a design which incorporated "a great gabled roof – even pedimented – like a temple – extending over the whole stage and with a secondary structure rising above it to house two descent machines and their loading platforms". But the 'official' design currently on the table – though now correct in size and orientation – still retained the separate "hut" structure. It was only when Theo Crosby, intrigued by Orrell's arguments, worked out a new version, based on what became known as the "Norden stage roof", that the question was reopened for discussion.

Both versions were presented to Gurr's 1986 Pentagram Seminar. The traditional Swan version was enthusiastically supported by Hosley and others. Debate raged around the comparative 'evidence' of Norden, Hollar and the Swan drawings and what they seemed to depict. In the end – as had been inevitable with so many decisions involving the design – it was the balance of probability that prevailed. Norden's pre-figuring of Hollar's view some forty years in advance finally carried the argument. The integrated 'Norden roof' was adopted as the 'authorised' version and, although much modified, became part of all subsequent versions.

The debates were by no means over but the main design points were being decided one by one. Which was just as well, because in April 1988 work began on the 6ft concrete diaphragm wall that would be sunk 40 feet below ground level to hold the whole Globe complex and keep the hungry Thames out. This, at least, didn't need support from Messrs. Norden, Visscher or Hollar. Even the Swan drawing, for once, could be left to one side. Authentic it wasn't but, in every sense, here was (as Orrell says) "concrete evidence that the project was under way".

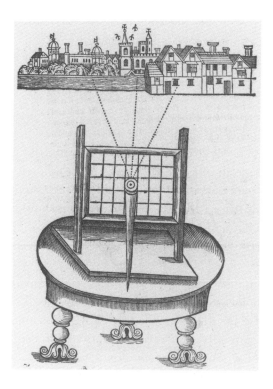

Topographical Glass from John Bates – The Mysteryes of
Nature and Art 1634

CHAPTER SEVEN

THE WILDERNESS YEARS
(1974 – 1981)

*...tragical-comical-historical-pastoral, scene individable, or
poem unlimited...*

Polonius, *Hamlet*, Act II Sc. ii

A près la déluge of 1973, with its rain-swept Cleopatra, superstition
surely suggested that the Gods were, if not angry then certainly
not best pleased. But then, in Sam, the Gods weren't dealing with
someone who paid heed to acts of Gods.

What did give him – and the project – pause was the state of the
exchequer. Cancelling the last week of *Antony and Cleopatra* had not
only involved the return of £6,500 in box office advance receipts –
the show had been a sellout – but paying the cast on their contracts.
(The disputes that had preceded the season did nothing to make the
actors more amenable.) When all the bills were in, it became
apparent that estimates had been of the fingers crossed, best
guesstimate variety. The cinema festival, the museum exhibition, the
summer school all lost money. The accumulated debt was just under
£50,000 and no amount of creative accounting could change that.

The Trust was bust. At the end of 1973 it was formally dissolved;
thus negating the rest of the debt. It was resolved that the work of
the Trust – particularly the educational programme – would be
continued to the best of its ability by the World Centre for
Shakespeare Studies. The rest of the 1974 Chairman's Report that
accompanied the year's accounts made sad reading:

> Mr. Wanamaker and certain members of the Council are convinced
> that if liquidation can be avoided, the main objective of the Trust – to
> build a Globe theatre on Bankside – would ultimately be achieved.
> Once present problems are resolved, it is planned that a Building Trust

be formed whose principal task will be to launch an international appeal for the necessary funds to build a theatre.

The use of the phrase 'certain members' was telling. It wasn't the first, and it certainly wouldn't be the last time on the odyssey, that some of the crew would choose to jump ship. Many of them argued that the last two seasons had been impossibly ambitious. There was talk of running before walking. It was 'Liverpool all over again' for the more critical. There was some truth in the criticism. The history of the project was to be conditioned throughout by the sheer size of Sam's 'vision' and by the unpredictable way he was inclined to embellish it. But then, who wants to follow small dreams?

Cabin'd, cribb'd and confined as he now was, defeat was never a consideration. He issued a statement:

"In the light of the present economic circumstances, however, the original timetable envisioned for the completion of the theatre has been set back to the end of the decade".

To which the sceptics asked – "*Which* decade?"

> ...the quick comedians
> Extemporally will stage us...
> *Antony and Cleopatra*, Act V Sc. ii

There was a lighter side, fortunately.

While Sam was in no position to stage a full 1974 'season', the idea was now so well implanted in the local Southwark culture that a series of events was still planned to celebrate The Birthday, one of which was a commemorative service to open the week in Southwark Cathedral. The oration *In Honour of Shakespeare* was delivered by Alf Garnett, the well-known East End working class TV character of somewhat extreme views created by writer, Johnny Speight and personified by actor, Warren Mitchell. Since his immediate predecessor in that particular 'spot' had been playwright, Christopher Fry, the contrast was marked and – until the ice was broken, in fact, shattered – distinctly shocking to an audience that had come in thinking itself a congregation.

Dressed in his Sunday best suit and clutching an umbrella (just in case of Acts of God), Alf found nothing sacred in this particular 'House'. He managed – as Hamlet would have it – to "cleave the general air with horrid speech". Leaning over the pulpit and gazing around the cathedral he let us know in no uncertain terms that ...

> Old Shakespeare would turn in his grave if he knew what they was doing with his theatre. Hot bed of Communism, innit? I mean, it's got to be... *(staring pointedly around the cathedral)* ...same as this place.

> Billy Waggle Dagger, as he was known in his native Wapping, and that is where he lived until he retired to Stratford-atte-Bow. He spent his summers down at Southend, where he wrote *The Tempest* on the pier. He used to sit there for hours with his fishing rod and his notebook, his feet dangling in the water. That's also where he wrote, *There'll Always Be an England*.

> In the old days, the Globe Theatre was more like a Palace of Varieties. As you went in they gave you rotten fruit to throw at the actors, sort of audience participation, which they enjoyed. That's why Shakespeare give 'em long speeches to do, so you could get yer eye in with yer fruit, have a few practice shots...

A number of clerics and scholars were seen to leave with distinctly bemused expressions.

> *Come on; thou art granted space.*
> *All's Well That Ends Well,* Act IV Sc. i

In early 1975 the Globe was approached by one Michael Cleary whose company, Sumaspace (pronounced Summer Space) offered to provide a permanent 'temporary' theatre on the site, seating and all, for a cost of under £20,000. Considering that a little further down the river the new National Theatre had already run up a bill of £12.5 million and still wasn't finished, the proposal certainly commanded a degree of attention. The structure was not to be of bricks and mortar but, said the proposal, "to be in tubular steel, high tensile strand, fireproof UPVC" and come with a certificate from the Department of the Environment. After the floods of 1973 – with the bills still bobbing to the surface more than a year later – this must have looked to Sam like the Ark, if not the Grail. And if the thing were *fireproof*, too...

Cleary's original design was an oval-shaped structure consisting of a skeleton made of hollow reinforced concrete beams, struts and columns, fixed to a central frame. These would form the basis for the sides and the roof. High tensile wire would then be threaded through the roof struts, so that the covering could be fixed to them. This do-it-yourself theatre – so the theory went – would last the two or three years it would take to get the real thing up and running. After which it would have a resale value and could easily be relocated.

After the events of recent years, even the establishment found it hard to be hard-hearted. The Greater London Council broke records in granting planning permission. Even the Arts Council dug into its pockets for a grant of £3,500 towards the project. The 1975 Summer Season would go on after all.

The deal was signed but, unfortunately, not read as carefully as it might have been. In the event, the Globe found itself paying for a number of building costs that everyone had 'assumed' were part of the Sumaspace commitment. The meter was ticking even before the show went on.

> As flies to wanton boys, are we to the gods;
> They kill us for their sport.
>
> *King Lear*, Act IV Sc. i

The comedy of the opening night takes on an air of farce when recounted in the typically understated English fashion of the Site Manager's subsequent notes to his colleagues.

"The Monday of the opening saw us in reality very little prepared for the evening's performance...", he says before cataloguing the disasters their understaffed little team face with not only the performance but the visit of the GLC inspectors imminent. With this in mind their first priority is to give the site 'a business-like atmosphere'.

"This in itself was somewhat complicated because rubbish was still being created... and there was nowhere for the waste material to go". At the eleventh hour – or 5:00 p.m., to be precise, when the Council finally removed the rubbish, there were the trees planted ("supplied by the Council") and the gravel ("which Mr. Cleary had arranged") to be spread. "Again, it must be stated that there was no help available of a contractual nature and there is little doubt that the sight of Miss Southam (the Globe Administrator) shovelling gravel in a temperature of 90°F was an encouragement to those less dedicated".

The intense heat had already prevented work being completed in the theatre itself until two fans could be borrowed from the National Theatre. "Just in case we were becoming complacent", continues the writer – in what is fast becoming an Alan Bennett parody of the curate reporting to his flock in the parish magazine – "there was a major breakdown in the switchboard... At this point a word of praise must be given to John Leventall, who was responsible for lighting the (opening) production, for his immense patience as various quantities of electricity to his lanterns went up, down or disappeared altogether over these successive days".

Enter the Government Inspectors... Exit the Inspectors, leaving behind two tight pages of notes of things to be done before the permit can be issued and the curtain can go up. The most daunting of which was a demand that the dressing room facilities be upgraded with particular reference to the toilets. In the event, the cast of the OUDS (Oxford University Dramatic Society) opening production of *Pericles* had to improvise, finally dressing in the nearby temporary cinema. Ironically, *The Guardian* had said (of a generally well-reviewed original production) that *Pericles* was "a great theatrical discovery of our time and the OUDS certainly do justice to its most moving moments". Little did they realise that on Bankside 'moving' would take on a whole new meaning.

"The performance on Monday evening went extremely well", reports our theatrical Candide, before noting that, "It is particularly fitting that, despite the efforts of the Oxford Company, the only good notices received from the Press in this week were those accredited to the theatre itself".

The following week saw the production of the Charles Marowitz *Hamlet.* "Whilst retaining much of the original workshop framework", the advance programme promised "this new production will also feature trampolines, which promises to add a new dimension to an already exciting piece of theatre". By this time the production had played in some twenty-five countries. None prepared it for its Bankside debut. It received a rather better critical reception than *Pericles*, although *The Daily Telegraph* found "the verse... fragmented and kaleidoscopically put together, often in the mouths of other characters, to make much nonsense". Although critic Harold Atkins, did come round to the conclusion that "...as a way of 'guying' the play the evening had its moments. Very near the scene of these goings-on Shakespeare guyed a few people in his time!"

Twenty years on it's impossible to disentangle who did what and to whom but Our Correspondent (the Site Manager) had his own conspiracy theory about the chain of events that led to the actors being reduced to access to "one WC and one wash-hand basin only... They are in considerably cramped conditions and they have to go completely round the site in order to obtain the stage entrance, making them visible to (the) audience leaving the theatre! It has been suggested by several reliable sources that this is, in fact, a political move directed against the Globe Theatre by the left wing of Equity..."

Whatever the militants may or may not have been up to, there was no doubt who was to blame for what happened on the day of the performance. God was doing one of His Acts. Having exercised His right to put a damper on the last two public seasons in 1972 and 1973, He went for the hat trick. "Torrential rain... left a four inch deep river round the exterior back of the theatre and created a virtual pool of water in the theatre itself, on the seats, in the aisles and on the stage". In the writer's view, the Almighty may have had a little help – specifically from "the painters on the roof, who seemed to have damaged some of the ceiling tape".

But the spirit that defied the Blitz wells up once more. "Nevertheless, with considerable work on everybody's behalf – including Miss Southam, who spent several hours baling out water, the desired effect was attained... in the cool evening sunshine and peopled with the first night audience, it once again became a live theatre".

The notices were kind and, once again, Britons proved there was nothing like a good bit of adversity to bring out the best in them ...

> ...do not put me to't,
> For I am nothing if not critical
>
> Iago, *Othello*, Act II Sc. i

The opening night slapstick aside, there was little that was genuinely amusing about the 1975 season. The theatre itself appeared to be a costly mistake, beginning with its unexpected and unbudgeted construction costs.

The third production – *This Wooden 'O'* – was intended to be a celebration in words and music of Shakespeare's historically famous Globe theatre... "a perceptive and amusing insight into the more unusual productions of his plays that have taken place through the centuries". Unfortunately, critics and audiences alike perceived it to be neither amusing nor illuminating. The multiplicity of slides, providing the background illustration and supposedly giving point to many of the lines, turned out to be so ill-lit that important details were often indecipherable.

The Times reviewer (Charles Lewsen) was particularly scathing, deploring "the heavy-handed vulgarity of Ron Moody, the genteel sonority of Marius Goring" and rebuking director, Douglas Cleverdon, "who lets them meander about the platform as though it was Crewe station on a go-slow".

Like so many of the under-funded, under-rehearsed productions that found their way to one or other of the Globe's temporary stages during these hand-to-mouth early years, *This Wooden 'O'* presented a supine target for critics. And to be fair, there was no programme note requesting: "Critics Be Kind: This Production is For a Good Cause!"

In many ways the most interesting aspect of Lewsen's review was the analysis of how he – and presumably he was not alone in his view – saw Sam at this point in the story:

> What an unruly, disparate lot these Wanamakers are; I mean the Sams.

He went on to enumerate them. Sam the Director, introducing post-war Britain to contemporary American drama with his "beautifully modulated productions" in which (Lewsen felt) Sam the actor – for all his 'musicality' and 'pantherine grace' – had looked strangely out of place. However, he clearly preferred either of them to Sam the Entrepreneur, who seemed to aspire to being a cross between impresario Bernard Delfont and the Chairman of the GLC. These 'posh' ambitions, Lewsen concluded, were in serious danger of sidelining the legitimate Sams' legitimate talents.

Lewsen wasn't the only one who was irritated by Sam at this time for hopping from one pigeon hole to another in his search for the ideal place to perch. In the 70's he was, indeed, Sam-of-all-trades as he sought to master the one thing he wanted above all others and which, mirage-like, seemed to move ever further from his grasp. The story of his search for the Grail that was the Globe was becoming more fantastical than any of the plays he tried to stage on that apparently benighted site.

What should have proved a financially successful season ended with a deficit of some £6,000.

> *Too little payment for so great a debt.*
> *The Taming of the Shrew*, Act V. Sc. ii

Nor was the Sumaspace Caper quite over when it was over. The original idea had been that the theatre, once erected, was to belong to the Globe and be worth in the order of £24,000. Erecting it was the responsibility of the Trust but costs were now much higher than anticipated. The 1975 balance sheet was in the red before the season was even under way.

Sumaspace, which was responsible for the structure itself, soon had creditors, some of whom came knocking on the Globe's door for payment. To make sure that the show went on, the theatre must go up and, in any case, it would all even out later. It wasn't long before Sumaspace owed the World Centre for Shakespeare Studies – the legal operating company now running the Trust's affairs – several thousand pounds.

After the season and the Second Deluge is over, Sumaspace hands over the structure, according to contract. By this time the £24,000 asset has turned into an unlimited liability. The storm damage has left the Globe with a mass of useless metal, quite impossible to sell or rent. The final indignity arrives when it's discovered that it will cost more to dismantle the structure than it will fetch for scrap.

> We see which way the stream of time doth run
> And are enforc'd from our most quiet sphere
> By the rough torrent of occasion
>
> Archbishop, *Henry IV (Pt. 2)*, Act IV Sc. i

There were other straws in the wind – all of them blowing one way and mostly matters that could be set aside in the short term when there were more immediate crises to be dealt with.

In any case there was a gale force wind blowing around the world called Recession that didn't award a high priority to the concerns of a few people trying to put up a wooden theatre on a neglected London riverfront. The Middle East oil crisis was now being felt in every aspect of daily life. What has seemed so far away began to come home as we learned, rapidly and painfully, the lesson of how inextricably the by-products of oil were woven into the way we chose to live. Anyone still cherishing a left-over 60's frame of mind was living in a bygone era.

...'tis true that we are in great danger;
The greater therefore should our courage be.

Henry V, Act IV, Sc. i

There were other rumblings near to home. Relations with Southwark Council had been reasonably cordial in recent years. Joint ventures had been undertaken during the soggy summer seasons and Sam was reasonably relaxed – for him. He felt that, although he still didn't have a site (let alone the money) on which to build, Southwark were committed to the extent that any development that did take place on it would only be approved if it included a rebuilt Globe. Thus, he could afford to file letters like the one he received early in 1974 from Mrs. Theresa Lewis, Secretary to the North Southwark Community Development Group.

Formed in 1972 with an urban-aid grant, the NSCDG had by now given itself the mission "to secure redevelopment which will primarily benefit, through low cost housing, industrial jobs, open space, shopping facilities, the traditional working class community of North Southwark, and working people in other parts of Southwark".

Sam was one of the first to approach the Group and apply for membership on behalf of the Globe Project. He was summarily rejected and it was made clear that the Group was opposing not only him but every other redevelopment project in their catchment area. As far as the Globe was concerned, they felt he and it were 'irrelevant'. Housing and industry clearly came before "fripperies like a Shakespearean revival centre" – particular when other perfectly good theatres like the Old Vic, The Mermaid and the soon-to-be-opened National Theatre were just a few steps down river.

In her letter, Mrs. Lewis returned the shreds of Sam's latest olive branch and enclosed the "Aims and Objectives" of the Group – as if he needed reminding – commenting that:

"At our last Group meeting it was felt that these Aims and Objectives are at variance with those of you and your organisation. I hope you will respect this decision and trust that you will wish to maintain a dialogue between North Southwark Community Development Group and your organisation".

Men of all sorts take a pride to gird at me

Falstaff, *Henry IV (Pt. 2),* Act I Sc. ii

It's highly likely at this stage that Sam didn't totally comprehend this typical piece of English circumlocution, which said only part of what it meant. (Later he would learn to read endless subtleties in the most innocuous communication.) But now... what 'decision' was she talking about? Southwark Council were the principals; he'd persuaded *them* – so where was the problem? And even when Theo Crosby wrote to him several months later to tell him that he'd been warned by one of their key supporters on the Council that "the Group are very much against us and have nobbled Councilors", he was too concerned with the problems of temporary theatres and tensile steel to let it worry him unduly. In any case, he had a deal.

He did lose his temper, however, when at the next meeting of the Southwark Planning Committee, and the Globe project came up for approval, the meeting was disrupted by jeers and heckling from the public gallery, which the Group had taken care to pack with their supporters. It was the beginning of a militant move to take over control of Southwark Council altogether. The Globe was simply a visible target and Sam could be counted on to supply the short fuse that led to helpful media headlines.

Being a man of the people, he was probably more worried by the kind of letter he received on the eve of the 1975 season from a Mr. Stevenson, a local ironmonger. It was addressed to The Globe Theatre:

Dear Sirs,

Before writing to local traders asking for money for another theatre project connected with Sam Wannamarker I would suggest that the £6,500 should be used to pay off some of the debts incurred by the late Globe Theatre Trust.

I do not think you will find much sympathy among us for your present cause.

The Stevensons of Southwark, after all, were the very people he was doing the whole thing *for* – for heaven's sake! And after all this time they could still spell his *name* wrongly!

Studying the incidents of Sam's life – and the odyssey of the Globe project, which became one and the same thing – one is struck by the *cinematic* quality of it all. I don't know if he himself ever saw it this way but it's hard not to view it as a screenplay with annotations for the film editor who would eventually have to put it all together.

Sam walks on to Globe site. Cut to his eyes. Dissolve to boy actor in Cleveland declaiming lines.

Sam on London stage... a front of house poster advertises *The Rainmaker* ...Rain teeming down on canvas roof which bulges ominously... an anxious Vanessa Redgrave eyeing roof and Antony simultaneously.

A 'Cancelled' notice over the prospectus for the 1976 Summer School – an event that had become a standby in the Globe calendar and through which several thousand students from all around the world had already passed. Those who had already paid their membership fees had the money refunded, since – realistically – there were no longer any benefits to be offered to members.

A 1977 letter, the New Year's gift from the GLC withholding their expected £37,500 because of further Government cutbacks. Now the World Centre for Shakespeare Studies must also cease to trade officially, although Sam refuses to give up the ghost entirely and insists on holding a ritual AGM at the Waldorf, after which the three surviving directors – Sam, Roger Sharrock of King's College and Diana Devlin – sit down to tea. Sam declares that he will continue to pursue the aims of the WCSS in his "personal capacity". And then there was one...

> *...and vast confusion waits, –*
> *As doth a raven on a sick-fall'n beast*
> King John, Act IV Sc. iii

Bulldozers at 40 Bankside as the new owners, Freshwater, demolish the remaining building, leaving the site derelict.

Now Southwark adds their twopennyworth of gloom and doom to the 1977 forecast. The museum is to close at the end of the current exhibition through lack of funds and The Birthday is cancelled.

In his 'personal capacity' Sam sends out a flood of letters to a variety of distinguished academics, inviting them to come and lecture at a Sunday lecture school he's thinking of starting. Reaction is positively lukewarm. 1977 veers more towards the worst than the best of times.

There was at least a diversion of sorts to occupy the rest of the decade. Although the WCSS no longer existed and the worldwide appeal for funds lacked a credible base, Bear Gardens was still intact and surely something could be done there to keep the dream alive and fly a small, if tattered, flag?

The Cockpit playhouse that caused much consternation when it was re-erected in the Bear Gardens Museum. It wouldn't fit until it was turned 90 degrees around.

In 1978 Sam persuades Freshwater to let him use their property, 58 Park Street – which backed on to the Bear Gardens Museum – as storage space and an extension to the museum. Freshwater agrees and the necessary paperwork is drawn up. For whatever reason, Freshwater never actually gets around to signing the agreement but Sam – determined to make something go his way – moves in anyway.

At about the same time Sam is introduced to a representative of the Cockpit, a theatre in Marylebone which claims to have been built as a ⅝ths replica of the original Drury Lane Cockpit, designed by Inigo Jones. If he couldn't wave a wand and have the Globe here and now, Sam reasoned, wouldn't it be at least the next best thing to have an 'Elizabethan-type' theatre inside the space he *could* call his own? He found there were enough like minds to make it happen.

Some of those like minds belonged to a theatre group called The Curtain – an educational resource used by the ILEA (the Inner London Educational Authority). They were happy to join forces with senior Globe members like Diana Devlin and a core group from the Rose Bruford Drama School in Kent to form an organisation – The Bear Gardens Museum and Arts Centre (BGM&AC) – with the specific purpose of installing the Cockpit Theatre into the Museum. The theory was that everyone would benefit from the arrangement. The Curtain players would have a home. The ILEA would have a place to stage educational performances and workshops. And Sam could point to a permanent theatre (of sorts) and a legitimate educational resource when he had to deal – as he inevitably would – with the Southwark authorities.

The exercise started with a nice piece of symbolism as the structure was dismantled and transported over the river – a modern echo of the Theatre being transformed into the Globe. But here the parallel ended.

The fit was not immediate and never perfect. There was an omen in the sheer physical problem of installing the theatre into the space on the first floor of the Park St. warehouse. It wouldn't fit – and several meetings were called to debate the problem before lateral thinking, as so often, saved the day. Someone suggested turning the thing around 90 degrees and after that the problem disappeared.

On the 1980 Birthday the Cockpit in Bear Gardens was officially opened.

It was a working educational exhibit – a combination of all the elements Sam held most dear. The ILEA had helped to create a charming exhibition of theatre models complete with information about the Elizabethan theatre. With their vast experience they were able to set up workshops for children and bring much needed professionalism to the project's presentation. And, indeed, there was a great deal of common interest to be served. Everyone pitched in. The Rose Bruford School provided the labour. The ILEA provided a couple of people by a complex system of secondment and made a modest financial contribution. What was never made entirely clear to all parties was the precise purpose of the BGM&AC. The ILEA staff saw their role as being that of educators bringing children to an appreciation of the theatre. Sam – now that the guests were in his house – saw them as *de facto* caretakers for his Museum. It was only a matter of time before the opposite points of view came into collision.

In mid-1982 the ILEA's Senior Inspector of Drama felt it was time to point out a few facts of bureaucratic life. One incident illustrates the broader canvas:

> I think it would be fair to say that College of Education lecturers have
> become accustomed to conditions of service that remove them from the
> need to undertake any menial tasks and concentrate on their academic
> pursuits. I trust you gather from my tortuous style that a direct
> instruction to remove a rubbish bin heaped with trash which has been
> used as a door stopper is not likely to receive unqualified agreement. In

local authorities we cannot be in the hire and fire business and the velvet glove business.

But though Sam knew the meaning of the individual words in the letter, it's doubtful if he ever fully appreciated the true meaning behind the tone of such a velvet glove letter. In the Chicago ghetto, who knew from velvet gloves? It was one more example of the Brits being obstructionist. In any case, he saw it from quite a different viewpoint. In his reply to the Inspector, he bemoans the condition the Museum has fallen into:

...dirty floors, rubbish at the front entrance, undusted cases, empty costume cases (for months), unused cases and equipment stored in a heap in an exposed corner, unreplaced burnt out light bulbs, exhibits (models) permitted to deteriorate without attempts to repair them, on the Cockpit staircase walls posters half falling down, and no fresh ideas, no work to improve the display of what we have, no attempts to acquire other materials or create them, etc. My litany is long and goes back a long way...

He goes on to restate the Mission ...

I realize all our problems of money and staffing shortages in these hard times for the arts and education but this enterprise has, as you know, survived against all odds and against the cynicism and hostility of many. But always knowing that what we were doing was to demonstrate the value of the total project which could lead to winning over the sceptics and doubters and foot-draggers. The 'image' had to be positive, poor but with pride in our poverty, like an impoverished housewife who will polish and shine the little she has and take pride in her home. It is that lack of pride in the place that seems to disturb me most. Or lack of awareness of its importance.

Unfortunately, things didn't improve because essentially the different groups were working to different agendas. A year or so later Sam is writing to Rosemary Linnell, the Chairman of BGM&AC, taking her to task for a series of housekeeping matters. Visiting the building over one particular weekend – as was his wont – during which auditions had been held... "I wish to report that all lighting in every part of the building was fully on all day for both days..." But the true horror is reserved for later.

I also discovered that there was no toilet paper or hand towels in the men's toilet and that a seat is broken in one of the cubicles".

It was the toilet seat that broke the camel's back, coming as it did after a whole series of disagreements. By the end of 1983, the BGM&AC was wound up in reasonably amicable fashion and the parties went their various ways. What Sam may not have adequately considered was that when the ILEA packed their bags those bags contained many of the exhibits – shabby or no – which currently adorned the Museum and had been brought in courtesy of the Curtain. With them went the "curators", leaving the place looking even more desolate.

Sam was back to a sad, damp, cold and barren set of rooms, a few forlorn models and a huge stuffed bear which he'd borrowed from the National Theatre after the production of David Mamet's *American Buffalo* had left it homeless. Now even the bear looked lost ...

Without making a formal announcement to that effect, the Museum was effectively closed down, except when the occasional party of Americans should turn up. Just in case they might happen to have deep pockets and good intentions, there would be a desperate phone call to the indefatigable Diana Devlin – "For God's sake come and tell them *something* about Elizabethan playhouses!"

By late 1983 it was back to square one. And with the rumblings from the newly-elected Southwark Council, it might even be a step or two further back than that. But still, he had a *theatre*. It just wasn't *the* theatre.

Sam (with a little help from Theo) opens his 'shoebox' and reveals his plan for the Globe project and the surrounding area to John O'Grady, then leader of Southwark council, Sir Philip Dawson and Sir Ove Arup, structural engineer. (1971) *Pentagram*

124

CHAPTER EIGHT

THE ARCHITECT'S TALE: PART ONE

(1969 – 1987)

Architecture in general is frozen music.

Friedrich von Schelling (1809)

Theo Crosby was sitting in a meeting of the Architectural Association quietly minding his own business when Sam Wanamaker erupted into his life.

A South African – one of the many talented people who had found apartheid too difficult to swallow – he had come to Britain in 1947 where he was now a respected designer and architect. He had no reason to suppose that this tense American with the hyperactive smile was about to infect him with his own incurable enthusiasm.

Sam was part of an agenda item dealing with possible redevelopment of the South Bank. It was 1969 and brave new urban worlds were the order of the day. When asked to make his presentation Sam proudly unveiled his 'model.' As someone who remembers seeing it at the time recalls: "You couldn't accuse it of being Disneyland – but it was definitely Mickey Mouse!"

"He'd had it made at Elstree Studios", Theo recalls, "it was so frightful everyone present laughed at him... it seemed to consist of a lot of shoe boxes arranged all over the Thames. It was so pathetic and he was so pleased that my heart went out to him. Not surprisingly, it cut no ice with that particular audience but after the meeting I took him aside and offered to help him at least get a decent brochure of the theatre together, in case he decided to do this again. That was my big mistake! He'd got me hooked. Over the years I saw him do the same to lots of people. It was a remarkable gift he had. That was over 25 years ago. Knowing what I know now, would I do it again? I *expect* so...!"

The next quarter century or so passed in something of a blur for Theo, as the amiable maniac with the shoe boxes drew him further and further into a universe of his own imaginings. A combination of a Lear – who would 'do such things,' if only short-sighted people would stop getting in his way – and a magisterial Prospero, who would assuredly put everything to rights in the last act, Sam moved Theo from tentative brochure advisor to centre stage in more ways than one. Before he quite realised that he'd agreed to anything, he found himself – as the 'official architect' of the new Globe project.

Like a lot of other people, Theo would look quizzical at the mention of 'official'. You weren't so much appointed as absorbed into Sam's team. "I started by putting a toe in the water and the next thing I knew – I was *swimming!*"

Sam, meanwhile, reduced his vision for the south bank from the incredible to the merely improbable. Today the Globe complex – tomorrow the rest of Bankside and Shakespeare's London.

His original master plan didn't include a replica of the original Globe. He had first settled for "a simple brick drum", a square modern building designed by architect, George Djurkovitch with a "Tudorised" gallery interior – not unlike the present Swan theatre at Stratford. This concept didn't last long and by the end of 1970 he was working with another architect, Ove Arup, on an authentic replica but with the addition of a plastic adjustable 'rain roof'. Many people who worked on the project with him in later years were never even aware that the Dream had such modest and 'un-authentic' beginnings.

> King Henry: Embrace and love this man.
> Gardiner: ...With a true heart
>   And brother-love I do it.
> *Henry VIII*, Act V. Sc. iii

Hollywood has a phrase – 'Meet Cute' – which means the scriptwriter has to find an unlikely way for the two protagonists to first get together. It's meant to hold the audience's attention while the plot gets under way. Then they have to work out whether they're suited to one another. The shoe boxes were certainly, though accidentally, cute but what Sam couldn't have calculated – since he'd never met or even heard of Theo Crosby – was that he was meeting a man not only qualified but instinctively attuned to what he was attempting.

There was one essential difference between their approaches. Sam wanted to recreate theatrical history and integrate it into a contemporary social context. Theo was fascinated by the changing attitudes of the community to city life and structure. And a resurrected theatre from the distant past inserted into a late twentieth century environment, come to think of it, would be an ideal experiment. Stanley and Livingstone. The meeting couldn't have been neater... or cuter. The fiery Mr. Wanamaker and the calm, bespectacled Mr. Crosby were to become the hub of this Wheel of Fortune.

Theo's fascination with the configuration of city life had been triggered by his time in Italy during World War II. As a soldier, free to wander the streets anonymously, he had the opportunity to see Roman antiquities in their natural context. He was also struck by the way the buildings were almost characters in a continuing plot, an 'outdoor theatre for commercial drama.' The city was a living, growing thing with structures from different periods taking up a natural role. It was as though a pattern had emerged, one that was sympathetic to the way people happened to live, rather than a singular view imposed dictatorially, which forced people to conform to the constraints of textbook theory.

The contrast with post-war Britain was stark. In this brave new proletarian world nothing was to be left to chance. Planning was the new credo that would rebuild a better Jerusalem. Like so many of his contemporaries, Theo threw himself with enthusiasm into building the New Towns that would be the answer to urban problems.

But the post-war Modernism had a stark, uncompromising quality to it. Not simply authoritarian and theoretical, worst of all it was displeasing to the very people who were supposed to live and work in it. We were destroying our heritage willy-nilly on the fond but speculative assumption that anything new must be better than what it replaced.

Theo was one of the first to realise the error that was being committed in the name of intellectual progress. He was to write:

> We have built so much since 1945 that old buildings are now in the
> minority. What we have built is so bad, without order or quality, that
> it has become imperative that we should hang on to every scrap of the
> pre-modern world. In fact, the problem is now to colonize, to civilize
> the new world in which we find ourselves. To be an architect in the

late twentieth century is to experience a moment rich in ambiguities. The experience is particularly acute to one nurtured in the rigours of Modernism with its puritanical imperatives, its unswerving traditions, its carefully manufactured history, its inevitability.

The pity was that the intentions had been largely good. The war had unleashed a flood of new energy. The problem was that – unlike the Italian model that had so impressed Theo – there was no guiding humanitarian vision to channel it. The thought that cities should fit people had little appeal to a new generation of Bauhaus-inspired, back-to-basics theoreticians that were flooding into the design business.

Nor did the administrators help. All this wonderful new planning must be *organised*. By the mid-1960s the largest architectural company in the world was the Greater London Council, which employed 2,000 architects, each 'marked' by an administrator. A machine like that demands to be used and its effect was felt – and is still visible across great swathes of southern England. The countryside was spoiled beyond repair, the inner cities gutted. Realisation of what was happening began to set in – but by then the damage had been done.

Watching the juggernaut advance cleared Theo's personal vision:

> The lessons of the Modern Movement are infinite and some are valuable; about space and light and form, and also about technology, practicality and social responsibility. They are impossible to discard. But, on the other hand, the buildings are largely disastrous, boring and tongue-tied.

It's one thing to admit error, quite another to decide what to do instead. The counter influences of conservation and environmentalism certainly stopped the mills of Modernism from grinding our remaining heritage even further into dust. Instead, things came to a halt, while a new theory of urban architectural coexistence was awaited. It was ironic that the environmentalists had discovered the environment through the destruction of it.

By this time Theo's own mind was clear about where he stood and by 1964 he had a mechanism of his own to experiment with, having set up with partners Alan Fletcher, Bob Gill and Colin Forbes a multi-discipline consultancy of graphic and product designers and architects, which was to turn in 1972 into Pentagram. More than almost any of his contemporaries, he came to represent what architecture was *about*. There should be "an attitude to architecture which sees it as a kind of language – that is, as a set of meanings, stories, directions which make the forms expressive."

Architecture, he believed, had been most successful by looking at both the past and the present. Again, the images of Italy beckoned. In the opening chapter of his 1973 book, *How to Play the Environment Game*, he wrote: "To make decent cities we must remake ourselves!"

He had clearly seen the error in the Modernist trial. Aesthetics meant nothing unless they were informed by humanity. Art – the unique expression of human individuality, the repository of its history over time – must be allowed its place in urban design. There had to be room for the product of the hand as well as the head. In a real sense this post-Modernist, while not ignoring the benefits of their disciplines, had also found his way back to the homely virtues of the Arts and Crafts movement. "Out of this conjunction", he wrote, "comes something new!"

That something new turned out to be a re-creation of something old but something that would also have the power to renew.

❖

"The project is now under way", he wrote in some personal notes – though not until the late 1980s – "an ultimate and rather terrifying test bed for a possible 21st century architecture; popular, monumental, eclectic, historicist, romantic, academic. All the forbidden words but where the challenge lies in a world with time and money to visit and enjoy buildings."

Though not written for publication, it sums up several of the fundamental themes that ran through his professional and personal thinking. There are and would continue to be plenty of people to ensure his designs would stay academically correct.

Theo's overriding concern was: how would the completed complex be *used?* Just as the Industrial Age had demanded its factories, he foresaw that the emerging Leisure Age would need places for people to *visit* and those should be places of grace and beauty. The problem, as he saw it, was that with our dependence on machinery, we had lost the art of decorating our buildings. He believed the Globe's surrounds should not be considered as an interesting diversion but a unique challenge in how to approach building in general and create a context. But were we up to that challenge?

...our training in the old skills has dissipated. We can only find our way by cautious experiment. The Globe is an attempt at popular architecture, with the admission that such a project is a very difficult thing to undertake.

Ruskin in his *Lamp of Life* essay in *The Seven Lamps of Architecture* equates the task of animating buildings with putting "voices into rocks". Theo was determined there would be a well-modulated chorus of voices in the context, too. With Ruskin he believed that buildings were "an expression of the human soul in material form."

An Architecte ought to understand language, to be skilfull of Painting, well instructed in Geometrie, not ignorant of Perspective, furnished with Arithmetike, haue knowledge of many histories, and diligently haue heard the Philosophers, haue skill of Musike, not ignorant of Physike, know the answers of Lawyers, and haue Astronomie, and the courses Celestiall, in good knowledge... all these Artes, Doctrines, and Instructions, are requisite in an excellent Architecte.

Vitruvius, *De Architectura (Book 1)*, (Translated by John Dee)

The project to rebuild Shakespeare's Globe seemed to fit all the criteria he had defined and, looking back twenty-five years later, Theo saw how the progress of the project has reflected the social, artistic and political shift of opinion of the times we've lived through.

Quite early in the game he attended a conference at the Royal Festival Hall organised by the Globe Trust where the options were still wide open. Should it be "a large hangar-like structure... flexible... multipurpose" or "a modern theatre with an authentic facade" or should it be "modern and flexible but reflecting the shape and facade of its 16th century predecessors?" A fully authentic reconstruction was only one remote possibility.

In 1993 – long after the site had been secured – he wrote about the project in the *Architect's Journal*: "...it became clear that the most interesting theatre to build would be the original, to test the staging and performance, to receive the sound and the reality of the plays. In short, to work for and with the actors, rather than provide another director's theatre. The Globe project was part of this taking of stock, not only of acting and theatre method but of scale and place within the city. The underlying function of the Globe is educational, to explore the nature and quality of performance, and to tell the

Theo Crosby, the Globe's
principal architect with the
final model of the Globe and
its surrounding complex.
Pentagram

extraordinary story of the Elizabethan theatre. Layered over this is
the experience of the place itself, a focus for innumerable tourist
journeys."

From the beginning – shining through Sam's many variations on
his theme – it was clear that there was much more to this than
rebuilding a theatre, even the world's most famous theatre. The
project even went beyond constructing a *second* theatre. What had to
be considered was the totality of the whole complex and how it would
fit into the surrounding landscape and appear to have grown out of it.

One major problem for Theo was how to treat the adjacent
buildings to give the site scale and visual impact. Even though it
would be London's seventh largest theatre when completed, the
Globe was still a relatively small structure by modern standards – a
simple white plastered building that could easily end up looking
insignificant. In Shakespeare's day the handful of amphitheatres had
dominated their surrounding by their relative size. There *were* no
other three-storey buildings anywhere near them on Bankside and
precious few anywhere else.

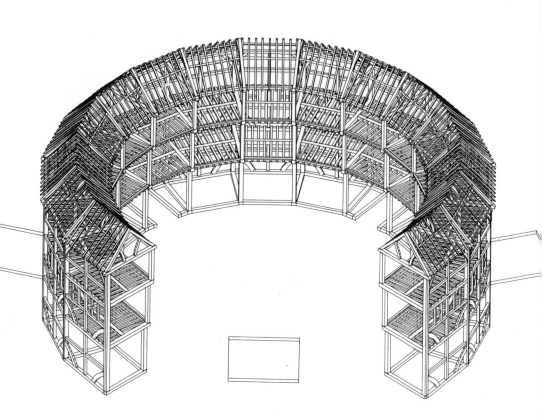

Computer axonometric projection of the Globe construction (1995) *Pentagram*

The Globe had to be placed in an appropriate setting, which meant that the surrounding buildings must be very carefully considered to emphasise the 'starring' role of the theatre itself. Theo felt he needed 'a complex visual background' against which the formal simplicity of The Globe would stand out. At the same time, the building must perform another function by becoming part of the context of the surrounding area in terms of 'scale and pattern'. No easy task because so much of it had been bombed and left to rot.

While the Globe would be at the heart of the complex, Theo envisioned towers, balconies – a whole range of shapes and textures that would bring life and colour to the area. While it made no sense to recreate the specific buildings of that time – even if records had existed – he wanted to design a setting of the kind of buildings that could have evolved around it.

The only buildings of substance left after the debris had been cleared were a double house belonging to Southwark Cathedral and a small house popularly known as the 'Wren House' which was literally next to the site and from which the architect (apocryphally perhaps) had watched his new St. Paul's rise in all its splendour. The former was a red brick terrace construction, while the Wren house was a medieval timber building, refinished in a white plastered brick during Regency times.

To the west of the site loomed Sir Giles Gilbert Scott's 1963 power station, grimly impressive in its own right, but threatening to overshadow the tiny Globe in every sense of the word. It was hoped – as the project went on – that the building would eventually go away of its own accord, become obsolescent and give way to another of the housing developments of which Southwark was always enamoured. Ironically, it was to prove more help than hindrance. It did outlive its function, stood empty for a while and was then taken over as an annexe for the Tate Gallery to house its collection of sculpture and contemporary art. Instead of standing like a giant hand raised against progress, by 2000 it would be a finger beckoning visitors to the new artistic heart of Bankside. An investment of £110 million would construct 120,000 square feet of gallery space.

The rest of the 'neighbours' were a dour lot; offices and warehouses, post-war practical and unappealing. Not a pretty sight and precisely the kind of structures that had disenchanted Theo with Modernism.

The Globe complex would have to re-establish a pattern for the area – one that had existed in Elizabethan times – of mixed domestic and entertainment usage.

Each building must have a character of its own, yet complement the others in the total design. The Globe itself, set on a piazza two metres above the Thames, higher than the nearby river wall, so that it would be visible from the north bank. By happy accident of geography the new Globe found itself exactly opposite the steps of St. Paul's and one day – Theo and Sam dreamed – there would be a pedestrian bridge that would allow the 2 1/2 million visitors who visit the cathedral every year – making it London's sixth most popular attraction – to walk over the water and end up at the Globe, a convenience denied to their Elizabethan ancestors.

Of course, a key element in planning the complex had not been a factor for builders of the original Globe. The new Globe site had to allow two siblings to co-exist, since adjacent to The Globe itself would be a building in a very different style. Their context had been consistent and of its time, in no way a hostage to the past.

Drawing by Theo Crosby
showing hypothetical reconstruction of the interior of the
Globe during a performance.
Pentagram

The Inigo Jones theatre, a perfect example of the enclosed 'hall' theatres dating from the 1610's, was to be built from the complete set of original plans.

The two 'jewels' – the Globe and the Inigo Jones – needed a carefully considered setting. Each of the remaining buildings, Theo felt, should have its own 'voice', which must be carefully chosen not to compete and "blur the individuality of the theatres by imitating their styles".

Contrast and unification would be the guiding principles of the project, itself the most dramatic attempt at 'popular architecture' in every sense of the word London had seen since the war.

On the Globe itself, Theo and Sam were soon as one. The early debates had convinced Sam that for the project to have any claim to credibility the theatre must be as exact a replica as the current state of scholarship would permit. But Theo took Sam's concept one important stage further. Not only would their version *look* like the original Globe, it would *feel* like it, too. It would be built only with natural materials and the finest craftsmanship – even if the craftsmen had to re-learn skills that had not been used in centuries. Man-made materials would be taboo. Using Elizabethan techniques and materials was not some modish affectation, devised for PR purposes. A building, even a new building, had a soul and this consistency,

Theo felt, gave them their best chance to conjure up a twin soul to the original.

The initial drawings were soon finished. But that was to prove the easy bit.

Revision followed revision but without a site on which one could visualise the buildings rising, the drawings lacked heart. That had to wait until after the 1986 court case. That Christmas, Theo celebrated by putting pen and line to paper in the knowledge that these drawings stood a very good chance of being turned into reality.

His previous master design, drawn up in 1981, needed serious modification. The experiments with sunlight he'd carried out in the summer of 1982 meant the orientation of the theatre had to be modified to be 48 degrees east of north. Then in 1985 Liddell had persuaded Theo that he should include in the revised plan a two foot thick concrete diaphragm wall around the whole site to form a waterproof box that would keep out the Thames ground water. Doing so would provide a significant bonus in the shape of a large basement that could house an exhibition. That exhibition soon became the main prop of the project's business plan. Visitors would enter the site via the exhibition, gain an overview of the Elizabethan social and theatrical context and then emerge into the glory of the Globe. Now we were talking!

Jon Greenfield pictures the scene in the Crosby home that Christmas of 1986:

> He set to his task with his usual energy and drew up the whole scheme at 1:100 scale; a total of eight double elephant size drawings. By anyone's measure, this is an achievement. He worked completely without assistance... He would work in an almost fevered way, his long body bent over his drawing board (propped up on bricks), fast movements of his set square and T-square, a quick brushing away of rubbings with his ink-stained duster and the frequent rattle of his electric pencil sharpener. His only concession to technology...

In his own journal Theo noted: "This marks the beginning of the serious work on the project" – seventeen years after he and Sam had first met.

CHAPTER NINE

THERE'S GOOD NEWS...
AND THERE'S BAD NEWS
(1981 - 1989)

Thus far our fortune keeps an upward course,
And we are grac'd with wreaths of victory.
Henry VI (Pt. 3), Act V. Sc. iii

Shakespeare doesn't have all the good lines. Dickens summed up the next phase of the Globe story when he began *A Tale of Two Cities* with the words: "It was the best of times, it was the worst of times".

After months of negotiation it appeared that they would finally have a site – the Greenmore Wharf site! As far back as 1973, Southwark had made it known that they felt the best use for the land would be to have a development of offices that included a Globe theatre as part of the complex and in 1979 came to such an agreement with a company called Derno Estates, a subsidiary of Freshwater. There was a nice irony here for those with long memories. Back in the early 1970's Sam had won the best of three falls with Town & Metropolitan, a subsidiary of – *Freshwater!*

The Council may have felt generous towards the project but the increasingly vocal North Southwark Community Development Group felt very differently. The land should be used for council houses. No, said the Council, refusing planning permission – the site is unsuitable. The water table so close to the river is too high and would make the cost of building the kind of houses they favoured prohibitively expensive. The NSCDG retire to lick their wounds and plan their next move. Derno files their application for planning permission for their offices, shops and restaurants – and a replica Globe.

Symbolically, on Shakespeare's Birthday 1981, a tripartite agreement is signed. Derno and the Council will be responsible for acquiring all the remaining third party land. When that has been done, Derno will pass the freehold over to Southwark and receive in turn a 125-year lease with planning permission to build their offices and fifteen residential units. Derno will then give the WCSS sufficient land on which to build their replica Globe, a restaurant, pub and shops for a similar 125-year lease at a peppercorn rent. The Globe's gain was also a 'planning gain' (or community contribution) for the developers. Derno also agreed to build a river wall and roadway – which they'd need anyway – and to buttress the adjoining Wren house. Everyone concerned was to come out smelling of roses. Events had not yet reached the point where the pun would seem double-edged.

> *A pretty plot, well chosen to build upon!*
> *Henry VI (Pt.2),* Act I Sc. iv

Now that there were pieces of paper with signatures on them and castles – or at least Globes – could be built on something more substantial than air, the need for funds became pressing. Like Puck, Sam would take it upon himself to put a girdle around about the earth in the shape of a fund-raising tour. But before he did that, he took the advice of the project's then lawyers, Freshfields, to turn the WCSS into the fund-raising arm of the enterprise – renamed the Shakespeare Globe Trust – and apply for charitable status. The new Trust's principal objective would be to "improve our understanding of Shakespeare" in both performance and education. The operational side would be run by a new company, the International Shakespeare Globe Centre (ISGC) with a board of directors. Sam would effectively run the latter and be a member of the former. It was a division of Church and State with which he was never to be terribly happy, even though he saw the need for it. He'd always enjoyed running Ad Hoc Unlimited and rather regretted its passing...

The process of change is set in motion, although the legal entities are not in place for another two years, by which time a complex situation is rapidly becoming impossible. Without consulting Sam, Southwark and Derno change a few small details. One is a stipulation that third party land must be acquired. The other is that the Council must relocate their road sweepers, who are presently using the abandoned site as a place to park their carts after working hours.

Oh, and there was one other small item. Clause 8 of this 1982 version specified that, if the conditions of the agreement had not been fulfilled within two years, it would be null and void. Two *years?* Good heavens, the Globe would be up and running by then. There was a lot of interest in America and the economy at home was picking up.

In May of that year the problems began to emerge. The third party clause hadn't seemed particularly onerous when it was drafted. People who owned parcels of land that were too small to develop would be glad to accept a fair, if not particularly generous offer. Some were and some weren't. The CEGB (Central Electricity Generating Board) had been lurking on the Monopoly board for some time and knew the rules. As a 'government' enterprise, their balance sheet wasn't the shrine it was to others. They were in no hurry and without their piece of the puzzle nobody was going anywhere. Say £500,000 an acre? Derno weren't about to say anything of the sort – particularly when they were finding it a lot more difficult than they had anticipated to pre-let their office space. They were running into the overbuilding situation that would eventually paralyse the commercial property market in London. They informed the Council that they'd like to look at the agreement again.

...do I tell thee of my foes,
Which art my near'st and dearest enemy?
Henry IV (Pt.1), Act III Sc. ii

Unfortunately, the Council was no longer the Council. In May local elections changed its complexion dramatically from a blushing pink to a choleric red and now some old scores could be settled. Down from their lair in the fastness of North Southwark came the hordes of the NSCDG and swept into the Council chamber. Sam was made aware of the implication for the Globe when one of the new councillors told him privately that the new group intended to try and undo some of the agreements that had been made by their predecessors but which they now found politically irrelevant to their present purpose. The Globe project had historically been high on their hit list. As far as they were concerned the 1981 agreement put the Globe in bed with the demon developers. "They thought we were just a front", Sam lamented at the time, "...that the Globe was spurious, a facade, something out of Disneyland".

As far as Bankside is concerned, Policy No. 3 in their published *North* Southwark Plan states that "Existing unimplemented planning permission will not be renewed". The river side "should be developed for public housing, industry, open space and social facilities and not for private gain". The writing was as plain as fresh graffiti on the wall. As far as the 'new' Southwark Council was concerned, all it had to do was wait. Two years was not long in the Marxist scheme of things.

Meanwhile, there were destabilising games that could be played. They had the obligation as their part of the 1982 agreement to relocate the road sweepers but these key public cleansing operatives – all fifteen of them – couldn't be asked to go just *anywhere*. Derno and Sam scoured the vicinity themselves and came up with site after alternative site. None of them was *quite* right. When there seemed to be agreement on one particular site, the Council moved so slowly that it was snapped up by someone else.

For Sam the dust carts were the ultimate insult. A derelict site could be seen to have a certain grandeur but a collection of rusting metal...! He would fume in private, Charlotte remembers: "He went bananas – but it was anger not despair" In public he took a more lofty view. "I don't *see* the rubbish bins", he told an interviewer, "they're a kind of haze – I see the *theatre!*"

1982 drags into 1983 and tempers are getting frayed. The project now has a set of designs that bring the theatre to life. You can almost touch it! They already have planning permission. What they don't have is peace of mind. Despite the nervousness he was undoubtedly feeling, Sam had no intention of showing any lack of confidence in public.

> *...your noble self,*
> *That best know'st how to rule and how to reign,*
> *We thus submit unto...*
>
> *Pericles*, Act II Sc. iv

In the theatre casting is, if not all, then most. As the WCSS was turning itself into the Shakespeare Globe Trust – and incurring a lot more legal responsibility to go with the gravitas in the process – they were fortunate to secure the services of Sir David Orr as Chairman of the Trustees. And like so many things in the Globe story, it happened by accident.

Orr was then Chairman of Unilever, the Anglo-Dutch conglomerate that made and sold just about everything from detergents to margarine, ice cream to cosmetics. Unilever House, his company's headquarters, was a converted hotel sitting on the northern approach to Blackfriars Bridge. The building itself had some of the remains of its art deco origins but when in 1982 the toll of decades of tramping feet decided the Board to refurbish, they determined to do it properly and restore the art deco detail or at least a fair replica of it. To do the work Orr called in the design firm, Pentagram and met the designer assigned to the project – Theo Crosby.

Both of them were quiet, contemplative men and they hit it off immediately. In the course of conversation one day Theo mentioned his work on the Globe and suggested Orr meet Sam. The meeting duly took place in Orr's newly-renovated eighth floor office. After the normal civilities had been exchanged, Sam drew him over to the window and said in apparent surprise: "Why, you can see it from here!" In fact, all that Orr could see was the dark, satanic power station, a lot of run-down buildings and a strip of waste ground with a few dust carts. He was not impressed but the picture Sam conjured up in his mind's eye was very different. "With eyes alight, voice becoming more impassioned, he expanded his concept of a Globe recreated as it had been when Shakespeare's company played there as a centre for education, research and theatrical experimentation. I could not remain unmoved... I thought: 'This fellow is going to do it!'" Orr was about to retire and thought he might have some time available, so he agreed to become Chairman of the Globe Trustees. He found the organisation he inherited – like the site – "a pretty ramshackle affair".

Luckily for the Globe, they had in Orr someone who was – in Trollope's words – "as useful as a great oil-jar, from whence oil for the quiescence of troubled waters might ever and anon be forthcoming".

It was as well for the project that David Orr joined when he did. Up to this point Sam had been involved in a series of minor skirmishes. He'd been like Robin Hood, except that he rarely seemed to come away with much money from the rich to give to the poor. But this was a serious power play. If Southwark were allowed to renege on their agreement, not only would the Globe not have this site – which had now been formally anointed – there was no chance of there being any other site that would make sense. The dice had to be thrown and the cost of even taking part in this expensive legal game worried about later.

Left to his own devices, Sam would have expended a great deal of unfocused energy, much of it verbal. That had traditionally been his way and it's likely that the new Council counted on more of the same. What they found themselves facing was the experience of a man who was used to playing in the big leagues of commerce and who could summon the support of like-minded contemporaries. To him the Southwark encounter was comparable to a troublesome local 'test market' – to be approached logically and attacked with all available forces. For once Sam was obliged to sit and take advice.

> *...now promises*
> *Upon this land a thousand thousand blessings*
> *Henry VIII*, Act V Sc. v

In any case, here was another performance to be staged – acting normally. Confidence in the project was fragile at best after all this time. Money was beginning to trickle in, particularly from the U.S., but it wouldn't take much to dry up the source and news about the legal spat would be likely to do just that.

There was the question of the dedication of the site. Before it became obvious that relations have deteriorated so badly between the three partners, it had been decided that the project's progress needed to be publicly demonstrated. What better way than to invite the major American donors over, show them a good time and, as part of it, let them help christen the spot which their money was about to transform? The site, after all, had been theoretically acquired and planning permission given back in 1981. What, a few donors were beginning to inquire, was taking so long?

By early 1983 it was becoming clear that feet were being dragged but Sam and the Trustees felt they couldn't afford to wait any longer. True to his belief that decisions invariably precipitated actions, Sam announced Dedication Week would take place between July 8th and 12th and the invitations went out. The week would cost £9,000 or so which, it was hoped, would be subsidised by various local donations in cash or in kind.

While the logistics were being worked out, Sam was busy arm wrestling with Freshwater. According to the agreement, he had no technical right to use the site without their agreement and Freshwater's concern was that such a visible event would give the impression of a *fait* that was by no means yet *accompli*. In the end a compromise was reached. The dedication ceremony could be held just *outside* the actual site but close enough so that the visitors would be none the wiser.

God save the foundation!
Much Ado About Nothing, Act V. Sc. i

The 28 American patrons or 'Founders' duly arrived on July 7th for what one of them in her letter home described as "five days of wonderful entertainment" leading up to the dedication ceremony on the 12th. Lunch at the House of Lords, dinner at Sutton Place, drinks at Samuel Pepys Pub, tea with Henry Moore ("who promised the Globe a sculpture when the time came"), receptions at St. James's Palace, the US Ambassador's Residence, Althorp House ("tea with Princess Diana's father and stepmother... One of the guests told Lord Spencer how very much she and her countrymen admired his daughter, to which he replied with a smile, 'She does come off rather well, doesn't she'").

And then the Dedication itself, where all the right people said all the required things – the Mayor, the MP, the Vice Chairman of the GLC, the Southwark Councillor, the US Ambassador and perhaps most importantly, the well known American businessman and philanthropist, Armand Hammer.

Hammer was a key figure at this stage of the project. Not only was he one of the world's richest men in his own right but his endorsement made it legitimate for other potential donors anxious to be seen to do the 'right thing'. Besides, Hammer knew everybody. He certainly knew Prince Philip, who had tacitly supported the project for some time now, since Sir Hugh Casson had introduced Sam to him in 1972. It was Hammer who persuaded him it was now timely to let his name be formally associated with the project. The reception at Buckingham Palace, which followed the dedication, was the Prince's first public appearance in the UK as Patron of the Globe.

One distinguished absentee was Lord Olivier. He declined on the grounds that he didn't want to have to get up and *say* anything! In trying to change his mind and persuade him that wouldn't be necessary, Sam went on to add: "...this project has not been brought to the point of realization by taking 'NO' for an answer – at least, only one 'No'!" (Olivier later agreed to serve as Honorary President on the assurance that it would be "a purely symbolic role").

In fact, Olivier's wasn't quite the only 'No'. Scenting the presence of the media, a group of local demonstrators turned up on site to protest that, while the champagne was (metaphorically) flowing, there were over 8,000 people on the Council's waiting list for homes. All of which the cameras caught, along with a scuffle in which Sam was seen to lose his temper, for which he apologised in his opening remarks. "The only thing these people have got", he said, pointing at the protestors, "is their history and their culture. We want to give them *jobs*". The incident couldn't have played to his purpose better if he'd arranged it himself...

The rest of the speeches were made, a prayer was said, Charlotte smashed a bottle of donated champagne against the neighbouring (Wren House) wall, a 50 ft hot air balloon rose with some effort and a flock of homing pigeons was released into the summer afternoon air. For once in the project's history, the Clerk of the Weather decided to be kind.

The next day the captains, kings and donors departed, the Globe's purpose suitable served. In writing home, one of the ladies expressed the verdict of them all:

"I feel that all my years of absorbing interest and study of English History and Literature were but a preparation for this experience – the most thrilling of my life. And so in the words of Shakespeare himself: 'I can no other answer make but thanks, and thanks'".

In a BBC TV documentary covering the event Armand Hammer assured the interviewer – who had suggested Hammer could guarantee the project's success with the wave of a hand or personal cheque – "I don't like failure. I won't let it down".

July 1983 left everyone feeling good but, as pageants went, it remained insubstantial. There remained a little matter of the law...

> *...I fear some ambush.*
> *I saw him not these many years*
>
> *Cymbeline*, Act IV Sc. ii

The Council's strategy was obvious – wait out the time and then invoke Clause 8. What could their 'partners' do about it? The GLC's 1983 decision to demolish the neighbouring power station and designate the space for housing also seemed to confirm the way prevailing political breezes were blowing.

The trouble with theoretical socialism is that it doesn't often come face to face with the brute force of the commercial imperative. Derno were running out of patience as well as time. Two could play at that game and they promptly informed Southwark in August 1984 that in their view "two efforts to relocate the Greenmore Wharf Depot (i.e., the road sweepers) in a two year time period is not a sufficient indication of the use of 'all reasonable endeavours as soon as possible to relocate the Depot'". Having led with the jab, a month later they delivered their uppercut by having their solicitors inform the Council that they (the Council) were now in breach of the 1982 agreement and that, if there was any attempt to invoke Clause 8, Derno would certainly sue.

Two months later the Council counter-attacks. Clause 8 *is* to be invoked. The Council has not been able to relocate the Depot and, in any case, Derno are themselves in default, since they have failed to acquire the third party land. Although the manoeuverings of the Council had occupied most of the Trust's attention, it had not gone unnoticed that Derno themselves were cooling on the whole development. At which point the Globe's lawyers advise the now active Globe Trust that they have an excellent case for suing *both* parties for backing out of the original 1981 agreement in favour of the 1982 agreement to which the Globe was not party. By year end, Derno are suing Southwark for £12 million in damages and the Globe is suing Southwark *and* Derno. Merry Christmas 1984! See you in Court...

> But though I am a daughter to his blood,
> I am not to his manners.
> Jessica, daughter to Shylock,
> *The Merchant of Venice*, Act II Sc. iii

Perhaps there's something in an actor's aura that encourages the theatrical. Certainly, at every twist and turn in the Globe's story dramatic personal touches abound and one was waiting in the chambers of the new Southwark Council.

As far as we know, Sam never played Lear but he did have three daughters. Abby, the eldest, had gone back to the States by now, married and living in the family home in Los Angeles. Middle daughter, Zoë, was beginning to emerge as a significant actress. Which left – Jessica.

If Zoë echoed the artistic side of Sam's personality, Jessica stood for the social commitment and her discussions with him on political issues were often heated. By this time she'd tried her hand at a number of occupations but had still to find her place to stand. She was inclined to be, in Dryden's words, "everything by starts, and nothing long". Her most recent commitment was to local politics and, being a true Wanamaker, it meant more than simply turning up. She found herself elected as one of the extremely extreme new intake, which meant going to work to vote the party line against Dad, then going home to break the family bread.

Her mother christened Jessica her 'Gucci Communist' and one wonders whether Sam, as he forced down the funeral baked meats, ever called to mind the passage from *Measure For Measure* in which Julietta says: "I do confess it, and repent it, father". To which the Duke replies: "Tis meet so, daughter...".

...being then appointed
Master of this design...
The Tempest, Act I Sc. ii

In March 1984 you could have seen the following ad in *The Times:*

"Museum Manager. Knowledge of Elizabethan Theatre an advantage; administrative experience not essential".

Patrick Spottiswoode did, applied and got the job. Six months later he almost lost it again. His first task was to work with Pentagram to create the new exhibition that would bring people back to the Museum, now rechristened the Bear Gardens Museum of the Shakespearean Stage – another of Sam's verbally unwieldy appellations.

Sam hated the exhibition. For him it was "history without theatre or poetry". For Patrick: "I was also nearly history!" To put back the element of theatre Sam so sorely missed he began to develop a programme of lectures that would bring the Museum to life for its visitors. He also started to book productions into the Cockpit, which turned it quite quickly into a 'fringe' theatre venue that earned a modest amount of money to pay the bills. An amateur group – the Bankside Theatre Company – became an unofficial resident company and the keystone of what became by 1985/86 an ambitious programme. A series of touring companies were brought in and the Cockpit's repertoire increased to include plays by Chapman,

Middleton, Tourneur, Ford "and the odd Arthur Miller for good measure".

In 1986 the court case closed the Museum for several months but by this time Spottiswoode had an infrastructure in place that could withstand the delay. If the gods of Justice were willing, the show would go on...

If the great gods be just, they shall assist
The deeds of justest men.

Pompey, *Antony and Cleopatra*, Act II Sc. i

Monday, June 16, 1986: Court 36 of the Courts of Justice, Chancery Division.

The opening day of the three way court case that had been waiting eighteen months to happen. It's all very well to say you'll see someone in Court. The question is – *when?* To anyone brought up on a TV diet of Perry Mason the actual trial probably seemed a mite dull, too, though impressive in its understated British way.

Junior clerks brought in the mountains of paper that would be used to justify the fees of their senior colleagues. Counsel bent bewigged heads to debate abstruse points in hushed tones. In serried ranks they sat, organised in absolute hierarchy – senior counsel, junior counsel, solicitors – all flanked with their fortifications of paper.

Towards the back of the Court the small Globe group sat literally on the edge of their seats, straining to hear the softly-worded arguments. As one of them described it later: "For the next five days it was as if the dream that had been going on for 16 years was being distilled, encapsulated and re-enacted in the court room".

Sam could hardly contain himself. Bit by bit and day by day he edged his seat forward until he was sitting behind Mr. Freshwater and looking over his shoulder to share the papers he and his lawyers were using.

For five days it droned on with the old arguments drily dissected all over again. By the time of the weekend recess, the Globe supporters felt they probably had an edge. But, then they weren't the judge and this wasn't TV. Even so, he *had* referred to the Leader of the Council as a *gauleiter*, which couldn't be bad...

Over the weekend a genuine ray of sunlight seemed to break through. The Southwark Council Labour Group, it appeared, had called an unexpected meeting for the Sunday. It was rumoured that their legal advisers were recommending a settlement. The rumour gained added credibility when the other lawyers were summoned and an adjournment was asked for until Tuesday... then Wednesday. Counsel were summoned to the Judge's chambers.

By the time Mr. Justice Harman finally entered the Court that Wednesday morning of June 25th, the show was certainly getting the ratings and the Judge was enough of an actor to keep his speech short. He congratulated all three parties for coming to a "speedy and sensible conclusion" and announced that terms had been agreed.

"A famous victory". Sam celebrates the successful settlement of the 1986 High Court case.

The Globers hugged each other or shook hands, according to their individual inclination. Sam's head was bowed on his knees. Whatever problems were still to be negotiated, at that moment he'd shed the accumulated weight of seventeen years. He'd won a famous victory. Looking at him from the back of the court Charlotte smiled the smile of a young girl...

The law hath not been dead, though it hath slept
Angelo, *Measure for Measure*, Act II Sc. ii

On the way back to Bear Gardens, the old Sam suddenly surfaced. The agreement revalidated the Globe's right to occupy and build on the site with a 125 year lease at a nominal rent of 5% of operating profits. But as he walked along with David Orr and Diana Devlin, Sam had nothing to say about that – it was all history. He could talk of nothing but the very small consolation bone that had been thrown to the Council in the agreement. The part of the Bear Gardens site that had belonged to Derno and had now been given to Southwark was to be returned to them in due course when the Globe was built. "Why couldn't they have been made to give us that, too?" he complained.

For once Orr was short with him: "For heaven's sake, Sam, we've got everything we could possibly have asked for. Count your blessings, man!"

"At that point," Devlin recalls, "I realised that whatever we accomplished, Sam would *never* be satisfied".

Orr had a point that any true businessman could appreciate. He and his fellow Trustees had taken a substantial business risk. At stake were legal and court costs in excess of £250,000 for which – since the Trust didn't have that kind of money – they would be personally liable.

"We'd have had to go round hat in hand", he recalls. As it was, "We came out with zero. Not a penny in compensation from Freshwater. We'd wasted three years getting back what we had in the first place but along the way we'd lost both credibility and momentum".

In the end the real losers were the citizens of Southwark. The price of their 'loony left' leadership turned out to be a bill for over £9 million and even with the inflationary prices of the mid-1980's, you could build a lot of council houses for £9 million. On that very day there were precisely 115 acres of building land available in Southwark. The three-quarters of an acre of land the fuss had all been about would have held just *twelve* houses...

The media, predictably, had a field day with the story. The legal minutiae were far too complicated to bother with, so the popular version of the story became the road sweepers versus W. Shakespeare. "Sweepers get the brush-off for the Bard", proclaimed *The Guardian.* And since one of the sweepers had been heard to remark that "the row is much ado about nothing" and the Leader of the Council that Shakespeare was "a lot of tosh", another headline read: "Trash v. Tosh!" Dignity was preserved by some of the more 'serious' publications. "Old Globe comes full circle" said *The Los Angeles Times*, while *The Times* contented itself with – "All's Well That Ends Well as Globe Goes Ahead".

"Going ahead", however, didn't turn out to be 'full Steam Ahead'. Although the legal verdict had gone the Globe's way, the small print required the Trust to reapply for planning permission. Although the Council had no way open to them to refuse it, equally there was nothing that said they had to be in a hurry to take the necessary steps. It was February 1987 – a full seven months later – before the paperwork was processed and, even though Sam might have been prepared to anticipate the inevitable, the Trustees were not. Not so much as a spade was to be set into that soil until the 'i's were dotted and the 't's crossed on the document that had caused them so many sleepless nights!

Time, of course, has many facets. Since the site was originally granted back in 1981, it had become increasingly difficult to explain why nothing seemed to be happening. In that respect the court case had had one unsought tangible advantage – everyone understood that *sub judice* tied your hands. But now that the case was over and won...? Were you *ever* going to start?

And when you can't start, it's easy for an enervating intellectual paralysis to set in. Quite simply, many of the core group were tired. Having screwed their mental courage to the sticking point for the trial, this further delay was more than some of them could take. Diana Devlin – one of the longest-serving supporters of the project and latterly the Administrator – took off on what turned out to be a sabbatical. As she left, she reflected on the inertia that had set in: "Ideas simply go round and round from one committee to another, as if in imitation of the circular structure which is our inspiration". The Wooden 'O' was at risk of turning into a wooden *zero*...

By this heavenly ground I tread on...
Henry IV (Part 2), Act II Sc. i

There was a Micawberish air about the 1987 festivities to celebrate the International Shakespeare Week in July. Forecast number of paid admissions – 20,000. Actual number – 987. Actual Deficit – £41,465. Once again, a series of events, intended as a launching pad for a £16 million fund-raising appeal that would start the work of actually *building* the Globe had turned out to be a 'lossleader', which had to be explained away as an exercise in "raising awareness".

Like so many of the events of this kind Sam planned over the years, it was imperfectly thought through and infinitely less than the sum of its variable parts, leading to frustration among those who had striven mightily to activate those parts. Sam summed it up as "a flawed but smashing success". Others were less sanguine.

An internal post mortem analysing elements varying from marketing, pre-planning, staffing and sponsorship through decision-making and publicity was littered with words like "inadequate", "unrelated", "unsatisfactory", "ill-defined", and "inferior". As an exercise in banner waving it was decidedly limp.

A Gala Shakespeare concert had the critics trying to be kind. *The Guardian* managed to find it "all very enjoyable" and then felt obliged to qualify that faint praise with "but not, I hope, an indication that the new Globe will be giving us Carry On, Merrie England".

The main purpose of the week was the Ground Breaking ceremony. Prince Philip drove in the first oak foundation post, taken from Windsor Great Park and the symbolic Wooden 'O' was completed by twenty-three other posts donated by Austria, Canada, China, Czechoslovakia, Denmark, East Germany, Finland, Hungary, Israel, Italy, Japan, Korea, Luxembourg, Malaysia, Mexico, Netherlands, Nigeria, Norway, Portugal, Singapore, Spain, Sweden, UK, US, USSR and West Germany, a tribute to the growing international awareness of the project. France abstained. Presumably the events of *Henry V* were still too recent... A few days later the timber was removed for safe keeping, its symbolic purpose served. It would be another five years before an oak beam touched the soil of Bankside – by which time it would have been decided that *twenty* would be all that were required...

As soon as "Oakhenge" was complete, a fire boat sent off a celebratory cannonade of water, the cue for the releasing of a thousand red, white and blue balloons – one for each of the invited guests.

The other significant launch that day was the international fund-raising appeal. The period up to the court case had caused a serious financial hiatus, particularly in the US. Why give to something that may never happen? Once again, Sam and his collecting box must be sent off on their travels.

> Opinion's but a fool, that makes us scan
> The outward habit by the inward man.
>
> *Pericles*, Act II Sc. ii

It was Terence not Shakespeare who wrote the line *quot homines tot sententiae sunt*. Roughly translated, it means that everyone has his own opinion and the Globe project, as it developed, brought a lot of conflicting opinions to the surface. Most of them were aired academically in seminars or the columns of learned periodicals. Some seized the high ground (*sic*) of the popular press. But there was the occasional exception.

Martin Clout was a self-proclaimed Shakespearean scholar and historian – mainly because other academics didn't consider him to be one of their number. His studies, he claimed, had brought him to a conclusion totally at odds with the advice Sam was getting from his advisors. They were quite wrong, Clout argued. The Globe had been hexagonal. What's more it was nothing like the simple wooden stage they were proposing to build. Instead, it had been more like the theatres of Inigo Jones and the Italian indoor theatres of that later Renaissance period – full of elaborate mobile scenery with "perspective" effects and artificial lighting.

The trouble was Clout didn't just claim it. He published his views in a private pamphlet called "The Globe that Shakespeare Knew" just before the ground breaking. A measure of the importance he attached to his pronouncements can be gauged by the inscription appended to the bottom of the title page – "Not for Sale in the USA" Since he'd only printed 24 numbered xeroxed copies, that didn't seem likely to be a problem.

Sam dismissed it as "a flea bite" and in the event the media gave it short shrift. In *The Daily Telegraph* Andrew Gurr called it "A flight of fancy. I wouldn't have given it an A grade as an undergraduate essay". It was one more piece of pseudo-news in an affair that, as far as they were concerned, had come to be about such a thing as would be done when 'twere done – one day, maybe... but probably not quickly. A couple of years later Mr. Clout was lending his insights to the Rose...

Much more helpful in the War of the Words was a young man called Adrian Hill. He made no claim to be an academic but he did talk more sense than many. He also talked himself into *The Guinness Book of Records* by conducting a "Bardathon" and reading the one million words of the Complete Works aloud. It took him 110 hours, during which his handlers fed him with NASA-approved food concentrates and dosed him with eye drops and Strepsils throat tablets. The worst part, he said later, was being washed with a Winnie-the-Pooh face cloth. ("After a while the bear frightened me").

He was sufficiently pleased with his performance that, when he'd got his breath back, he answered the inevitable media question: "What next?..." with "Oh, *The Bible,* I suppose... Shakespeare's a hard act to follow!"

❖

The project was never short of symbolic events. There was the ceremony of dedication and the International Shakespeare Week of 1987 – not to mention a host of minor celebrations in lieu of actual spadework.

There was even the family of gypsies who briefly camped on the empty site and made their own headlines. But this was merely by way of Prologue. On The 1988 Birthday an official start was made. In a special service at Southwark Cathedral 424 children – one for every year since Shakespeare's birth – lit ceremonial candles and a child from each of 26 countries said: "Happy Birthday, William Shakespeare" in his or her respective language.

Later, on the site Dame Judi Dench, looking fetching in a yellow hard hat, gingerly coaxed a huge earth mover into scooping up the first official load of earth. As she smiled her relief, there was the sound of cannon fire, the "whoop" of a fire boat shooting out a jet of water, and a cloud of confetti drifted down over the crowd, the most cynical of whom could scarce forebear to cheer. "It's a tremendous day!" the lady Mayor of Southwark was overhead to say. "To think that this could happen in *Southwark!*" It was the kind of day when it would have been churlish to point out that it could have happened in Southwark a lot sooner and £9 million cheaper...

> *The cloud-capp'd towers, the gorgeous palaces...*
> *The Tempest,* Act IV Sc. i

There was one other new aspect to the project at this time that was to have a serious effect on its future viability. Until the court case the plan had been to build only the theatre. "*After* the case", David Orr recalls, "we suddenly found ourselves talking about the *complex* – the pub, the flats, the whole thing". As a businessman, he at least had a grasp of the financial realities. Taking stock of the project to date, he was concerned to see the growing scale it was assuming. Weren't they trying to run before they could even crawl?

Discussions were long and hard. Orr would have much preferred to see a 'temporary' Globe built on the site for £2 -3 million. At least there would be something for people to *see*, something the fund-raisers could point to. It could then be replaced in due course by the real thing. But there were other agendas to be considered. For different reasons Sam and Theo both needed a monument – Sam his theatre; Theo a major project to call his own, which a theatre alone would not satisfy. His "visionary dialogue" was well argued (Orr remembers) and the complex carried the day. But looking back, there are those who wonder even now whether the decision taken in the heady excitement produced by the court victory to pour what turned out to be several million pounds into the ground was the correct one. Once taken, there was go going back. It would be all or nothing and how could it now be *nothing?*

CHAPTER TEN

BRUSH UP YOUR SHAKESPEARE...

THE VIEW FROM THE USA

If you cannot understand my argument, and declare, "It's Greek to me", you are quoting Shakespeare; if you claim to be "more sinned against than sinning", you are quoting Shakespeare; if you act "more in sorrow than in anger", if your "wish is father to the thought", if your lost property has "vanished into thin air", you are quoting Shakespeare; if you have ever "refused to budge an inch" or suffered from "green-eyed jealousy", if you have "played fast and loose", if you have been "tongue tied", "a tower of strength", "hoodwinked" or "in a pickle", if you have "knitted your brows", "made a virtue of necessity", insisted on "fair play", "slept not one wink", "stood on ceremony", "danced attendance (on your lord and master)", "laughed yourself into stitches", had "short shrift", "cold comfort", or "too much of a good thing", if you have "seen better days", or "lived in a fool's paradise", – why, be that as it may, "the more fool you", for it is a foregone conclusion that you are (as good luck would have it) quoting Shakespeare. If you think it is "early days" and clear out "bag and baggage", if you think "it is high time", and that "that is the long and short of it", if you believe that "the game is up", and that "truth will out", even if it involves your "own flesh and blood", if you "lie low" till "the crack of doom" because you suspect "foul play", if you have "teeth set on edge (at one fell swoop)", "without rhyme or reason", then – "to give the devil his due" – if the "truth were known" (for surely "you have a tongue in your head"), you are quoting Shakespeare. Even if you bid me "good riddance" and "send me packing", if you wish I was "dead as a doornail", if you think I am an "eyesore", "a laughing stock", "the devil incarnate", "a stoney-hearted villain", "bloody-minded", or a "blinking idiot", then – "by Jove!", "O Lord", "Tut, Tut!" "For Goodness' sake", "What the dickens!" "But me no buts" -"It is all one to me", for you are quoting Shakespeare...

Bernard Levin

"The cloud-capp'd towers, the gorgeous palaces" – "No, you're still running into each other. Douglas, you say the line, then Cleo picks it up as a sort of echo. Then, when you come to 'the great Globe itself', you look at each other and speak it as one. Then you, Douglas, *slowly* begin to move back..."

The setting was not a deserted London theatre but an elegantly furnished suite in a New York hotel belonging to Leona and Harry Helmsley, at that time one of the country's leading property managers, as well as one of its richest men. That evening there would be a Shakespearean entertainment or, as Sam put it, "something like a court *masque*". ('Court' clearly pleased the Helmsleys. The hotel, after all, was the Helmsley Palace but they probably never quite understood 'mask').

The 'gig' was part of a 10 city fund-raising tour of the U.S. that took place in the spring of 1983, shortly before the appointed date of the Dedication ceremony on the Globe site. Sam had appreciated from early days that he would need American money to fulfil his dream and, as the realities of British life sank in, he began to believe that *most* of the money would have to come from there – "British culture – American money", he used to say ruefully.

"Americans are much more generous with their money. The British are by nature much more reticent and suspicious, much slower in making decisions of this kind. Also, they've not yet accepted certain aspects of their own culture. They're just getting round to it".

This wasn't his first foray but it was the most serious to date. He now needed to attract and focus serious transatlantic attention on the project and he didn't want to be seen as the impecunious swain with his hand out. The idea of a troupe of wandering players seemed particularly appropriate. Wealthy donors or potential donors could host an elegant supper party, after which a group of famous theatrical folk would entertain with Shakespeare-related material. Ian McKellen had done his one-man Shakespeare show a couple of years earlier with Princess Grace of Monaco in attendance. She'd offered to appear at several more evenings this season but then came her tragic death the previous autumn.

The speech Sam was rehearsing was Prospero's soliloquy put to music as a two-hander for Douglas Fairbanks, Jr., and jazz singer, Cleo Laine.

The strolling players had a core group of Laine and husband, John Dankworth, Fairbanks, Millicent Martin, Michael York and

Nicol Williamson (who turned out to have a singing voice pleasantly reminiscent of Hoagy Carmichael!). The audiences loved mingling with the celebrities – the contributions began to come in, "although we never *asked* for money", Sam was quick to point out.

Very occasionally he got more than he bargained for. John Dankworth recalls three silver haired ladies approaching Sam and asking nervously: "We're just three little widows, but if we made up a half a million dollars between us, would you accept it?"

❖

Sam had set up the North American Chapter of the Shakespeare Globe Centre as far back as 1974 – appropriately enough, in Chicago, where the Dream had first reached out to him. By 1982 he'd enlarged his original concept. Now the "national" organization was to be in New York with "regional" offices in Chicago, Denver, Houston and Los Angeles. The South East and Toronto would soon follow. Moreover, the Shakespeare Globe Centre Inc. now had tax exempt status, making it easier and financially more efficient for wealthy Americas to donate.

Though in no way an 'organisation man' himself, Sam quite liked *organisations* and was in his element opening a branch of this or congratulating a new chapter of that. All these people were living proof of a dynamic popular movement gaining momentum. At the same time he was well aware that, valuable as their efforts might be, the Globe was not going to be built by the accumulation of small contributions. The presence and the sheer decibel level of the organisation would provide the project with credibility but to bring it to completion would require a few big fish in the net. And the biggest fish undoubtedly swam in American waters.

> I cannot do it; yet I'll hammer it out.
>
> *Richard II*, Act V Sc. v

Of these the biggest was Armand Hammer. Industrialist (head of Occidental Oil), philanthropist and reputedly one of the world's richest men, Hammer was unique, even among billionaires. When Sam had first introduced himself, at the suggestion of the Palace, in 1981 Hammer was 83. He made it his business to know everybody who was anybody – or might become somebody – and his friends went right back to Lenin. In fact, he'd created something of a market for himself as a self-appointed diplomat, specialising in US-Soviet relations and his personal contacts did seem to keep certain doors conveniently ajar. He liked being famous and there were those who said that he conducted his activities with one eye on the Nobel Peace Prize that would complete his collection of citations.

He certainly gave generously and visibly to a variety of charities and his cultural credentials were impeccable. It was a happy day for Sam when Hammer consented in August 1982 to head up the North American chapter, because it made the Globe project legitimate for other potential major donors. Hammer set the tone by becoming a "Founder" and pledging $50,000 a year for five years and cajoling others to do the same. When, soon after, Gordon Getty – another of "the world's richest men" – signed on as *Vice Chairman*, Sam could be forgiven for thinking he'd just set foot on the Yellow Brick Road. The *names* would surely be bankable enough. And to start with it seemed as though they would.

In September 1982 Hammer threw a party at the Beverly Wilshire at which the guest of honour was Prince Philip and the rich, pledging $10,000 or more each, rubbed shoulders with the rich and famous, such as Cary Grant, Elizabeth Taylor and Richard Burton. The glamour on show that evening was in marked contrast to what the guests would have seen, had they been transported to Bankside, where grit was more in evidence that glitz.

With typical Hammer panache the coup of the evening was to have Prince Philip announce in public that he had now accepted the ten year old offer to become the project's Patron.

To commemorate the occasion the Prince was presented with the 'affiliation royalties' from eleven US Shakespeare Festivals and – on behalf of the academic community – with a facsimile edition of the *Shakespeare Quarto*. Unfortunately, the presenter had neglected to check the tonnage of the weighty volume he had to present. As he tried to pick it up after his speech, it flew out of his hand and the guests were treated to the unexpected spectacle of Prince and don trying to field the Bard like baseball players.

In the excitement of the evening it apparently went unnoticed that Hammer had not actually *signed* his quarter million dollar pledge...

...and all alone
To-night we'll wander through the streets and note
The qualities of people.

Antony and Cleopatra, Act I Sc. i

The following spring came the road show. Raising money was certainly an objective but there was another important agenda item and that was keeping up morale. There was precious little progress to report in terms of actual building, although the site was supposedly secure, and some donors were beginning to ask if things were still on course. The Dedication ceremony loomed as an important symbolic event which must set any doubts at rest.

As we've seen, it achieved its purpose. As Chairman of the Trustees, Sir David Orr reassured the American donors who had made the trip they could tell their friends back home that "It will be as much *their* Centre, *their* Globe, *their* Museum as those of us who happen to live in the country where the Globe originally existed and where it will be resurrected to live once again". He went on to emphasise the fact that, quite apart from the reconstructed playhouse and the appreciation of the plays in performance, the project was to become an educational focus for Shakespearean studies worldwide. To sharpen that focus it had been decided to set up an International Council, which Armand Hammer had consented to chair in addition to his North American duties.

Dr. Hammer, after listing a few of his own achievements in bringing the peoples of the world together, related this to the current project: "It is through strengthening world understanding by promoting a mutual appreciation of the arts, poetry, drama, music and literature that we can arrest the rush to doomsday". The Globe, he felt, would become "a powerful force able to transcend the artificial barriers which are erected between people".

So the occasion more than passed muster but Hammer was far too beady not to have read the signs. Early in the year he had warned Sam that, unless he felt that things would go well, he would certainly advise Prince Philip to call off the promised reception at the Palace. And no one was in any doubt that he could and would do just that.

Although he declared himself satisfied with the week's events, there were troubling signs that true Hammer watchers might have detected. He prided himself on running a tight organisational ship and at a London Board meeting that coincided with the dedication he was clearly not impressed by what he saw of the project's financial administration. Record keeping was inadequate and precious funds were dribbling away. He offered to send in his own financial people to tidy things up. The tone of subsequent correspondence was a little less cordial and there was an emotional episode caused by Tim Halford (Hammer's man on the UK Globe Board at the time) sending in a report critical of the Dedication ceremony, which caused Sam to sulk in his tent for a time. It almost certainly stayed Hammer's hand from signing the funding pledge at that time. Many other potential donors shared the reason he gave – that he didn't want his money to be used to fund the bureaucracy of the Trust; it was only to be used for the actual work of building and, since no building was yet under way, what was the hurry? It was hard to argue, though Sam certainly tried.

> *...as rich men deal gifts,*
> *Expecting in return twenty for one?*
> *Timon of Athens*, Act IV Sc. iii

In retrospect it seems likely that the writing was on the wall from that point. Hammer had no time for ventures that might not succeed and the Globe was rapidly falling into that category in his mind. While the legal wranglings were taking place, there was nothing for him to do but sit back but, once the verdict was in, his letter of congratulation was one of the first to arrive on Sam's desk. Unfortunately, it also contained less welcome news: "The funds which I originally pledged to the Globe Theatre were, when the project went into abeyance, naturally obligated to other charities". Those "many new charities" to which he had attached himself since 1984 "are taking up my time and energy and available resources". In short, he felt he should resign his Chairmanship of the International Committee and withdraw his local consultant from the directorship of the Trust.

One of the new causes was the recently discovered *Mary Rose*. Prince Charles had enlisted his support personally and in Hammer's scheme of things a Prince with a wooden ship to preserve outranked an actor with a wooden theatre still to build.

Sam was devastated. "Your leadership, enthusiasm and contribution have been the principal rock on which the enterprise has been anchored", he wrote, begging Hammer to remain Chairman

Emeritus, "so as not to damage the Globe's chances to raise further funds by implying with your resignation your disapproval of the Project ... I am writing this in my personal capacity and without the approval of our Trustees who are as deeply disappointed as I am but would not express themselves in such an emotional and frank manner as I have done here".

There is no evidence that Hammer ever answered this or any other of Sam's impassioned letters. Eventually Sam resorted to asking Hammer's onetime lawyer, Louis Nizer, to intercede for him and Hammer agreed – at secondhand – to retain a titular role for the time being and pay $100,000 as a once and only contribution. Sam was deeply hurt. Hammer's commitment had been vocal and public – but you didn't sue the Armand Hammers of this world. Gordon Getty took over as President of the International Committee.

Hammer's defection can be attributed to a number of causes. He had little regard for Sam's administrative skills after the London meeting and for his penchant for spending hard won funds on setting up committees here, there and everywhere, most of which cost upwards of $100,000 a year to run before a red cent had come through the door – not to mention ill-planned events that came in over budget and produced a similar result. To him this was amateur night. But more worrying than that – which he could have disciplined, if he'd had a mind to – was the sound of time's wingèd chariot at his back. Hammer was an old man in a hurry. Once the court case became a factor, he couldn't afford to wait. The cause was still a good one but it was less and less likely that it would come to fruition in the time he had left. He wasn't a man who was easily satisfied with promises of posterity, so he picked up most of his chips and left the table...

> Noble patricians, patrons of my right
>
> *Titus Andronicus*, Act I Sc. i

The Hammer episode was in many ways symbolic of the problems Sam faced in enlisting and retaining American support. Culture and geography change perspectives. As far as the Globe home team was concerned, when he took off on one of his many crusades, it was Daddy going out to earn the money. He was going back to talk to his own people and who knew them better than he did?

But it wasn't quite as simple as that. To begin with, he wasn't one of 'his own people' any more. By this time it was thirty years since he'd lived there; he was now a professional expat. And for some of the older monied families his social and ethnic background meant that he never had been and never would be 'one of us'. The social stratifications that conditioned American society were every bit as subtle and excluding as their British equivalents. And Sam could never expect to be absorbed there either, despite the many good friends he was to make. He was to remain a citizen of no city. His passport was the Dream – and that would have to do it all...

❖

One of the abiding problems the project faced was that potential American donors were never quite sure what the Dream *was*. A replica of the original playhouse, fine. But that would be over there and they would be over here. When they'd helped to build it, what would they be – tourists like anyone else but with privileged ticket prices? No, there had to be more to it than that, something *permanent*.

Lee Freeman, one of Sam's early advisors in Chicago, cut through the rhetoric early on by pointing this out to Sam. *Education*, he argued, was the key to unlocking American funding. Build up the academic element, the access to worldwide Shakespearean knowledge. And for heaven's sake, get academic *Americans* on board!

Not that Sam needed persuading. For him, the study and understanding of Shakespeare had always been almost as important as actual performance. Shakespeare was an international language and the Globe a theatre for the world. The theatre would provide the glamour and draw the crowds; the educational aspect would provide a solid underpinning, both intellectually and politically. It was all part of a master plan that constantly grew and expanded in his mind and threw off impassioned language. The sadness was that in the twenty or so years he played the US fund-raising circuit he never found a way to harness those words to describe the Dream clearly and succinctly.

Late in the 1980's, when the project at last seemed back on track, an American advisor had written to him, expressing his own concerns:

The difficulty is that I do not sense a clear program policy. I hear you refer to various possibilities – i.e., visiting companies, a scholarly center for Shakespearean research, children's theatre, community activities, but none of this seems to have been fully worked out.

How could it be, when it was always changing for *him?* Nonetheless, Americans were understandably concerned at what they saw as lack of clarity. They had, after all, contributed a good third of the money and at times their contribution had made the difference between carrying on the fight or closing up shop.

When the letter arrived, Sam had just left on another fund-raising tour. This time he would take in *twelve* cities. Action, lots of *action*, that's what was needed.

> O! this learning, what a thing it is.
> *The Taming of the Shrew*, Act I Sc. ii

Although Sam never managed to allay American concern fully, he was made well aware of it and always sought to disarm it.

He wooed academia as he had in England from the outset. Professor John Styan of Northwestern University became his Glynne Wickham at an early stage, his place taken in time by Professor Hugh Richmond of the University of California at Berkeley. So those credentials were soon in place. By 1982 there was an academic council of more than 40 top scholars in North America. In some ways that was the easy part. North American scholars were as much Bardophiles as their English equivalents – perhaps more so in some ways. Shakespeare was an imported delicacy, to be sure, but appreciated all the more for that – and certainly never to be taken for granted, as he could easily be in a more blasé British culture. (As one scholar pointed out: "One word that never haunted him this side of the pond was – *Disneyland*. Perhaps because over here many of us realise that it's a pretty well-run operation!") In his speech at the Dedication ceremony, Armand Hammer took care to point out that there had been more than fifty Shakespeare festivals in the US in the last year alone! If the Bard and what he stood for didn't belong to the *world*, perhaps we should debate that subject now?

> If money were as certain as your waiting,
> 'Twere sure enough.
> *Timon of Athens*, Act III Sc. iv

Despite the reservations, the work of fund-raising went on.

Chicago – firmly convinced that it was still *de facto* the centre of the American Globe universe – went on acting accordingly, staging event after successful event, often under the most adverse circumstances. If there was one Shakespearean theme that ran through so many of the Globe's early activities it must surely be *The Tempest* and the windy city could tell tales to match the horrors of *Antony and Cleopatra*.

One St. Patrick's Day event saw a gust of wind showering the stack of programmes into the green-dyed Chicago River, forcing a rapid reprint in the half hour left to the organisers. The ink was not much drier than the copies floating gaily downstream. Another occasion found the Chicago loyalists on the flight deck of the visiting British destroyer *HMS Fife* during another storm. While actor, Nicholas Rudall competed with the blowing and spouting of the 'cataracts and hurricanes', guests clung to anything solid to prevent themselves being washed into Lake Michigan, while trying to deal with soggy sandwiches and diluted drinks. Time and again, the Bard proved a demanding taskmaster.

But not everyone was as steadfast as the Chicagoans.

A number of eminent American names had originally been drawn to the Globe's fire. Many of them heeded Hammer's call and brandished their bright cheque books. The money didn't exactly roll in but it kept up a healthy pace.

And then at the end of 1984 came the news of the court case.

At which point Jerome Link, (a businessman who had become Chief Executive of the US Globe in 1984) made the reluctant decision to freeze the funding drive. In his view it was improper to continue to solicit funds for a project that might no longer exist, should the Globe lose their case!

"But we *shan't* lose, we *can't* lose!" Sam kept insisting. Link, backed by an American Board with a knowledge of accepted local business practices, stood firm, permitting only the release of small amounts of funds already accrued to finance the legal costs required to actually fight the case. "I'm sure Sam considered my attitude negative", Link recalls. "In fact, it was just the opposite: I was concerned that we should live to fight another day!"

It was to prove a wise decision.

The moratorium or hibernation lasted for three years. After the court victory Sam renewed his pleas but Link and the US Board were clear. When the new planning permission was granted, then – and only then – could purse strings be legally untied. They didn't want somebody suing *them*. In the UK the situation was a mirror image with Sir David Orr writing to Sam in October 1986 urging him to delay the major fund-raising drive for precisely the same reason.

Hammer was gone and with him a large measure of the project's visibility and social credibility. And when the dust had settled, it could be seen that significant names, such as the Cabots and others for whom Sam had had such hopes – had also failed to reappear. Nor did the economic climate help. Worldwide recession was looming and those who knew about money matters were getting an uneasy feeling, which the stock market lurch of October 1987 only served to confirm. These were *real* events, whereas that business over in London... would it *ever* be built?

One thing that kept the Anglo-American relationship on a reasonably even keel during this period was the stability of the personal and professional relationship between Link and Michael Perry, the London Chairman of the ISGC. Perry was well aware the cash flow – or at least, trickle – from America was necessary to keep the project ticking over, while Link perfectly well appreciated that, should the UK end collapse, there would be no US operation. Their interests were extremely mutual.

> I gave it freely ever; and there's none
> Can truly say he gives, if he receives
> *Timon of Athens*, Act I Sc. ii

Through it all a handful of people kept the faith – despite the fact that, as the 80s ended, they were among the few, that precious few, who had the image of a depressing concrete swimming pool firmly in their minds and who *still* believed...

One of them was Douglas Fairbanks, Jr. Fairbanks remains typically modest about his own involvement but what attracted Sam to him was obvious enough. They were both Americans who had become Transatlantic Men. ("We both used to bounce back and forth all the time", as Fairbanks puts it.) And there the resemblance ended. Sam hovered between the two countries. Fairbanks was at home in both, accepted at the highest social levels and a personal friend of people like Prince Philip and Lord Mountbatten, who could make all the difference to the outcome of the project. Sam made sure

Fairbanks was invited to become one of the original Trustees... Fairbanks declared himself glad to be "a small spoke in Sam Wanamaker's wheel".

Occasionally, a surprising new champion would emerge. One such was the Ambassador Foundation, an interdenominational religious group based in Los Angeles, which came through with a pledge for half a million dollars.

The continuity of the precious few, such as Fairbanks, the Freemans, Herbert and Audré Mendel, Roberta Nelson-Walker, Gene Andersen, Sam Scripps and Rhoda Pritzker – supplemented by Sam's increasingly frenetic visits – undoubtedly kept the project afloat in the sea of troubles that engulfed it after the court case.

The tide turned with the building of the bays, and once again, the Americans came to the rescue. "How much?" they said, when the idea was first mooted in early 1991. And when they heard the figure – "Done!" Jerry Link and Nancy Knowles-Kolden sponsored them personally and work commenced. If there was one point when final success was assured, this can now be seen to have been it.

Learning is but an adjunct to ourself
Love's Labours Lost, Act IV sc iii

Another – though necessarily less dramatic element – was the quiet but constant underpinning of the educational side of the project. During the worst of the wilderness years, overshadowed by the drama of external events, the work had gone on.

Even from across the Atlantic it was clear that Sam meant business, even if he was in a small way of business as the decade ended. There were lectures and workshops on offer as well as a couple of university courses. In 1989 he could claim that some 5,000 students had visited Bear Gardens for classes.

What American ears could not overhear were the board room discussions at which several members consistently argued that an organised educational effort at this parlous stage of the project was a waste of time and money. Standing firmly in opposition, like Horatius guarding the bridge, was Sam. The Globe *must* develop its educational profile. The world must be made to see the educational importance of the new Globe for all nations and all ages. Shakespeare belonged to the world, etc., etc.

As usual, he carried the day and, by winning this particular argument, he probably saved the project. Education was the visible and indisputable tip of the Globe iceberg. Uniquely, education preceded the actual theatre. With the National and the RSC, educational departments were 'after-thoughts'. In the difficult years ahead the Globe team could point out that their venture had its *roots* in education. Symbolically, when the complex was finished the Education Department would be physically located beneath – i.e., supporting the theatre.

In the last couple of years a clearer and more comforting message has come through. The project would be a mix of Theatre, Education and Exhibition, acting interdependently. As always, Shakespeare would provide something for everyone...

❖

For many years the American education programme had been marching in lock step with its British equivalent. Conferences were organised on such topics as "Multi-Culturalism and Shakespeare in the Non-English Speaking World". There were teacher training workshops and activities devised specially for inner city schools, where teenagers used the plays to explore issues like gang violence – shades of *West Side Story!* – and AIDS. Without fail the wisdom of Shakespeare's words provided new insight...

Another statistic created a little perspective. At the time of the Globe's dedication Hammer had quoted fifty Shakespeare festivals as proof of American interest and commitment. Had he been speaking in 1996, he could have said – *110!* It was a 'Shakespeare industry', complete with marketing.

The California Shakespeare Festival in Berkeley caught the imagination of their particular audience by advertising a casting call for a dog to play in *The Two Gentlemen of Verona*. The response was overwhelming and the part went to "a goofy-looking mutt" which, according to the artistic director, "was a better actor than some of the actors". The Heart of America Shakespeare Festival in Kansas City arranged with the local paper to run a comic strip version of *The Tempest*, while their production was playing in the park. But perhaps the subtlest device was the one devised by the Utah Shakespeare Festival with its somewhat eclectic catchment area. By using the slogan "Let's Play!" they caught the attention of the Las Vegas gambling fraternity, while the straight-laced Mormons of Salt Lake City said, "Why, that sounds like a family event". What it *didn't* say was much about Shakespeare. But then, as the Stratford Ontario Festival director put it: "Shakespeare's voice is so loud that you have to be deaf to ignore it".

Over the years the Globe has done its own share of marketing. As the financial corner was finally turned at the end of 1995, the New York Bar Association was holding *Hamlet on Trial*. A judge and two prominent attorneys (whose combined fees could have built a bay or two) cross examined the characters, who answered only in the lines from the play. The audience, fresh from the complexities of the O. J. Simpson trial, found the process riveting and were clearly disappointed when the jury found Hamlet guilty of second degree manslaughter and they saw him taken off in handcuffs to serve his "twenty year stretch ..."

CHAPTER ELEVEN

THE COUNCILLOR'S TALE

...by the holy rood,
I do not like these several councils...
Richard III, Act III Sc. ii

At the dedication of the Globe site in July 1983, the then Mayor of Southwark began his speech by explaining the meaning of the badge of office he wore, the official symbol of the Borough.

On a shield there is an Elizabethan ship, a stone barbican (or round defence tower) and figures of hop flowers and a hop cane. The shield is supported by two men and beneath them is the inscription – "United to Serve." (Sam's face would have made an interesting study at that point, since he was feeling particularly *ill* served).

The Mayor went on to discuss the detail and score a few points for the home team. When the Romans founded Londinium some nineteen centuries earlier, they had had the good sense to settle on the south side of the river, leaving the locals to occupy the other side that became the City of London.

The *shield* was the symbol of defence, as was the stone tower or defence work ("wark"). The hops represented the beer brewing that was one of the area's ancient industries, "now entirely and tragically moved to the countryside." What the Mayor couldn't know was that the nearby Courage Brewery site now acquired by the Hanson Group, would be found six years later to be sitting on top of the original Globe foundations.

Another of Southwark's "once great industries" was represented by the *ship*. From Rotherhithe, a short distance downstream, had embarked the *Mayflower*, "on which the forefathers of some of you sailed to America early in the 17th century." *(Emotional applause from the American donors)*

169

As for the two men... on the right is the Esquire from Chaucer's *Canterbury Tales*, since the pilgrims started their historical journey to Canterbury from the Tabard Inn in Southwark's High Street... while on the left, holding a shield in his left hand and a skull in his right is Hamlet.

Thus, the Mayor concluded, Southwark's badge "is the symbol of our proud heritage, our industry, our craftsmanship, our great cultural past. We are determined they shall not be lost."

At which point, Sam was seen to nod...

> *I am Southwark born. I heard you and*
> *I want the theatre..!*
>
> Mrs. Emily Braidwood, Southwark resident

When you talk about a group of people, it's easy to find yourself referring to the people who talk for them, assuming that the one stands for the other. In referring to 'Southwark' opinion during this narrative, the opinion expressed has invariably been that of the Southwark Borough Council and has fluctuated according to the political make-up of that Council at different times. From inactive to passive to mildly supportive to wildly antagonistic, finally to enthusiastic, the official mood swings have occupied two and a half decades.

But the correspondence generated by the knowledge of this book's preparation suggests that many of the unelected citizens of Southwark didn't necessarily share their sometime officials' sense of the project's 'elitism.'

Emily Braidwood recalls going to a local meeting in the mid-1970's where housing was to be discussed. The meeting was less than satisfactory with the then Labour MP, Bob Mellish, finally beating a tactical retreat, leaving a seething room of people behind him:

> Incredibly, at last, a hush, then a softly-spoken man stood in the middle of the crowd, appealed to be heard, and said Southwark should remember and acknowledge the greatest scriptwriter in the world and build a Globe theatre to his memory. William Shakespeare was unique. The crowd yelled their obscenities. Sam was vilified. My friend, Winnie, a tall lady but of a nervous disposition, tugged at my coat, urged me *not* to get involved, saying to me, 'Don't I know this bloke from somewhere?' I said, 'It's Sam Wanamaker, in lots of films, you know.'

The crowd, still on their feet, were extremely nasty. I said to Winnie: 'This can't be right.' I stood up and pushed my way through the crowd followed by Winnie ... I stopped short of Sam, because a young woman stood in front of him, leering, tugging at the back of her hair and said: 'Go back, bleedin' Yank – we don't want your bleedin' Globe!' She turned, yelled over her shoulder to someone in the crowd: 'What do you want me to say next, Joe?'

With alacrity, the penny dropped; the rent-a-yob mob had obviously been orchestrated to fill the hall, to abuse.

I then pushed in front of the 'lady', took hold of Sam's hand, said: 'Hello. These are not Southwark people. I am Southwark born, I heard you and I want the theatre.' Then to Winnie – 'Come on, Winnie, shake his hand.' She did. I said: 'Well, keep going. Bite on the bullet...'

It was that kind of grass roots reaction that kept bullets a staple part of Sam's diet for the next twenty years – As for Mrs. Braidwood, she was invited to unveil the ninth bay of the rebuilt Globe in 1994.

> It was the people of London who inspired
> Shakespeare to such reflection on human nature.
>
> Mark Rylance, Globe Artistic Director

The Southwark Sam found in 1970 – the year he first approached the Council – was not so very different from the kind of cohesive working class community celebrated in so many post-war British films.

In many ways the locals were still dealing with the effects of that war. While other parts of London had raised or been given the money to re-generate themselves, Southwark had not been so fortunate. Much of it still suffered from the industrial ague of half-demolished buildings and overgrown waste land caused by wartime bombing. But while those depressing relics of recent history remained all too visible, other, less tangible things were changing with bewildering speed. With the closing of the Surrey Docks and a number of local factories local jobs were vanishing into thin air. And you might well find yourself not only out of a job but without a proper place to live. Eleven thousand people had their names on Southwark's waiting list in that year.

Local luck was most definitely out, because at that very moment the property speculators, who had picked over much of London in recent years, turned their eyes south of the river, giving Southwark a glimpse of what Prime Minister Edward Heath was to dub 'the unacceptable face of capitalism.'

It didn't take Sam long to realise that his timing was off. Land values were rising at such a pace there was no way he and the Globe could afford to pay a full commercial price. Could the Council – *would* the Council – help him to find a site as near as possible to the original and then come up with a formula for acquiring it without putting the project into debt for the *next* four hundred years?

The then Council would and eventually did. Contrary to later perception Southwark Council's acceptance of what Sam was trying to achieve was both immediate and enthusiastic and many of those early supporters remain so to this day.

One of them was Councillor Ron Watts, who took over as Chairman of the Planning and Development Committee in 1973. An expert on planning law, Watts was able to find the way to turn Southwark's *would* into *could*. Sam's heart had originally been set on building as close to the original as possible but Watts soon convinced him that not only was that not possible but that there was a lot to be said for choosing a more dramatic setting on the river itself. He personally involved himself in the negotiations for the site on which the Globe now stands.

Local authorities have never enjoyed the degree of omnipotence they often like to imply – as another Southwark Council were to discover to their cost a decade later. But the Council of the early 1970s worked in an altogether more subtle and sensitive fashion. They'd seen all too clearly from a very early stage that Southwark's fate could easily be to have a series of ugly derelict factories replaced by a series of ugly concrete office buildings as an overspill from the overcrowded City across the water. In anticipation, they'd been quietly buying small parcels of land in strategic spots. When you happen to own even a few square yards slap in the middle of a potential development, you are likely to get the developer's serious attention. More to the point, you are likely to be able to negotiate significant 'planning gains' from the developers that will benefit the community. Such a bargaining chip was already in place on the East Bankside site Watts was suggesting for the Globe.

Even so, the calculations were complex. Despite owning a crucial strip of land, it was to prove difficult to persuade the other landowners involved to co-operate. In 1974, however – while the piecing together was in progress – the co-conspirators were handed a bonus. The newly-returned Labour Government passed the Community Land Act, which gave a local Council the power to acquire land "for schemes that benefitted the community." The Council immediately applied for a Compulsory Purchase Order (CPO) for the East Bankside site.

Not for the last time was the Globe project to be a guinea pig. The law was brand new, there was no precedent and the developers couldn't afford to roll over. They forced a public enquiry which, as these things do, inevitably dragged on. When Labour lost power in 1979 there had still been no decision. At which point hearts collectively sank. What chance would a piece of what was essentially bureaucracy, however helpful, stand of surviving in Margaret Thatcher's brave new Britain with its 'free market forces?'

In fact, it did somehow survive, though it was to take another three years before all the details were worked out and John O'Grady, as Leader of the Council and Ann Ward, as his deputy, were able to sign the agreement with Derno (a subsidiary of the Freshwater Group). The Globe Trust, while not a signatory, was a 'third party beneficiary' under the terms of the arrangement.

The final signing took place on April 30th 1982. A week later on May 7th local elections returned yet another Labour Council but this time of a very different political complexion. The Globe's troubles – as already described in Chapter 6 – were just beginning ...

So, in other ways, were Southwark's.

> Faith, I have been a truant in the law,
> And never yet could frame my will to it,
> And therefore frame the law unto my will.
>
> *Henry VI (Pt.1)*, Act II Sc. iv

Throughout London and much of the rest of England the Labour Party had been moving to the far left as a reaction to the right wing politics of a Thatcherite Tory Party. In constituency after constituency moderate Socialists were being challenged – often to the point of being de-selected as candidates – in what became known as the 'politics of confrontation.' Pragmatism, the cornerstone of post-war Labour politics, was to be a thing of the past in the new era.

In the eyes of the new men and women who took control, reducing the moderate faction in Southwark to a mere rump, this was a return to true Labour dogma and an end to wishy-washy compromise.

Ironically, the group that took effective control – the North Southwark Community Development Group – had been heavily subsidised by the Council for many years. They now took exception to almost all of the policies of their previous patrons. They were particularly opposed to office development in the area that included the Globe. The land, they claimed, should be used for housing. And indeed, their point of view was broadly popular; the only problem being that the high value of the land in question made it unrealistic for it to be used for that purpose, according to the cost limits agreed by both successive Labour and Conservative governments. In any case, *land* wasn't the problem; the Council had plenty of that available. What it didn't have was money to develop the land and the only way it could obtain the money was through the income that office development would provide. Catch 22.

> "Shakespeare... a lot of tosh!"
> Tony Ritchie, Leader of Southwark Council, March 1986

The issue rapidly became personal as well as political. Facts were soon irrelevant. The Left saw Sam as an American who – *because* he was American – must be in it for the money. His own left wing credentials and the personal damage he had received for standing by convictions very similar to their own during the McCarthy era went for nothing. Of course the man had an angle. All this stuff about a community gain and an educational charity was so much hot air. Even when Sam went to the lengths of providing the Borough Treasurer with full details of his personal finances, which showed that not only was he giving his time and effort free of charge but also putting money into the project that he had no hope of recouping, the Council declined to be convinced. Sam was a foreigner, he was in bed with the Demon Developers, Shakespeare was 'elitist' – and that was that.

The new leadership of the Council, spearheaded by two NSCDG activists – Alan Davies as Leader and Geoff Williams, the new Chair of Planning – took a *kamikaze* attitude towards any opposition, though they naturally hardly saw it in that light. Supported by Ted Bowman, as Chair of both Bermondsey Labour Party *and* the NSCDG, the group's policies were to determine all planning decisions for the next four years. As far as the Globe affair was concerned, beyond a point political bloody mindedness appeared to dictate the agenda.

Their attitude was typified by the ludicrous episode of the road sweepers. Before he left office Ron Watts had made sure that under the terms of the 1982 agreement there would be no problem about finding alternative accommodation when the time came. He had even begun negotiations with British Rail for a nearby railway arch in an area zoned for 'light industry'. The new Council chose to refer to the application as being an "inappropriate use in a residential area" – a definition Mr. Justice Harman was to question with the scepticism only a British High Court judge can command. Only Flanagan & Allen had been known to *live* "underneath the arches".

The plot thickened. In early 1983 the Council received a report from the Deputy Town Clerk warning of the consequences of defaulting on the 1982 agreement. Few councillors were even aware of its existence until too late in the game. In a memo to the Chief Executive of April 7th the Borough Valuer wrote that the Leader of the Council (Davies) had instructed him not to submit the report to the Committee. The politics of the twilight zone continued for the next year or so. On May 22nd 1984 there was a meeting of the Labour councillors who were members of the Planning Committee at which it was decided to summarily reject the Derno agreement. No members of the opposition were invited to the meeting, nor were Derno or the Globe informed, so that they could present a point of view.

For the two years since the signing of the agreement and the changing of the guard both of the other interested parties had been trying through their lawyers to find out what was happening behind the closed doors of the Southwark Council chamber but without success. By July they learned that a "political decision" had been taken. At no time had there been a public discussion. From that point things degenerated into black farce. In a last ditch attempt to save the agreement both Freshwater and British Rail wrote to the Council offering alternative sites for the road sweepers. Their suggestions were rejected out of hand. The NSCDG juggernaut was now out of control. Political face was at stake.

At another closed meeting of the Labour Group in October the few members who bothered to attend voted in favour of voiding the agreement. Ann Ward was the solitary dissenting voice and hand.

A month later the full Planning Committee dutifully voted along party lines, many of them having never been made aware of the potential legal risks. All that remained were the consequences...

It had taken the Globe twelve years to find a home. It took its opponents just two to undermine its foundations.

Derno carried out its threat to sue, which surprised many of the Labour councillors, who thought they were the only ones who were licensed to bluff and bluster. The Globe's position, however, was less clear cut. It had a strong legal case to sue *both* sides, even though it was not signatory to the 1982 agreement. Money for legal fees would be and was a problem but an even bigger one in Sam's eyes was the need to explain to the people of Southwark just what all this confusing legal wrangling was about. He decided to organise a public meeting in May 1985.

By this time the Globe Board was in two minds as to what course of action it could responsibly pursue. Could they even risk taking High Court action, despite the strength of their case, knowing the likely costs involved? While the Board was actually in session, Diana Devlin, then the Administrator, received a phone call which made the decision for them. It was from Ann Ward, offering not only to speak at a public meeting but to give evidence in any court case that might ensue. If a leading Southwark Labour Councillor was willing to stand up and be counted for the Globe, well...

Ann Ward, a longtime Southwark councillor who became one of the Globe's most loyal supporters.
Robert McBain

When the public meeting finally took place, Ward was the opening platform speaker. It was gratifying to find that, as far as the public were concerned, support for the Globe was overwhelming – the exceptions being Bowman and a claque from the NSCDG who came to heckle and were clearly perturbed to find themselves in such a small minority. At the end of the meeting thirty or so of the audience found themselves lingering to continue the discussion. Before they left they exchanged addresses and agreed to set up what became the Southwark Friends of Shakespeare's Globe. By the time the Globe was built the Friends were strong and had raised over two hundred thousand pounds towards the cost.

From the day of the meeting Ann Ward became a leading counter-revolutionary. Quite aware that her political position was now untenable, she informed the Council that she would be standing down at the next election in May 1986, bringing to an end a fifteen year career in local government. The Council's loss was the Globe's gain as she refocused her considerable energies to help the project.

> I do suspect this trash
> To be a party in this injury
>
> *Othello*, Act V Sc. i

One of her first activities as a 'private' citizen was to satisfy herself as to precisely how much disturbance the notorious road sweepers actually caused to the surrounding area:

> I got to the site at 6:30 on a lovely summer morning when the only sound was that of the birds. The first man arrived on foot at two minutes past seven and the rest of the fifteen trickled through the gate by 7:35. Some came on foot, a few on bicycles and two came sharing a car. They went on the site, assembled their trolleys, had a mug of tea and were quickly away for the rest of the day ... Throughout the early morning the song of birds continued without interruption and was the loudest sound to be heard... Yet the reason put forward for not moving the depot was the noise and disruption it caused!

Ward gave her log and file of photos to the Globe's lawyers. She also spoke to *The Sunday Times*, which subsequently published a half page of pictures of the road sweepers arriving for work under the headline: "If Shakespeare moves in 'ere, I'm moving out!" Many a true word...

With Ward's encouragement Sam decided to canvas local opinion for himself. The NSCDG's case was essentially based on the argument that the people of Southwark were against the rebuilding of the Globe. But how true was this? Two petitions were organised, the most important of which was restricted to the people who lived in Cathedral Ward, which covered the area in which the Globe was to be built. The Friends of Shakespeare's Globe acted as poll takers. Armed with voters' lists, they went from door to door, making sure that all those who signed really did live there. With considerable effort they managed to contact over three-quarters of the registered voters and found, once again, that support for the project was overwhelming. Wherever Councillors Davies and Williams (who represented the ward) obtained the statistics on which they based their vehement opposition, it certainly wasn't from their *constituents!*

> And be these juggling fiends no more believ'd
> That palter with us in a double sense,
> That keep the word of promise to our ear,
> And break it to our hope.
>
> *Macbeth*, Act V Sc. vii

From then until the case finally came to court, the Council fought a bitter rearguard action. The Globe project had never been debated at a full Council meeting and even now, despite deputations from the entertainment industry and with the Friends anxious to present the results of the several petitions, agendas were so arranged that the contentious item appeared down among the wines and spirits. At the critical Council meeting the vote was finally taken at 1:30 a.m. Inevitably, it was lost. Even the Globe's most loyal supporters had to sleep some time. There was nothing for it now but to wait for the case to be heard.

The rest, as they say, was history. After two days in Court it was clear that the Council's case was a poor thing of threads and precious few patches.

When the judge insisted on taking the Court off by bus to tour the area and inspect the possible sites the Council had rejected for the depot, there was a distinct hint of surrealism in the air. By the end of the bus ride it was clear that the defence had no credible defence. The lawyers retired to negotiate an out-of-court settlement.

> *"Southwark was never against Shakespeare*
> *per se...our North Southwark plan just*
> *registered a different priority for Bankside."*
> Geoff Williams, sometime Southwark Councillor

In true British tradition at least some of the losers congratulated the winners. After the verdict Sam called an impromptu press conference on the site. Ann Ward's memory of the occasion is the image of Sam, champagne bottle in hand, surrounded by back-slapping road sweepers.

"If Shakespeare moves in here, I'm moving out," said one of the road sweepers. But before he did, he and his mates helped Sam celebrate his Court victory. (1986)

In the end, although the Globe won back what it had had to begin with, there were after-effects that served to sour the victory. In the shuffling of parcels of land that resulted from the Court's final decision, Southwark was given a few bits and pieces, which it hoped – by way of saving face – to use for house building. It soon became apparent that this was not going to be possible. The huge costs that had been incurred because of the case meant the land had to be sold right away. The Midland Bank bought most of it and promptly built its cheque clearing headquarters there. So, as a result of its Council's own folly, Southwark's would-be house owners were once again disappointed and, funnily enough, so were Sam and Theo. They'd always hoped to see the Globe surrounded by houses, as it had been in Shakespeare's day. A bank on Bankside didn't fit the scenario at all...

This isn't the most important issue in
Southwark ... The camera crews should be
here when homelessness is being discussed.
Southwark Councillor

The Council elections of 1986 did much to restore the balance of commonsense to Southwark politics. Although the NSCDG and its supporters continued to fight every inch of the way, in due course all the necessary processes were completed and along the way a few fences were mended. At the 1987 ground breaking ceremony the Lady Mayor made a point of riding to the site side by side with Sam in an open horse-drawn carriage and celebrating the new relationship with a very public embrace on the platform.

Two years later, when the Rose remains were discovered, the new leader of the Council, Anne Matthews, was among the first to commit the full support of the local authority. As far as Southwark was concerned, Shakespeare and Bankside were firmly back on the local map.

There was an uncomfortable nakedness of spirit about much of Thatcher's Britain. The sight of the unfettered entrepreneur brought out the worst in the kind of people's politician who is determined to defend the rights of his people, whether they like it or not. The Globe affair was simply one manifestation of that sorry social divisiveness that began early in the decade with the feeling that anyone could do anything they could get away with and which began to peter out as the realisation grew that everything had its price, even if the currency wasn't always simply cash. There was much to be forgotten in a lot of people's behaviour.

Today – unless you fought in the trenches on one side or another in the mid-80s – it's hard to comprehend the pointless bitterness of those years, the appalling waste of time, temper and money.

The Globe management team now works closely with the Council in the preparation of the Council's strategic plan for the area – a plan which now includes the future impact of the Tate Gallery taking over the Bankside power station next to the Globe and, increasingly likely, the fulfillment of Sam and Theo's dream of a pedestrian river crossing linking the site to the steps of St. Paul's.

Without the initial support of Southwark there would have been no site for the loony left to argue about and, thus, no Globe project to be writing about. The four year hiccup, though upsetting, didn't turn out to be terminal and history will no doubt see it in context. In the end the power lay, as it always does, with the people. And the people of Southwark got their Globe...

As good to chide the waves as speak them fair
Henry VI (Pt.3), Act V Sc. iv

It would have given Sam a wry smile to read an article headed, "Smiling All the Way to Bankside" in the *Evening Standard* in July 1995 in which Jeremy Fraser, Southwark's 'persuasive Labour Leader', was quoted as saying: "If you act like King Canute, it rarely works. We aren't going to get big manufacturing to return. The Docks won't re-open. We must rebuild a local economy. The Tate Gallery and the Globe are essential to all that." "Amen to that good wish."

Amen, amen to that fair prayer...
A Midsummer Nights' Dream, Act II Sc. ii

CHAPTER TWELVE

SHAKESPEARE'S ROSE V. WANAMAKER'S GLOBE

> So we grew together,
> Like to a double cherry, seeming parted,
> But yet an union in partition.
> *A Midsummer Night's Dream*, Act III Sc. ii

Laurence Olivier's farewell performance was at the Rose. The official biographies may determine otherwise but on June 11th, 1989 at the main rally for the Rose Campaign that familiar voice asked the crowd – estimated at anything from one to five thousand – whether a muse of fire could exist under a ceiling of commerce. "It seems to me terrible", he said later, "that one's heritage can be swept under the concrete, as though it had never existed". The words were written and recorded with feeling from the Brighton sick bed, where he died one month later to the day without ever seeing the site. Had he done so, the grim reality of the bulldozers might have answered his first question for him. Art's slender chance of survival in the late 1980's required if not the ceiling, then at least the umbrella of commerce.

And could the echoes of that rhetorical question have somehow drifted back over the centuries to when the Rose was new, its original owner, the entrepreneurial Philip Henslowe, would have thought it absurd. How *else*?

❖

Far from being a Binkie Beaumont, a Joseph Papp or Cameron Mackintosh – someone with the theatre in his blood – Henslowe was a man who could easily have put money into anything that would give him a good return. (In the 90's he would almost certainly have been knighted!) Having come up to London as a young man to be apprenticed as a dyer in 1577, he'd finished up ten years later marrying his master's widow and was now a rich man with money to invest. He put it into a playhouse venture and had the foresight to pick Bankside, having watched the problems his competitors were encountering from the Puritan City Fathers in the City.

At that time, of course, Mr. Theatre was James Burbage. The Queen had been pleased to grant him and the Earl of Leicester's Men a licence back in 1574. Burbage and his troupe – which included his sons Richard and Cuthbert – had gone from strength to strength, building the Theatre (1576) outside the City bounds, an example followed a year later by the Curtain. But since the safe distance also had the drawback of inconvenience, Burbage eventually looked for a hall playhouse (the Blackfriars) closer to the heart of things. In this – as we've seen – he was initially frustrated and, his lease on the Theatre being in jeopardy, the troupe decided to 'pick up sticks' and make the move to the now fashionable Bankside. But this is to jump ahead. By then James Burbage was dead. They were now the Lord Chamberlain's Men and the century was about to close.

For the previous ten years Henslowe and the Rose had had Bankside pretty much to themselves. To open a playhouse there back in 1587 was a gamble – but then Henslowe was as a man of business. In the diaries he left behind there is much talk of numbers but little of the dozens of plays he presented in those few short years. We know, for instance, that he was prepared to pay between £6 and £10 for a play – more than most people earned in a year – but many of those 'investments' repaid him well over time, particularly those he commissioned from the young Christopher Marlowe, among them *The Jew of Malta* and *Doctor Faustus*. None were performed more than two or three times a month. Twenty performances a year for any single play was considered a real hit. In 1594/5, a typical year, the Admiral's Men presented thirty-eight different plays at the Rose, twenty-one of which were new.

Southwark in those days was a dangerous place with some of the glamour later attached to free ports like Tangier, Hong Kong or Macao. Outside the jurisdiction of the City, accessible by water, Southwark was as free as any part of the emerging metropolis, a melting pot from which anything might emerge. Why not a new playhouse?

In fact, the Rose wasn't quite the first. That 'honour' went to a rather ramshackle construction way out in Newington Butts, built in 1576 and too far away to worry Henslowe. His real competition came from a host of alternative attractions from bear-baiting to prostitution – and worse still, the *Plague*.

Starting in 1563, the Plague swept the country in two to three year cycles, being particularly lethal in the crowded streets of London. It also played into the hands of the anti-theatre faction since, when the numbers of dead rose above thirty a week, the theatres had to close by law and the players take to the road. The players who visit Hamlet may well have been on one such 'tour'.

In such turbulent times, very little is recorded about the early years of the Rose, until Henslowe substantially remodelled it and increased its capacity in 1592 – the year he started keeping a diary. The assumption must be that he used it for staging plays rather than the more 'bestial' pursuits. He was certainly not the man to let it stand empty, not when he would hear daily of the great success that Burbage, his chief rival, was enjoying north of the river. Whether Burbage saw Henslowe as a rival is more debatable. North and south of the river, they operated in different worlds. Acting was at best a hand to mouth affair and the composition of the troupes was permanently in flux. Groups would merge and splinter again. One of the more prestigious companies of the late-1580's was undoubtedly the Lord Admiral's Men with its rising star, Edward Alleyn (a man who would later give up acting and found Dulwich College in his search for a more 'legitimate' calling). At the beginning of the 1590's the troupe split up and many of the players went on tour. Alleyn, as it happened, joined up with the Burbages in a new company, the Lord Strange's Men, and played at the Burbages' Theatre. Thus, playgoers of 1591 had a chance to see Edward Alleyn and Richard Burbage on the same stage, "two such actors as no age must ever look to see the like". The moment, however, was to be brief. The playhouse was Burbage's and *he* would decide how the profits were to be divided. After a quarrel, Alleyn walked out. Friendly professional rivalry turned into a family feud, which would eventually affect the Rose.

Such news looked nothing but good from Henslowe's point of view. He welcomed Alleyn and Lord Strange's Men to the Rose with open arms. It was February 19th, 1592.

Alleyn's arrival inspired Henslowe to completely refurbish his intimate but decidedly cramped playhouse. It had been built at a

Edward Alleyn, actor – star of the Rose's most successful productions.
Dulwich Picture Gallery

halfway point in the development of London theatres and now he could gain from the experience of Burbage and others. He built a stage roof, for instance, which would include a 'heavens'. He plastered, he painted, he even enlarged the auditorium, superimposing a new playhouse on the old. His improvements gave considerable pause for thought to theatre historians when the remains were uncovered nearly four hundred years later.

The next few years were a drama in themselves – what with legal arguments and the recurring Plague closing theatres for unpredictable periods, none of which pleased Henslowe the businessman. What should have warmed him was the quality of the troupe that his theatre housed. In that first year Lord Strange's Men boasted not only Alleyn but several actors who would become the backbone of Burbage's Lord Chamberlain's Men and lead the way to the Globe. Shakespeare, as far as we know, never *acted* there, although his *Henry VI (Pt.1)* was one of the Rose's first productions.

By 1593 the Rose was back on its financial feet. Alleyn was indubitably the country's leading actor. Not only that, he was now Henslowe's son-in-law! Kit Marlowe was writing leading roles for him – Faustus, Tamburlaine – and the money was pouring into the box office. Even when – in 1591 – a splinter group, which included Shakespeare, defected to join Burbage at his Theatre, Henslowe and Alleyn weren't unduly worried.

Far more worrying was the death of Marlowe, killed in mysterious circumstances in a tavern brawl. Who would write Alleyn's hits now? Shakespeare's *Titus Andronicus* tided them over the spring of 1594. It was, however, to be his last play for the Rose.

Then, in May 1594, came the ruling that henceforth only two companies were to be licensed – one at the Rose performing Marlowe's plays; the other at the Theatre performing Shakespeare's.

From then on competition was intense. The bright young men from the universities were heading for London to try their luck as 'wits' and playwrights, full of new ideas. Up to the point when the playhouses were forcibly closed, more than two thousand new plays were produced. Of the many new plays, by the law of averages, few of them would be outstanding. The Lord Admiral's Men alone are recorded as putting on six different plays a week. Few of these were carried over into a permanent repertoire. The verdict of the box office was as decisive then as it is today on Broadway or Shaftesbury Avenue. But, of course, what raised the stakes considerably for everyone was the prolific success of Will Shakespeare, once he'd settled in with the Lord Chamberlain's Men.

In those first three years between 1594 and 1596 he wrote – and possibly even acted in – *The Taming of the Shrew, The Two Gentlemen of Verona, Romeo* and *Juliet, Richard II, A Midsummer Night's Dream* and *King John*. All the Rose had to compete with was Alleyn, *The Jew of Malta* and *The Spanish Tragedy* – and since Thomas Kyd was also now dead, there would be no more from that source.

For a time the emerging realities were obscured by good receipts and, of course, the frequent interruptions caused by the Plague. Inevitably, competition increased. Bankside earned good word of mouth in the theatrical community and the first tangible sign was the news that another major playhouse – the Swan – was being built nearby, sparing no expense and adding a touch that was to impress everyone and find its place in the influential De Witt drawing – fake marble stage posts! From now on no playhouse could afford to be bare again. New playhouse interiors with their wealth of vivid decor had a lot in common with a later popular art house – the movie palace.

Tastes were changing and the change was accelerated by the kind of subtlety Shakespeare was bringing to the drama, the more realistic depiction of character that spoke to Elizabethan audiences and gave Richard Burbage a platform for his talents. Alleyn's barnstorming, declamatory style was beginning to look a little old-fashioned.

The balance of theatrical influence continued until the end of 1596, when James Burbage made an abortive move to take over the Blackfriars and ease the problem the winter months brought to his 'country' playhouses – the Theatre and the Curtain. Thwarted, he took his company to the temporary comfort of the Curtain, a move that can only have irritated Henslowe. Bankside was now theatrically chic... but there was only so much business to go round.

The tide was turning against Henslowe and the Rose. There was a permanent risk of defection of actors from the Admiral's Men to other companies, unrelenting pressure from the authorities, who missed no opportunity to create new anti-playhouse proclamations. The behaviour of some of the actors gave them a lot to complain about! A proclamation in 1598 confirmed the earlier 1594 arrangement by ordering that the only two companies that would henceforth be officially licensed should be the Admiral's Men and the Chamberlain's Men – one north of the Thames and one south of it.

This pleased Henslowe mightily, since his rivals were still having playhouse problems. The lease for the Theatre was up and the landlord refused to renew it.

At the end of 1597 Edward Alleyn retired at the age of 31. Perhaps he felt his best parts were behind him with the death of Marlowe. There were other good playwrights coming along – Ben Jonson, Thomas Dekker, Thomas Nashe – but none with the versatility of Shakespeare. He may also have tired of a profession that attracted so much official hostility and perhaps, felt that by removing himself from it, he would make it possible for the Queen – his great admirer – to knight him. If that was his motive, he was to be disappointed. There would be no theatrical knight until Sir Henry Irving in 1895.

By this time, however, Alleyn was a rich man and he could afford to diversify his interests. He moved into theatre management, helping Henslowe as company manager and playhouse landlord and later commissioning the building of the Fortune to compete with the upstart Globe.

April 1597 saw the expiration of the lease that led to the building of the original Globe, as the Burbages – with the aid of Peter Street – crossed the Thames with the timbers of the Theatre and reassembled them a hundred short yards from Henslowe's theatre door. It was several months before they were able to open and become a commercial threat to the Rose but from the start of 1599 Henslowe had to face the harsh facts. Just as the Swan outstripped the Rose as the 'latest thing' in playhouse design, so must the Globe have outshone the Swan. The Rose's days – not to mention its lease – were numbered.

Ever the man of business, Henslowe knew when he was beaten. He saw no point in ploughing yet more money into what was basically an outmoded structure. Instead, he waited until the Globe was ready, confirming his worst fears, and he and Alleyn promptly commissioned Peter Street to build them a new playhouse "like unto... the said Playhouse called the Globe". It was to be built north of the river in an attempted reversal of fortune and called – the Fortune. So in 1600 north had come south and south elected to go north.

Though Henslowe's activities took him to new territory, the Rose soldiered on, enjoying an honorable Indian Summer. Although the Admiral's (now Nottingham's) Men had decamped, there were a few glory days as the new incumbents – Worcester's Men – took over and introduced the work of some exciting new writers at the Rose, men such as Thomas Heywood, Thomas Middleton and John Webster. But the curtain – had there been one – would have started to fall slowly from the time Henslowe began to half-heartedly renegotiate his lease, which was due to expire in 1605. The terms asked by the landlord were such that Henslowe wrote in his diary that he would rather pull the playhouse down. Perhaps he was justifying himself in print for posterity, perhaps he had just lost heart and interest in his firstborn. In the event, of course, he couldn't bring himself to tear the old place down. Instead, he consigned it to that fate worse than theatrical death. Apart from an occasional rental, he let it go dark.

It was 1603... a few weeks after the old Queen died. The Rose was active as a playhouse for just over a decade but it lived in a lot of hearts and minds for much longer. Even when the Globe was in its heyday, many a seasoned playgoer would tell you that Burbage and Shakespeare were all very well but they weren't a patch on Alleyn and Marlowe in their prime.

Which is the stuff legends are legendarily made of...

A window on the world of big business,
corruption and greed.

A message written next to a gap in the fence surrounding
the site of the Rose excavation (1989)

"Developers, both public and private, just hate the idea of having to postpone the rate and rent revenue from a new building for a day longer than they have to – and there are no powers, other than publicity, to force them to wait".

So wrote Simon Jenkins, a crusading young journalist on the *Evening Standard* in the 1970's, in one of a series of articles attempting to shake Londoners out of their apparently permanent state of lethargy where their heritage was concerned. But twenty years on the fundamental question remained unanswered – when there is a conflict of interest between conservation and development, who pays? The Government or the Developer? And what are the priorities in a city "awash with sites in need of excavation"?

The latest chapter in the Rose saga to unfold at the end of the 1980's was only incidentally about an historic theatre... except for a few enthusiasts, the argument had little to do with irregular polygons, 'misplaced' or tapered stages, or the angle of rake in an auditorium.

The news was of government bureaucracy, commercial greed and media hype – in short, with the way we live now. And the drama itself was over in less than a theatrical season, as the moving media finger – having writ – moved on to write about something else.

But it did bestir the theatrical community to look outward for once – even though there were opposing sides on related issues, once their attention *was* engaged. All this both helped and hindered the Globe project. The Rose itself – having come out of retirement to make a brief charity appearance – ended up where it had begun, hidden from view, waiting for that next uncertain booking. All in less than a year. And once again – in a parody of history – the Rose had broken the ground for the Globe.

❖

It's only in recent times that the present has cared about its past. The archaeology business as we now know it, glamourised by the media, is a recent invention. Until the post-war period most of the work was undertaken by amateurs with whatever financial support they could muster. Legislation was more a statement of intent than a binding force. Finds were random and what was important was a matter of opinion.

It had been that way for centuries. To get to the Elizabethan Rose meant sifting your way through the domestic debris of Victorian Southwark, which covered Dr. Johnson's London and so on. Henslowe himself in building the Rose did no favours to Chaucer's Southwark, let alone Roman Southwark.

Paradoxically, there were those who would rather leave things alone altogether. Too much expedient development, they felt, was changing the townscape without proper regard for the past. Suddenly old looked good. "Until very recently", one journalist wrote, "the dirty alley ways and gloomy 19th century warehouses of old Southwark reeked of history". He was expressing a privileged minority view. Most of the people who actually lived in that particular vicinity would say it just reeked. Historically, Southwark had gone its own way since Elizabethan times. In 1839 the locals decided that their 13th century St. Saviour's – from whose tower Norden drew his famous map – was too expensive to keep up. So they tore it down and sold the pieces! The present Southwark Cathedral is a Victorian manifestation.

It was only as recently as 1954, with the discovery of the Roman Temple of Mithras in the City that Londoners felt some of the vibrations of their past and made enough public fuss to get some action from those in charge. Momentum grew until – in typical British bureaucratic fashion – by the time the Rose was found there was enough red tape in place to gift wrap it several times over. The tortuous logistics of preservation in a democracy can be wearing.

The logic of making money, on the other hand, had become very simple. In the post-war property boom, for instance, you picked up a piece of land for a song and slapped an office building on it. It wasn't built for looks. It certainly wasn't built to last – or the Rose story would have ended earlier. As it was, the most recent phase actually started in 1957, when the first rumblings of the conservation debate were being heard. Knowing full well that it was in all probability the site of the Rose, Southwark Council gave planning permission for Southbridge House to be built on it.

We pick up the story thirty years later. During that time various committees have given birth to sundry acronym-laden sub-committees... by some freak of bureaucratic biology, the separate Ministries of Housing and Local Government, Public Building and Works and Transport and Planning had managed to beget the DoE (Department of the Environment), which in turn – begat a "quango" (a quasi-autonomous non-government organisation) called English Heritage. Which is another way of laying off the odds. The Government doesn't have to decide because it has its 'official advisors on conservation law concerning the building environment' (English Heritage) to advise it. And the 'advisors' can't decide. The Arts Council (mentioned earlier) was another quango.

Meanwhile, at local level was the Museum of London's Department of Greater London Archaeology with a staff of 160 archaeologists by 1989. Founded by the recently-defunct GLC (Greater London Council), the Museum of London now relies for most of its funds on English Heritage, which relies for most of its funds on – the Government...

Such complex machinery was bound to seize up, particularly with the number of calls on its services. English Heritage was responsible for about 400 properties and in the financial year of 1989 that included the Rose and the Globe discoveries the Museum of London's team (led by Harvey Sheldon) took on the investigation of more than 70 very varied sites.

The archaeology business, it might be said, was booming. Partly because we were becoming more aware of our environment and preservation of the past was a *kind* of ecology. But that cut little ice with a tired ten year old Tory government, wearing somewhat thin at the edges and infinitely more concerned with the problems of Europe than South London.

Ironically, the real impetus for the archaeology came from the developers (who kept trying to tear up the past all by themselves) and a voluntary 'Code of Practice' that insisted that a site must be properly investigated before they were allowed to do so. At which point the Obsolescence Factor became a factor...

Southbridge House had been built on top of the Rose – or *probably*. In fact, thirty-six concrete piles had been driven straight through it to prop up the seven-storey pencil box, which became the home of the Property Services Agency, which became a department of the DoE! Thirty years later it was a diminished return. Refurbishing made no sense for a building of that vintage. It wasn't built to take the air conditioning considered obligatory for contemporary office blocks and, besides, the land it stood on was now worth a great deal of money.

The only good thing to be said about it was that, if it had to be built at all, 1957 was as good a date as any. Ten years later any building erected on that site would have included a massive underground car park – and that would have been the end of the Rose. In late 1987 the site was sold to the Heron Group. But before any binding development deal could be signed, Heron suddenly sold the site to another developer, Imry Merchant, who wanted – and were eventually granted – a ten-storey permission. After a process of hard-nosed haggling that was to become the norm, Imry agreed to a 10-week archaeological investigation as part of the deal.

While Southbridge House was being demolished, excavation went on in parallel, as the Museum's archaeologists moved in just before Christmas 1988.

Soon it became apparent that the site fell into two parts. In the north there was nothing of interest; in the south there might well be. And on February 2nd it appeared there was. Part of a wall built of chalk and brick appeared – the first sighting of an Elizabethan playhouse for some 350 years.

Enter the actors, *fortissimo*... many of them bearing roses.

Cut to the building across the street. Move in to a window where a man with silver hair and a craggy face stands looking down at the activity with a thoughtful expression. Sam's feelings were mixed. Joy at the discovery, since it vindicated his message of this being the Elizabethan theatrical heartland. Concern that, if these relics turn out to be authentic – and the state of their preservation is surprising all the experts – this may draw the credibility and somewhat fragile support from the building of what is, after all, to be a replica. On the other hand, if the two houses could somehow become *one*...? At this early stage, on balance, Sam's theatrical instinct was to do what he could to help. He even came up with a specific suggestion, once the debate moved from excavation to preservation to presentation. Why not bury the Rose in the basement of whatever building was finally allowed to be built over it and have the access to it from his Bear Gardens Museum? There is no evidence of how seriously this scheme was taken. There were many who questioned his motives – even though the most likely eventual solution to the problem is likely to be of that order.

For the next few weeks, the Rose performed an archaeological striptease. First the stage, then a wall (*which* wall?), then *another* stage. Which bit belonged to the 1587 Rose and which to the 1592? Get rid of some of that damned mud and perhaps we can tell...

And the rains came... and the media came... followed by the public – many of whom weren't quite sure *why* they'd come but they'd heard it was historic and something to do with Shakespeare, so they'd brought the kids. And wasn't that *Peggy Ashcroft* over there? And Ian McKellen? And Judi Dench? For some it was magic, for others it was a few bits of stone emerging from a sea of London winter mud.

And the scholars came... and some of them couldn't believe what they saw. One archaeologist remembers seeing theatre historian and artist, C. Walter Hodges wandering around with a bemused expression, clearly wondering why the things he'd drawn so often over the last fifty years weren't where they were supposed to be. "A lot of academics seem to have thought there was just one prototype Elizabethan structure and everything would conform to it. The Rose made them realise the individuality and accept that every one was probably going to be different". When the first shock wore off, like the rest, Hodges took it in good part. To be there was enough...

English Heritage managed to negotiate an extension with Imry but it was hard won. May 14th 1989 was the day the bulldozers would come in, so do all your looking and measuring and photographing before then... After that Imry promised only to 'mothball' the remains under a layer of sand and rubble before they got on with their building. Then, one of these days, when *their* building was also obsolete... well, who knew?

At this point public opinion began to be heard. English Heritage, anxious for a settlement and without power to impose one, felt such a solution would be acceptable. "No", said the growing group of Rose supporters, "it's a cop-out". The 'backfill' technique, as proposed, was never intended for remains as fragile as these and, according to Imry's plan, pilings will be driven clean through what we now know is the Rose's stage. At first, this reaction was very much an undercurrent but, as the days to the deadline shortened, the tiny but vociferous campaign to Save the Rose gained more and more momentum.

> *As for you, interpreter, you must seem very politic.*
> *All's Well That Ends Well*, Act IV Sc. i

Central to it, whether he'd initially wanted to be or not, was local MP, Simon Hughes. Elected as a Liberal in 1982 for the newly-combined Southwark-Bermondsey constituency, he didn't have an easy situation with two-thirds of his constituents on social security. Any project that might create new jobs, particularly in north Southwark, was a straw to be snatched. He and Sam had never got on well enough for him to be particularly close to the Globe project but now the Rose would caterpult him into national prominence and provide him with a platform. As a new 'Liberal Democrat', he was used to balancing acts and uphill battles. *The Times* political columnist, Matthew Parris, once wrote of him (perhaps a little unkindly): "No sparrow falls in Bermondsey without a Hughes eulogy; and should the cheeping have disturbed a constituent, there will be a Hughes diatribe against sparrows too".

Few MP's were better equipped for sitting in the House of Commons until the wee small hours, waiting to plead the Rose's case – and receiving the Government's predictable response – moral support, etc., etc. After all, Virginia Bottomley (Under Secretary of State for the Environment) reminded the House, with true Thatcherian sweetness, that we must be careful not to turn all our cities into museums, mustn't we? London had to choose between being "a modern living city" and "a square mile of archaeological remains".

To his credit, Hughes stuck at it. So did the rest of the hardening 'core' group. The media – always partial to a story with a deadline countdown, particularly when it involves little (preferably famous) people taking on big business *and* Whitehall – decided to feature the Rose Saga and splashed the story.

The situation wasn't particularly helped by some of the accidental casting. The Minister in charge of the relevant ministry (the DoE) happened to be Nicholas Ridley, a politician who had more feet than his mouth could comfortably hold. The Rose was not his finest hour. Would he 'schedule' it under the 1979 Ancient Monuments and Archaeological Areas Act (AMAA), as was his privilege, and put everyone out of their misery? Well, he might... no, he wouldn't... then, when the emotional temperature rose, he'd 'buy' a bit more talking time with a £1 million 'grant' to Imry. His late uncle, the architect, Edward Lutyens, must have heard the sound of elephants trampling his grave. In July, Mrs. Thatcher 'rescheduled' Ridley in her Cabinet reshuffle.

Government indecision in the early stages and its insensitivity to the public nerve that was being touched undoubtedly contributed to the later tension. The Rose affair did not fall into the comfortable category of 'letting free market forces have their way'. Then, when the media spotlight swung on them, a little self-justification started to take place. Hadn't they put a mechanism in place called English Heritage just to prevent this sort of thing? Schedule the site and Imry would be round with its hand out claiming serious compensation – £40 million was being mentioned. The bigger fleas began to bite the smaller fleas... and so *ad infinitum*. Nobody left the show at the Rose looking or feeling as good as they'd expected to when it began...

In those last few days the campaigners began to see some result for their efforts. Prime Minister Margaret Thatcher – who was suspected of preferring Kipling to the Bard – felt obliged to answer the persistent Hughes in the House that in her view "everything must be done to preserve those remains so that one day they may be on public display". The next day, *The Times* carried a letter of support signed by the theatrical great and good.

By now it was Friday, May 12th and Imry Merchant and English Heritage were in the same position – between the proverbial rock and hard place! What could they do that made business and political sense to satisfy a lot of emotionally charged people who had little idea of what was either practical or possible?

> Things in motion sooner catch the eye
> Than what not stirs.
>
> *Troilus and Cressida*, Act III Sc. iii

That last weekend saw more 'theatre' than Bankside had known since the time of Elizabeth I. The cover over the site had been removed, ready for Monday's start to construction and the exposed remains looked like a series of discarded dental charts. Already the fragile remains were visibly drying and cracking. Hoses wetted them constantly. In the background heavy equipment hovered. Then, steadily, on that last Sunday the streets filled as the Actors – McKellen, Ashcroft, Rosemary Harris, James Fox, Peter Hall – the Politician, (Hughes)... the Bureaucrat and a crowd that ebbed and flowed as the evening wore on... all gathered to put on a show. Professional and amateur alike, they spoke their piece, sang it or mimed it – or simply applauded. Many came with camping equipment, determined to keep an all night vigil. All the time the cameras clicked and turned... One of the people *not* asked to speak was Sam. He sat in his office waiting for the call that never came. The next day he left for the States...

The media event that Sunday turned into had its intended effect. Afterwards Imry said they had always intended to redesign their building – and perhaps they had. English Heritage certainly realised they couldn't be seen to roll over. Talks were resumed.

Next morning – Deadline Monday – was something of an anti-climax... Imry's lorries began to move. Some of the crowd determinedly linked arms and prepared to stand their ground. Peggy Ashcroft publicly threatened to throw herself in front of the bulldozers but there *were* no bulldozers. An Imry executive was heard to remark wryly that the sight of the Dame throwing herself in front of a *wheelbarrow* would hardly have the same impact! The lorries backed off. So did everyone else.

> Cry, God for Harry, England and the Rose!
>
> Lord Olivier, in a recorded appeal to a Rose rally
>
> 11th June, 1989

Imry Merchant *did* change their office design at a quoted cost of some £10 million. Shortly before being bought out themselves, a building was finally constructed, perched awkwardly on stilts like a stork waiting to give birth. It stood empty for several years. Beneath it the Rose was carefully re-covered and packed "as carefully as a porcelain doll". As a gesture the building was christened – Rose Court – which had a nice irony to it.

The campaign became The Campaign. The interested parties – led by Hughes – trooped off to the Globe offices and formed A Committee, which begat numerous sub-committees, all of which talked themselves hoarse. And like almost all committees everywhere, it gave itself undue importance and attracted varied and militant opinion. And most of the Good Guys, having achieved what they could, packed their tents or sleeping bags and departed, leaving the Committee to debate such overly optimistic matters as whether they should buy the whole site and turn it into a sort of shrine. So they started a Fund... just in case.

But by this time discussion was, in reality, *post facto*. The Rose was relatively safe, which was the important part. Some day, somehow there would be funds to awaken the sleeping beauty and the state of archaeological preservation techniques would have improved to the point where it would be safe to expose the fragile remains and treat them, so that man's discovery didn't destroy in its enthusiasm what Nature had accidentally kept safe for centuries. But that day would have to wait. (In 1992 it was duly but quietly scheduled and thus protected from further commercial intrusion.) And by now there were many who felt that justice had been seen to be served. The Save the Rosers had won a famous victory, so it was time for life to go on and other crises to be faced. After all, as someone said – it wasn't *Stonehenge*, was it?

> Come, gentlemen, we sit too long on trifles,
> And waste the time, which looks for other revels.
>
> *Pericles*, Act II Sc. iii

Once again, the Rose and the Globe became rivals – which was both a Good Thing and a Bad Thing. A good thing, because (a few months later) just as the dust from the mud was settling, it turned out to be a rather long-winded prologue to the discovery of the Globe. Bad because tempers were lost and positions were taken from which retreat became difficult.

Sam and the ISGC found themselves sitting on the sidelines – not entirely of their own volition. For the brief duration of the debate they acted like good neighbours, since that's what they were. Being literally next door, Sam hastened to offer the Bear Gardens premises freely to the emerging Rose group for their councils of war. Indeed – at least to begin with – he considered himself a leading member of their supporting cast. After all, wasn't this for the greater good of Shakespeare's Bankside?

But when the campaign turned remorselessly into the "Rose Campaign", talking importantly about fund raising, Sam had second thoughts. From bitter experience he knew there was a very definite limit to how much money public interest in Elizabethan theatres could generate – and two into one very definitely wouldn't go. Every pound the Rose raised – he reasoned – was a pound the Globe lost. So they might both lose. And it wasn't as if the Rose could ever be a proper *working* theatre...

Why not merge the two organisations and call it the Globe-Rose Trust and campaign jointly for funds? Of course, the money would all go to the Globe until it was finished, after which... But the Rose supporters didn't see it that way at all.

Sam had already given his reluctant blessing to the inclusion of Jon Greenfield (to represent the Globe's architects) and Jennifer Jones (his Marketing and PR Officer) to keep an eye on things from the Globe's point of view. The Rose had also been 'lent' an office, although Sam insisted it had to be reached via the Globe Museum. The address read accordingly. The hand was helping but the gesture was half-hearted.

Nor did it help when he was excluded from the Rose Committee, even though it seemed to consist of just about anybody and everybody else.

Insult was added to injury when one day he and fellow actors, Ian McKellen and Tim Piggott-Smith – also 'non-members' – were asked by Chairman, Simon Hughes, to leave a 'confidential' meeting, even though it was being held in his own conference room!

> ...it oft falls out,
> To have what we would have, we speak not what we mean.
>
> Isabella, *Measure for Measure*, Act II Sc. iv

It was the wrong way to handle someone like Sam – volatile, suspicious and passionately committed to whatever point of view he happened to hold at the moment. Who *were* these Elizabethan *arrivistes?* He answered his own question in an irritated interview at the heated height of the affair: "A bunch of over-enthusiastic actors seizing any reason to give importance to the Rose other than its own inherent significance". It was a view many people now shared but it didn't sound convincing coming from someone whose motives might easily be questioned. From equivocal collaborator he turned *agent provocateur*. Why have *two* competitive groups? Why couldn't they join forces? After all, the ISGC had an "established infrastructure". "At the Rose you will see the stones of an Elizabethan theatre", he told one interviewer. "At the Globe you will see the stones come to life". With his sense of what made a good story, all he had to do was hold a press conference, talk to the media and it was as good as done. He was to go on doing it for months. As late as September – when it was all over bar the moaning – the *Evening Standard* reported: "The Rose goes to Wanamaker..."

Sam claimed he was setting up a working party consisting of English Heritage, the Museum of London, the Rose Theatre Trust and the British Museum. A month later nobody was speaking to anybody else. But then, nobody had *agreed* to speak to anybody in the first place. Sam then broke off diplomatic relations and left further conversation to others. Those who weren't with him were, by definition, against him...

The idea of being 'sharers' had never appealed to the Rose faction, anyway. Their crusade had nothing to do with what they considered to be an American pseudo-Disneyland. The Rose was an all-British show and they were taking it on the road. Well, not exactly on the road – more to the media. And for a while the media indulged them in the dog days of a silly season when journalists pray for another Loch Ness Monster to fill their space. It was only when some of the actors started to declaim their declamations for the second or third time that the photo opportunities were cut back. And, in any case, by June there were other stories to cover – like the death of Ayatollah Khomeini, what to do about dangerous dogs, not to mention the unfortunate things happening to a lot of real live people on the other side of the world in Tiennamen Square.

> *A fine volley of words, gentlemen, and quickly shot off.*
>
> The Two Gentlemen of Verona, Act II Sc. iv

However sincerely it started, the Campaign eventually became incestuous and many of the protagonists more than a little silly. For a few *part* of the point was to be anti-Wanamaker. When the Campaign had moved from the important matter of when to hold the next meeting to the vital question of the logo on their T-shirt, Sam objected to their use of Shakespeare's head on the grounds that it would be confused with the Shakespeare's *Globe* appeal. The head was omitted. Could they perhaps use *Sam's* head, someone asked? Around the same time a graffitus appeared on the wooden hoarding that surrounded the Rose excavation. "Shakespeare's Rose v. Wanamaker's Globe", it proclaimed. As we walked past it one day, he eyed it laconically: "I suppose that's fame of a sort", he said, "and at least I get equal billing!" A remark that disturbed his academic supporters rather more was when he was quoted as saying: "There is not a shred of evidence that Shakespeare ever had anything to do with the Rose". "Is he saying", one of them asked, "that Shakespeare didn't write *Titus Andronicus*" – a play known to have been performed at the Rose – "or *Henry VI*?" No, he wasn't *really* saying that. He'd just said it in the heat of the moment, trying to defend 'his' Globe. For anyone who knew him, it was just 'Sam being Sam'. At one point he flatly refused to believe that *Henry V* hadn't been written for the Globe. After all, it contained the definitive speech and Larry had set his *film* version in the Globe. It was pointed out that the Globe wasn't the *first* amphitheatre and, in any case, there was nothing to stop him from opening his Globe with it, either...

In truth, there was no need for an argument, because there was no real comparison. The Rose had the emotional significance of being the actual remains of the first Elizabethan theatre anyone had ever seen. Theatre people could stand where that stage had been and let their imaginations soar – and many did.

Understandably, a few of them *over*-stated their case, even after the point had been made and accepted. *The Sunday Times* described the Campaign as a "strange one... a kind of madness-for-art" and even Rose historian, Christine Eccles, reflected later that it was symptomatic of the 'Our heritage' syndrome, which "has come to represent the fraudulence of nostalgia divorced from history". Julie Burchill in the *Mail on Sunday* expressed the same thought in a pithy Betjemanesque lampoon:

> Come, friendly bulls, and doze the Rose –
> It's only there for those who pose

As for the Globe – that would recreate the *experience* of the Elizabethan playhouse. Both were part of the same thing... a celebration of Shakespeare's London. There was plenty of room for those whose hearts were in the right place.

Yes, there had been a moment when the Rose – effectively put out of business by the Globe all those years ago – looked on the point of returning the compliment. In the end, by firing up the debate, it proved a valuable ally.

The site of the original Globe looking East. The second piece of a complex puzzle that remains largely unsolved. (1989) *June Everett*

CHAPTER THIRTEEN

THE ARCHAEOLOGIST'S TALE

Tis you must dig with mattock and with spade,
And pierce the inmost centre.

Titus Andronicus, Act IV Sc. iii

The Rose affair taught a lot of people a lot of lessons. It certainly reminded the archaeologists employed by the Museum of London's Department of Greater London Archaeology that finding yourself squeezed between commerce and politics could be an uncomfortable position to be in – especially when it's not of your making.

Robin Densem – who was involved with the negotiations for the Globe excavation – carefully defines the terms of reference: "We only do that which we are commissioned to do within the regulations... Most of the work we do now is funded by the developers". In those few carefully-chosen words he touches upon two of the key issues facing the 'archaeology industry' in the mid-1990's – regulations and money. And one dictates the other.

The ethics of organised archaeology swing between two poles. Excavation or preservation? Do you dig it up – in the knowledge that, by uncovering some historical treasure without having the means to conserve it properly, you are effectively destroying it for all time? All that's left will be your records, however complete you've made them in the time you've been allowed? Or do you conserve what you find, identified but protected until improved techniques are available to preserve it indefinitely?

The early British archaeologists of the 18th and 19th centuries – invariably gentlemen of private means – were almost always concerned with domestic *preservation*. Abroad was a different matter.

As late as the 1940's Sir Mortimer Wheeler – better known to the public at large for his charismatic, moustachioed appearances on early TV shows like *What's My Line?* – was carrying on the great 'amateur' tradition around London with his band of enthusiastic unpaid assistants. The Gentleman Archaeologist lived...

The dubious windfall that turned the hobby of the few into the occupation of quite a few can be traced directly back to Adolf Hitler and the Blitz. Bomb sites in the capital yielded fascinating secrets and gave impetus to post war interest in archaeology. Property development began to boom and that also helped, if only accidentally. Before we build on it, let's see what we've uncovered. Soon demand exceeded supply and the game of professional archaeology started in the early 1970's. As money became less of a problem, it wasn't long until more than 1,000 archaeologists were in full-time employment, rescuing information about sites before the developers moved in and obliterated it for good. There had never been fieldwork on that scale in Britain before.

When English Heritage was set up in 1983, 'rescue' archaeology – a distinctly contradictory term – was still the cornerstone of their activities (*"Recording* discoveries was our priority"): a priority understood by all concerned but it took another seven years for this policy to be promulgated. In November 1990 Planning Policy Guidance Note 16 stated that "wherever possible ancient remains should be preserved for the benefit of future generations, when archaeological techniques will be better and there may be more time and money available..." "In other words," Densem translates: "We shouldn't just rush in and dig everything up now to get instant news and leave nothing for the future". What he might have added was that of the 350 sites the Museum had "rescued" in the fifteen years up to the discovery of the Rose 344 had been destroyed in the process. All that remained were 344 tidy reports. On the positive side, things hadn't worked too badly since the last piece of major legislation – the 1979 AMAA (Ancient Monuments and Archaeological Areas Act) which had stipulated that before a developer was granted planning permission for a site of possible interest, he must agree to a reasonable archaeological survey. What was considered 'reasonable' was a question of negotiation. As Densem points out – with both the Rose and Globe in mind – "Under the old system a developer would have been allowed to plough ahead. There may or may not have been a cursory dig but then the thing would have been up and whatever might have been there would now be under a big underground car park, probably". Even a 'trial dig' didn't fall within the province of the archaeologists; that decision was the prerogative of the local authorities. Based on the archaeological report, they would decide whether what had been found was something they really wished to preserve for the future. It was, one might say, something of a trade-off...

> Archaeology is the science of destruction...
> Unless you record it to a standard, you're the only
> person to have seen it — and it's gone!
>
> Simon Blatherwick, Museum of London archaeologist

Simon Blatherwick, a senior Museum archaeologist who worked on both the Rose and the Globe, is clear about the business any professional archaeologist is in: "Archaeology is the science of destruction... Unless you record it to a standard, you're the only person to have seen it — and it's gone!... It works as a sort of reverse removal of deposits. As you remove the layers, you make a written record, a drawn record (on a scale of 1:20) and a photographic record... You can't repeat the experiment".

The kind of 'field evaluation' used in the case of the Rose — where documentation such as maps and sewer records pointed to its likely presence on the site — was typical, if rather more thorough than usual. It involved supervised trenching with machinery until you got down towards the bottom of the overburden — the modern build up from the mid 18th century onwards. This could be up to two metres and sometimes more. Removal by hand takes far too long and the developer's taxi meter will already be ticking...

After the two metre mark you edged your way down inch by inch until you reached 'significant archaeological deposits' — or didn't as the case might be. All of which took time, if it was to be done properly, and in what turned out to be a 'classic' site in the case of the Rose, the two months originally granted for exploration was pitifully short for what was involved. But then, Imry Merchant came to the party with their planning permission in their pocket and only a voluntary 1968 code to observe. As far as they were concerned, two months was plenty. Later developers wouldn't find things so easy. The Rose helped change things — if only because it made the process public. The kind of publicity Imry received was not to the taste of developers anxious to get their building up and sold before the property boom ended.

> Ay, the most peerless piece of earth, I think,
> That e'er the sun shone bright on.
>
> *The Winter's Tale*, Act V Sc. i

Everyone approached the Globe on tip-toe.

The Globe site benefited from the experience of the Rose in a variety of ways. First, no developer wanted to be cast as another Imry, particularly when he didn't have planning permission to start with.

The site had been part of the old Courage brewery, bought by Hanson plc in 1986 and subsequently knocked down. The urbane Lord Hanson operated in a different league and saw from the outset that there was both political and public goodwill to be gained here. He was in no hurry to build. The site wasn't going anywhere and the value was certain to rise. He also knew the value of good PR and had enjoyed plenty of it. He didn't employ Michael Shea (formerly the Queen's advisor) for nothing.

The part of the site that was the focus of everyone's attention was the former car park, now standing deserted. The Museum was given from July to September for their trial dig, plus a strong hint that more time and money would be available, should the need arise. If 'serious archaeology' was likely to be needed, better to embrace it willingly and publicly than have 'another Rose situation'. Hanson even funded the operation.

Harvey Sheldon put Simon McCudden in charge of the excavation.

The stated purpose of the dig was to investigate "the archaeology of the whole site" – not merely to look for the Globe. "We'd done a lot of work on the southern part of the Courage site", Blatherwick recalls, "and found some Roman remains... So, although we approached the new work as a routine evaluation exercise in one way, we made sure we were looking at a larger sample than normal – just to make sure. I'd say we felt that the probability of finding the Globe was high. Our uncertainty was to what extent anything might have survived. In that sense the Rose gave us reason to hope..."

As team leader, Simon McCudden began by taking into account the height to which it was now definitely known that the Rose had survived beneath street level. After which it was slowly, slowly... July to September stretched into October. Most of the site had been examined and so far all that had turned up were some medieval remains, a Georgian cesspit and a Charles 1 penny. The only land left unexplored was a tiny piece with the site hut on it and the vehicle access ramp. They had literally dug themselves into a corner.

On October 11th 1989 they struck archaeological gold. It was McCudden's decision how far to go with the cutting machine. "Another foot and we'd have chopped right through it – and my career as an archaeologist would have been over!"

Had they been around, several people would have been profoundly pleased to have their work justified at long last. Theatre historian, W. W. Braines had pinned the site down definitively (for him) as long ago as 1924 – though that didn't stop the debate. And, of course, Norden's inset on his *Civitas Londini* drawing was also vindicated. He'd been right about the Rose, too. Even the famous blackened plaque that had started Sam's quest and which he later used to say was wrongly placed turned out to be 'close enough' – only 20 metres away from the spot that was uncovered that October afternoon.

Good Neighbour Sam was in his office at the time, discussing the final plans, as he later told the media – for *his* Globe. "We literally rose up in the air at the news", Sam was quoted as saying, as he appeared "in Prince of Denmark black to lead the applause for the men and women on their knees in the mud".

Once again, the Rose reached out a proverbial helping hand. It was the layer of hazelnuts McCudden uncovered that clinched it in the minds of the archaeologists that what they'd reached was the floor surface. By now it was generally agreed that – despite the media's insistence that they were the Elizabethan equivalent of popcorn for the spectators – the nuts had become a proven ingredient in the flooring surface, helpful in draining and probably with acoustical properties, too.

That was the good news. The bad news was that they'd only struck gold in a very small way. Theo Crosby summed up the thoughts of many of the interested parties when he said, "It reveals just enough to be irritating". As for the rest of what could now be reasonably defined as the site of the original Globe... 10% had already been destroyed by 19th century construction work on ground due for redevelopment (now the Unisys building)... 20% was a narrow strip of empty land... 30% was under Anchor Terrace, occupied by a row of empty buildings – of which much more anon! – and the rest lay under the restless surface of Southwark Bridge Road (built 1814-1819). The problems were obvious but before they could be addressed, first things first...

> Lest too light winning
> Make the prize light.
>
> *The Tempest*, Act I Sc. ii

This time there was total unanimity. A recommendation was filed for the site to be scheduled as an Ancient Monument and with Chris Patten now at the Department of the Environment, nobody was inclined to doubt that commonsense would prevail – which it duly did. It was not often a *developer* asked for a site to be scheduled but on this occasion Hanson did.

He also put out a press release congratulating all concerned and offering to donate another £250,000 to help further investigation. The Museum also produced one which was careful to restrict itself to the facts. The area of the Anchor Terrace car park site that had been evaluated covered 2,000 square metres "but approximately 60% of the area had been badly disturbed by concrete bases and intrusions from previous buildings... The area in which the Globe has been revealed lies in the north-west corner of the site and is about 10m x 6m. To north and south of this area the archaeology has been destroyed by modern intrusions. The surviving walls form the eastern part of the theatre, most of which is lying beyond the edge of excavation under Anchor Terrace. The remains consist of three wall foundations, the middle wall being about three metres in length and made from chalk blocks with associated timber stakes. This is likely to be part of the first Globe Theatre. Two metres to the east of the chalk is the outermost brick foundation of the theatre. An area of gravel metalling lies outside this, possibly representing an external surface. Four metres to the west of the chalk there is a more substantial brick foundation, one metre in length and largely 'robbed out'. A layer of crushed hazelnuts may be associated with this and together this wall and the hazelnut surface may represent part of the second phase of the theatre".

Well, that was their view and the academics would have a word or two more to say about that, when they'd got their breath back...

After the jubilation... the problems. What next?

What had been done and destroyed in the past was spilt milk. The Road was the road and nobody seriously thought there was any chance of stopping the mighty roar of London's traffic – and losing the commuter vote. *But Anchor Terrace...?*

What stood between Sam, the scholars and other interested parties and the Globe foundations was what stood on Anchor Terrace – a row of unoccupied but 'listed' (Grade II) 1830-ish Georgian buildings. Unless English Heritage and Southwark decreed otherwise, they would continue to stand there. Nor could anything be done in their immediate vicinity that might undermine their foundations. The Rose Affair had been Developers v. Preservationists. The Globe was to be Elizabethans v. Georgians and the Georgians felt just as strongly about preserving their version of our heritage. (What they felt about the Georgian cesspit is not recorded!) As a spokesman for the Georgian Group – which fundamentally had more sympathy for Sam's point of view than he did for theirs – put it: "I'm against demolishing something old merely to reveal something older".

> *He says he has a stratagem for't.*
> *All's Well That Ends Well*, Act III Sc. vi

Not surprisingly, Sam didn't see it that way at all. In a November letter to Sir David Orr, as Chairman of the Trustees of the Globe project, he lays out the scenario as it seems to him. Hanson, he feels, won't be a problem:

> Hanson have said they wish to obtain planning permission for the site and sell it to a developer. Their objective is to exploit the site commercially and profitably to its maximum value – namely office development. Provided a sympathetic scheme could be designed around the fully excavated Globe foundations we, the champions of the Globe and the Elizabethan Bankside theatrical heritage, would not object.

He then went on to suggest what might be done...

> It is possible to excavate at least 60%-65% of the Globe remains, provided Anchor Terrace, except for its facade, could be demolished. There are thousands of examples of excellent late Georgian terraces in London and hundreds of thousands in Britain. The interiors of the Anchor Terrace houses have, at least 50 years ago, been structurally converted and joined together to make the headquarter offices of

Courage's. Little of heritage value has remained. There is no conceivable justification for retaining these interiors at the cost of preventing a complete archaeological investigation of the world's most important theatre. The facade could be incorporated in a new development.

Thus leaving it open to charges of both desecration *and* 'facadism' – a social and aesthetic sin very much on the increase at the time.

The ending of the letter is very much Sam, as he sends his knights Sir David and Sir Evelyn Rothschild out to do battle. As they ride off to confront Lord Hanson, his brief is clear:

> It could be first suggested that in the present circumstances, at the relatively low value of the site without change of use to offices, Hanson PLC might wish to consider donating it to the Shakespeare Globe Trust... It could also be suggested that any commercial profit they might realise from the sale of the Globe site with office planning permission to be contributed by Hanson to the Shakespeare Globe Trust.

There was nothing like travelling hopefully and with all your options open. The conversation, when it took place, was on more circumspect lines.

Other Globe supporters were more realistic in their suggestions. Gurr and Orrell argued for sacrificing the back parts of Anchor Terrace, so that both parties might be satisfied. English Heritage thought not. Over at the Museum Harvey Sheldon was trying to balance the conflicting demands of his own mind. He called them "Problems and Risks..."

1 Partial demolition of Anchor Terrace – even if it were allowed – would 'further interfere with Southwark's townscape'.

2 There was the worrying lack of preservation technique. 'Until a technique can be shown to work for the Rose, it might be better to leave the Globe undisturbed... It's come to some equilibrium with its environment. Once we start fiddling around with it, we could start trouble!'

3 Elsewhere there were dozens of sites that needed to be excavated prior to development and a shortage of trained archaeologists. Every 'non-threatened' site that was excavated – like the Globe – deprived 'threatened' sites of vital personnel.

The debate went on but nobody budged. The lessons of the Rose were too recent and too salutary. Feet stayed firmly in place. That way they couldn't be put wrong.

In November English Heritage issued a press release in which it spoke of "a reduction in the need for expensive excavations, the costs incurred by developers, and the kind of crisis which occurred over the Rose Theatre". Whether it was a move designed to save face or protect its back was not entirely clear. With the Curtain already destroyed by developers, there weren't too many Elizabethan theatres left to worry about...

Hanson offered English Heritage the cost of a full excavation in return for an agreement that in due course it would be allowed to demolish Anchor Terrace and, therefore, secure the planning permission it had always wanted.

> The stones... are being treated as objects of worship
> not information... But the trouble with idolatry is
> that it conceals ignorance about what you worship.
>
> Andrew Gurr

In February 1990 a scheme that involved significantly less proved decidedly more acceptable. Again with the benefit of Hanson funding, and after consultation with its 'joint venture' partners in the project – English Heritage and Southwark Council, the Museum commissioned research not commonly used in their more routine investigations. When a doctor wishes to examine an inaccessible part of the human anatomy that he doesn't wish to disturb unnecessarily, he asks for an x-ray. The Museum brought in GeoSpace – a company that had worked on York excavations a couple of years earlier – to conduct a 'sub-surface sonic scan' over the remains as well as the basement of Anchor Terrace. The Georgian Group had no objection to that. It was the first time that a scan had been done inside a mid-19th century building – but then this wasn't just any mid-19th century building. It was also the first time it had ever been done in Southwark.

The scan seemed to suggest that there were indeed further remains worth looking at under the foundation but that was hardly a surprise. As to what they were exactly... The one thing that *was* clear was that they would have to think of something else or call it a day, until either the political climate changed or an Act of God took the listed buildings into another dimension.

The something else turned out to be some limited 'test bed' or 'keyhole research', as it is sometimes called. Test pits would be carefully dug to look at the state of the foundations of Nos. 1 – 15 and examine what little might also be seen of the Globe beneath. The priority was clearly restated: don't do anything to disturb the status quo. If there looks like being any risk to Anchor Terrace, stop at once!

English Heritage were in favour of three test pits. The Museum suggested ten. In the end a compromise was reached – four but slightly *larger*. There was to be no accidental straying beyond the agreed limits of the pits, no matter how promising the view appeared. Hanson again funded the search, which took place between July and October 1991.

The first thing they discovered was more than a little embarrassing. What the scan had totally failed to reveal was that the entire Anchor Terrace construction floated on a concrete 'raft' some one and a half metres thick – presumably to provide greater stability against the treacherous Thames clay. It wasn't an isolated example in the area. In fact, it had been a technique known to have been employed by some 19th century architects. They just hadn't expected to find it *there*. The irritation Theo Crosby had spoken of turned to frustration because the glimpses through the 'keyholes' confirmed that the Globe *was* there. One thing Anchor Terrace and the old Courage brewery had contributed to the cause was to sit there quietly during the years when the site would have been most vulnerable to the unsupervised assaults of the developers and their mechanical predators.

What they saw may have been a pier base for the playhouse. It certainly looked like the right kind of construction. And a Nuremberg token found nearby dating from the late 16th century seemed to add further confirmation. If you were a believer in the 80ft diameter theory, it might be part of the inner wall. If you went to the 99ft hypothesis, well... There was also what might be a part of a stair turret. The archaeologists reported on what they saw and are still understandably anxious to point out that "we would be the first to advise you that we can't prove this goes with that". They needn't worry. There would always be plenty of other people to do that for them.

Where archaeology begins, art ends
Oscar Wilde

And that was effectively that. Mindful of the deterioration they'd witnessed in the short time the Rose had remained exposed, the tiny portion of the Globe that had been excavated had long since been wrapped up – like the Rose – in a shroud of plastic sand and concrete to await – who knew? Monitoring equipment was buried with it to keep a check on its 'vital signs'.

It's likely that several of the parties at least breathed a sigh of relief when the embalming was over. The Museum was certainly relieved at official level, although individual archaeologists in their private capacity would like to have done more. Could more have been done in the then state of technical knowledge, had the legislative climate been different? Robin Densem's current view is that "it might be possible to undertake a full excavation if a sufficiently well-funded research design could be produced and published. More work would depend on economics, on how valuable people perceive that piece of land to be... There's a big bill attached to it!"

Simon Blatherwick muses on the then and now: "If we did that in the mid-1990's, we'd do a better job than we'd have done in the late 1980's... But we'd do a better job in five years time!" In 1995 Sheldon believed the necessary new technology was "3-4 years away, no more". But the political problems could well take rather longer to resolve...

The public scrutiny that was focused on the way we treat our past – a direct result of the Rose and Globe episodes – was helpful if not necessarily welcome in every quarter. It revealed, even if it didn't resolve, all the tensions inherent in a system that had grown like Topsy.

In Harvey Sheldon's view the episode surfaced "the very short term commercial view" that had been prevalent in the City and commercial circles since the 1950's. There were "definitely elements of the old-established hostility to archaeology in all this". He did not see the subsequent change of public stance on anyone's part as "a conversion on the road to Southwark". More a media *force majeure*. Some might say a *farce majeure*.

> That opportunity,
> Which then they had to take from's to resume
> We have again.
>
> *Cymbeline*, Act III Sc. i

For Sam and the new Globe the whole episode provided both a problem and an opportunity.

By the time of the discovery he had his site, the ground had been broken and the concrete diaphragm was virtually complete. During the latter part of that unpredictable year a real enthusiast had the opportunity to peer into *three* muddy holes within the space of a couple of hundred yards! Now there was some genuine evidence to check against their best guess design. Not much but surely there would be more quite soon, unless the gods were really spiteful?

What was already more than a little perturbing was the way those few hard won clues were beginning to suggest that the 24-sided structure they'd celebrated with token beams was incorrect. And with the complexity of the design involved, reducing it to 20 involved a lot more than carting away four large bits of metaphorical wood. It was back to the drawing board for Theo Crosby and his team. And then, what *else* might they find?

Luckily for Sam, one of his great skills was his ability to weave a successful PR event out of a few threads of fact. Welcoming the discovery of the Globe and publicly assuming there would be plenty more information still to come, all of which would further validate his own project, he announced grandly that the Trust had decided to halt the actual building until that evidence should become available. It made perfect sense and omitted only one small fact – the Trust had no money to continue building anyway...

> Strange it is
> That nature must compel us to lament
> Our most persisted deeds.
>
> *Antony and Cleopatra*, Act V Sc. i

Of the many postscripts to the Globe episode there are a few worth recording.

A bureaucratic implosion at the Museum shrinks the infrastructure still further. Harvey Sheldon's job disappears at the end of 1991 and he goes off to work freelance, teach – and become Chairman of the Rose Trust. On February 28th, 1992, the Rose remains are quietly scheduled.

❖

Imry's building – Rose Court – is duly completed in January 1991, then stands there even more quietly for another three and a half years. It was finally occupied in August 1994 by The Health and Safety Commission.

❖

In 1993 a small story tucked away on an inside page of *The Times* had some disquieting news. Mike Corfield, English Heritage's Head of Artifact Conservation and Technology, reported to the Committee for Conservation of the International Council of Museums that, "We have been concerned to see unusual changes in pH and increases in dissolved oxygen; we have also had considerable sulphate crystallisation". In simple terms, the soil moisture probes that were buried with both of the recovered sites were indicating that – in the case of the Rose at least – a chemical change was taking place that may lead to deterioration of the remains that had been buried 'for safe keeping'. It seems that the chemical stability the site achieved accidentally over 390 years had been disturbed by uncovering it for those few short weeks. While the idolaters were arguing, the object of their idolatry was catching the archaeological equivalent of pneumonia... The race was now on to develop the equivalent of an antibiotic.

Failing that? "We'd have to dig out the remains", says Sheldon, "treat them, put in a water-resistant membrane, then put them back". Would that still be authentic? "As near as you can get!"

❖

While in early 1995 the story seemed to be coming full circle, as the 'Shakespeare in Shoreditch' Society announced plans to excavate the site of the Theatre. "Seventy-one per cent of the site is on open land, mostly car parks", said a spokesman, "which should make archaeological exploration comparatively easy". There might be more than one point of view on that...

❖

Whatever the mixture of motives, the political-economic-archaeological balance had been irrevocably changed by the mid-1990's. And although no one was rushing to put it in quite those terms, it was one more area in which Britain had been forced to move – with much dragging of feet – towards European practice and the mainstream of conservation thought. And there was one other factor which had finally begun to weigh with financier, councillor and politician alike. The Multinationals – those alternative governments *de nos jours* – were busy deciding in which capital city to place their one centralised European headquarters operation. It must be in a place that had all the facilities and those facilities must include the cultural as well as the commercial. Now, should it be Frankfurt? Paris? Or have you heard about the wonderful way they've developed Bankside in London? *That* sounds different.

Nobody making those decisions would remember there had been plans on the table to do all this as far back as the late 1960's, proposed by an amiable American eccentric called Wanamaker...

CHAPTER FOURTEEN

THE THEATRE HISTORIAN'S TALE: PART TWO
(1989 – 1996)

When we mean to build
We first survey the plot, then draw the model
And when we see the figure of the house,
Then must we rate the cost...

Henry IV (Pt.2). Act I Sc. iii

In February of 1989 John Orrell received a fax in Canada from Theo Crosby. It was short and to the point: "They've found the Rose. Come soonest!"

The demolition of an outdated office block had revealed what had long been suspected – it was indeed the site of Henslowe's Rose theatre.

There wasn't much to look at in the winter drizzle once he did arrive: "I found a couple of small trenches with a few Elizabethan bricks, all flooded and very cold... But it was unmistakably the Rose, and those cold bricks had been warmed in their time by Marlowe, Jonson and Shakespeare!" The vibrations kept the rain at bay.

Andrew Gurr – in America at the time with Sam and on a sabbatical at UCLA – didn't get back to London until April, by which time it was possible to see an outline of much of the theatre etched in the mud. There was certainly enough for the two men to come to some tentative conclusions, which they published in June in the *Times Literary Supplement*.

For both of them the over-riding question was – what did the findings mean to the design of the new Globe, already so far advanced?

As we've seen, it complicated the argument about the positioning of the stage. It also confirmed that the circular appearance of both theatres in the all-important drawings really mean *polygonal*. The Rose was revealed as basically a regular 14-sided polygon most definitely set out *ad quadratum*.

It was, as expected, smaller than the Globe with a diameter of 72ft. The ground layout gave no indication of a stage tower within the yard – but then, Norden hadn't indicated one. What was clearly visible were the 1592 alterations, presumably to create more space for the audience, as well as to add a stage roof. Not only was the stage in the 'wrong' place, it had clearly been tapered towards the front in both phases, unlike the squared Swan or the present plans for the Globe.

A bigger surprise was the *yard*, where the groundlings had stood. The Globe design had opted for a flat surface, whereas this one was most definitely raked. And while brick had been chosen as the yard surface for the Globe, there was no sign of brick here. The 1587 yard appeared to have been laid with mortar, while the 1592 version seemed to consist of hard black ash containing crushed hazelnut shells.

> Let time shape, and there an end.
>
> *Henry IV (Pt.2)*, Act III Sc. ii

Of all the revelations the shape of the Rose mattered most.

In every discussion over the past three hundred years or so scholars had been divided into 'Rounds' vs. 'Polygons'. The classic drawings suggested round and hadn't Shakespeare spoken of the "Wooden O"? So argued the Rounds... Fine, replied the Polygons, but the Elizabethan builders simply didn't have the techniques to construct a circle in wood. And besides, there was another drawing – Claes Visscher's 1616 depiction of an *eight*-sided Globe, a structure which many modern builders feel would probably have been architecturally unstable.

The circle could be 'squared', however, once you accept the fact that a structure with many sides will appear circular and certainly will appear circular from a distance. Norden (in his inset drawing) and Hollar both drew a circle because they *saw* it as a circle.

The Rose remains proved a polygon, leaving the question – how many sides might the *Globe's* polygon have been? Why not fourteen, like its immediate neighbour? Twenty-four, said Richard Hosley, citing the Swan drawing. He had already incorporated that number into the model that had initially sparked the interest of Orrell and others. As a result of that, when the ground on the new Globe site was broken and the first symbolic posts put in place and unveiled by Prince Philip in 1987, there had been twenty-four.

But in the light of the Rose, did that number still make sense? All the permutations were tried again by Orrell and others. Six or eight-sided constructs were too angular and lost the 'roundness'. Thirty-two dictated a bay size that was impossibly small. The debate was open again and Orrell concluded that, faced with the 14-sided reality of the Rose: "It was obvious that the 24-sided plan... was not only speculative but decidedly open to question".

❖

And then in October they found the Globe...

Another fax from Theo to John Orrell read: "The Globe was found this morning. Back wall along Park St. and thank God, no sign of the stage so far. Keep you posted".

At 9:30 a.m. on the morning of October 12th Hanson plc made the announcement that those in the know had been expecting for several days. Once again, Gurr and Orrell were the first Shakespearean scholars on the site. Orrell was a little disconcerted to find it 14ft further north than his original calculation – or Hollar's, come to that. Not that there was much to see – far less than the treasure trove of the Rose. Little more than a solitary bay, in fact. The rest of the Globe lay under the adjacent Anchor Terrace or Southwark Bridge Road, which was now one of London's traffic arteries.

The joke was that Nos. 1/15 Anchor Terrace not only had a Grade II listing to protect them but they also had a grade one *list* – some nine degrees from the vertical over the nearby road!

In truth, what *was* visible really wasn't much to go on. Part of the front of one bay, some remains of a radial wall and a few traces of what might be the outer wall – although the archaeologists weren't too sure about that – leading into an adjoining bay. The lessons of the Rose, however, had prepared them to look at these traces with a more open mind.

On the positive side, the depth of the bay they could see was definitely 12ft 6in – the same as the Rose and precisely the dimension quoted in the Fortune contract for a playhouse to be built just like the Globe. It was also possible to draw some tentative conclusions about the overall plan, assuming – as was true of the Rose – that the polygon was regular. Undeterred by the early projection of a computer expert (briefed by the Museum of London) that the Globe had been round with a diameter of 80ft – presumably based on the reading of the inner wall as the outer? – Orrell took a more systematic approach, based on what he could now see. If this segment was replicated in the total structure, you were looking at a theatre about 100ft in diameter. Once again, Hollar would have been right.

But even Orrell had to admit that he was still dealing with possibilities, not even probabilities. There were still too many imponderables to be sure of anything – except that even a tiny miscalculation would have a major effect on the overall plan. It was tantalising to have a few facts in your hands and those sufficiently well preserved to suggest that the rest of the puzzle was within feet of where you were standing, waiting to speak to you – yet likely to remain indefinitely silent and out of reach.

In the next two years the frustration increased. Archaeological 'keyhole' research – carefully controlled probes in the basement of the Anchor Terrace building – had confirmed the existence of more remains but thrown no further light on the all-important layout. Nor were their researches helped by the existence of the concrete 'raft' that sat beneath the whole of Anchor Terrace and which acted as an effective 'umbrella' for the Globe! Unless and until circumstances

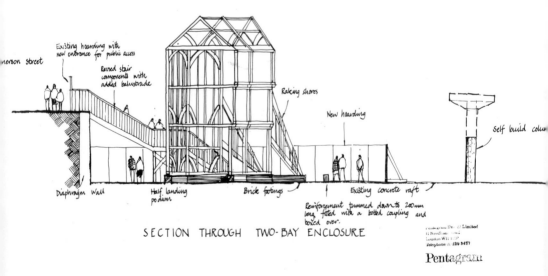

SECTION THROUGH TWO-BAY ENCLOSURE

Section through a two-bay enclosure. Pentagram

changed drastically, the scholars had learned all that "Shakespeare's factory" (to quote Gurr's description) chose to tell them.

Ironically, after all the years that had passed, time was now becoming a problem. There was now enough money in the kitty for the Board to have decided to erect two experimental bays on site in June 1992 based on the best thinking to date, Orrell's geometrical projection. The most pressing question now came from the architects: "Can somebody please tell us if we're right before we go any further?" It was time to resolve the academic debate and come to a practical conclusion.

Gurr and Simon Blatherwick (the Globe archaeologist) decided to flush out the present state of academic opinion once and for all. In the June 1992 issue of the archaeological journal *Antiquity*, they published the arguments for both the 80ft and 100ft alternatives, a means of focusing the debate they could anticipate at the forthcoming seminar to be held in October – the latest in a series of six such meetings that Gurr had organised.

This one was crucial. The ivory tower had to put down some foundations.

> *...were the whole frame here,*
> *It is of such a spacious lofty pitch,*
> *Your roof were not sufficient to contain it.*
>
> *Henry VI (Pt.1)*, Act II Sc. iii

The trial bays that were erected in the summer of 1992, using 18 tons of green English oak, were designed by Jon Greenfield (Theo's associate and eventual successor) from specifications provided by Orrell – 100ft diameter and 20 sides. The point of the exercise was partly for builder, Peter McCurdy, to try out his techniques in practice and then submit them to other experts on timber framing for their professional critique. That purpose was admirably served. Greenfield remembers: "We impressed the pros that we were going to do it right!" The other purpose was to focus the academic discussion on the detail of design. If not *this* – what?

There was no shortage of suggestions. 18-sided and 94ft... 18-sided and 90ft... 21-sided and 100ft. Even 32ft-sided! Support for 24 sides dwindled rapidly. In the end it came down to a vote between 20 sides and 99ft (Orrell's revised recommendation after discussion with Peter McCurdy) and 18 sides and 90ft. Orrell was supported by fourteen of the twenty votes and all the participants agreed to accept

the conclusion in the light of probability but by no means certainty. The new Globe would now be built to those dimensions.

One thought continued to nag at the back of Orrell's mind, even after he had left the seminar. There had – as usual – been much talk of the Fortune and the specific instructions to the builder of the later playhouse to replicate the Globe. The Fortune probably had 20 bays... but that argument, for good or ill, was behind them. Well, then, should the similarity perhaps be in the *width*? Should the Globe's "round" be 80ft to match the Fortune's 80ft square? But that, too, had been decided. Then it struck him. The similarity was in the *audience capacity*; the shape was irrelevant. The approved ground plan for the Globe would yield 270 running feet of bays, each bay 12ft 6in deep. When he came to calculate the Fortune's dimensions, it was precisely the same – or, at least within the dimensions of a single seated spectator. Orrell could breathe a sigh of relief and put the issue from his mind once and for all. The unities were being observed. The Fortune was simply the Globe squared.

Drawing of the Globe complex from the River Thames by Dennis Bailey. (1992) Pentagram

There remained the question of framing the tiring house. As things stood, it was incorporated in several of the bays of the main construction, extending a little to the front to the decorated *frons scenae*. The Rose findings were inconclusive in this regard. No sign of *frons* footings and equally no proof that the tiring house was a separate structure. Yet the Fortune contract was specific about separation and the Hope's tiring house and stage – built later than the other theatres – was portable.

Orrell felt his comfort level rise considerably when Peter McCurdy gave his opinion. Throughout the whole odyssey he had leaned instinctively towards the requirements of the craftsmen. For structural reasons – McCurdy argued – the tiring house and the roof that projected over the stage needed to be framed independently from the rest of the building. The balance of the documentary evidence tended to support him. The Red Lion (1567) certainly had a separate stage tower and the Swan drawing (1595) seems to suggest the same.

Just as important – so did the Theatre. It would be reasonable to speculate – the design team concluded – that in the intervening years the independent tower formula had merely evolved into something more integrated and functional – without fundamentally changing. The design they produced showed the tiring house as a separate entity, slotting into a gap left among the regular bays of the polygon, so that (as Orrell poetically put it) "the auditorium enclosed it as a hand might grasp a painted jewel box".

Wrought he not well that painted it?
Timon of Athens, Act I Sc.i

How should the jewel box be decorated – plain or fancy? It would, after all, be at least partially exposed to the elements. Many pet theories had been thrown up in the air by the findings of the Rose and Globe excavations, limited though they had been.

The yard surface of the Rose had been one such. Not even brick, it was made of heavy duty mortar. Functional but hardly elegant. Was that the theme that linked other aspects of surface design? What about the playhouse's most distinctive feature – the mighty pillars that supported the stage roof? The Swan drawing depicted Corinthian columns of what architects call a 'giant order', about 25ft high, a Renaissance feature newly introduced to England and then only for outdoor use.

Orrell surmised that the Globe would have followed that indoor/outdoor tradition with a rough surface underfoot for the groundlings and 'giant order' columns supporting the stage. This robust 'exterior' look would be softened by the 'interior', which Orrell considered should be highly decorative. Time enough to debate that when the structure was built.

❖

Having made the decision to have a self-standing tiring house, what would the face it presented to the audience look like? The space again offered plenty of scope for conjecture and academic debate.

Orrell was convinced – as he had been about the builders' techniques – that the answer to most, if not all, of the design questions would be found in the realms of the practical: "My own view was that the Elizabethan public playhouse was a conscious attempt to reproduce in the vernacular the glories of the ancient Roman theatre and the tiring house front was a modern version of the ancient *frons scenae*", which traditionally represented the facade of a classical palace.

The design of this front surface is key, because it contains the doors through which the actors come and go, a 'discovery space' to bring on large props or special effects and an 'above' sometimes used by the actors. Should it have two doors or three? There were contemporary precedents for both but Hosley's case for the superior aesthetic balance of three easily carried the vote.

By this time, in any case, Orrell was coming to another conclusion about the doors. Close study of the texts and stage directions had convinced him that the Shakespearean actor invariably entered on to the stage through the door he had previously left by. Most of the action, then, passed through the two flanking entrances, leaving the double main doors for processions and dramatic entrances.

Should they open inwards or outwards? It was tempting to imagine dramatic entrances where the doors burst open on to the stage. Three pairs of outward-opening doors were part of the projected design until 1981 but it became clear that they would interfere with the stage hangings. Nor were they present in later stage designs such as those of Inigo Jones. The 'inward' choice was made for them by the New Zealand project to produce real hangings. If further evidence should ever come to light which proves otherwise, it would be a relatively simple matter to correct. But until then...

> Of excellent discourse,
> Pretty and witty, wild and yet, too, gentle.
>
> *A Comedy of Errors*, Act III Sc.i

The 1992 Pentagram seminar resolved some other outstanding matters. One was the stage itself. Despite the Rose, the stage of the Globe would be rectangular and as wide as four of the bays – or 44ft. It would thrust forward to the middle of the yard. This was comfortingly close to the Fortune's dimension. The Seminar gave its blessing. It also voted for something Orrell didn't agree with – he wasn't to win all the battles! – the height of the stage balcony. No higher than 9ft above the stage, said the seminar, for the safety of the actors required to negotiate a tricky manoeuvre. How could Romeo be expected to climb a balcony or Cleopatra lift a dying Antony to a greater height? Perfectly easily, grumbled Orrell, convinced that the separateness of the tiring house changed the rules of symmetry as far as varying the storey heights went. In any case, didn't the later and smaller Cockpit set its stage balcony at 10ft or more? And by the way, Romeo was never required to climb Juliet's balcony in the Globe, since the play pre-dated it. He still lost the argument... A more practical post-script was that, in the light of the decision, the New Zealand hangings – already well advanced – would no longer fit without some fairly major surgery!

Where would the two great pillars go? For once there really was so little historical evidence to go on that it was anyone's guess. It was agreed to let structural considerations dictate the decision – at least for now! Theo went away and came back with "a great unified roof that seemed to shrug its shoulders and get down to business" in Orrell's view. Peter McCurdy was less enthusiastic. He worried that it might unduly denigrate the design, as well as being difficult to build...

The design of the *frons* was something else altogether. Lowering the dimensions of the balcony had created a lot of other problems in terms of height and proportion. Late in 1993, Theo made his own kind of statement. As Orrell recalls: "He circulated an astonishing scheme: the three-door pattern had gone and every good piece of historical evidence seemed to have been ignored in a design for an open colonnade intended to be flexible and of maximum use to modern actors. This was also the first occasion when he raked the platform stage. I think now that Theo was merely being provocative, as was his wont".

It was also Theo responding to the demands of certain members of the Artistic Directorate for a more 'convenient' Globe and saying: "OK, if that's how it's to be, *this* is how it will look..." He made his point. The Players backed off. The Authentics carried the day and Orrell caught the first plane to London. A few days later the design was back on track.

Much upon this riddle runs the wisdom of the world
Measure for Measure, Act III Sc. ii

Designing the new Globe was a thriller. Dozens of characters, even hundreds, coming on stage – some of them centre stage – and then retreating to the wings. Messengers – usually with bad news. Spear carriers and serving men. Even the occasional clown.

Clues. The infamous "drawings" that one witness would triumphantly produce to prove one theory, only to have the next witness use them to argue a contrary case. The few crumbling bricks that said different things to different people.

The flirtatious Rose, promising to reveal all, then coyly demurring...

And in the midst of it all – capable of being swayed by every new theory in turn – the restless figure of Sam, coaxing, cajoling, bullying in his quest for the ray of light that's sooner or later permitted to shine through the gloom in all the best dramas and illuminate The Truth.

Piecing the jigsaw clues laboriously together – the Five Just Men. Wickham, Gurr, Orrell, Crosby and Greenfield. They had a picture but a few key pieces were still missing...

> Thy charge
> Exactly is perform'd but there's more work.
> *The Tempest,* Act I Sc. ii

American football parlance has a dangerously deceptive colloquial phrase – "It isn't over 'til it's over". The theatrical design may have been decided but that was in the study and on the drawing board. The Summer of 1995 would have something else to say about certain aspects of those decisions. The "Buts" were but waiting in the wings...

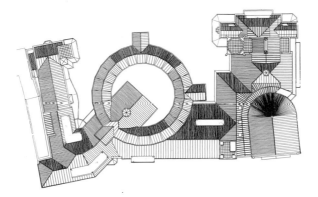

The roof plan shows the complexity of the project. *Pentagram*

CHAPTER FIFTEEN

THE GREAT GLOBE ITSELF
(1989-1993)

...the great globe itself,
Yea, all which it inherit...
The Tempest, Act IV Sc. i

The discovery of the Rose and then the Globe was a mixed blessing to the Globe project. On the plus side it validated beyond the possibility of further debate the concept of Bankside as the cradle of Elizabethan theatre, the Shaftesbury Avenue of its day. Many people who had been genuinely puzzled as to what Sam was about now at least understood the basis of the Dream.

Even the down side had an accidental, if temporary advantage. As soon as the fragment of the original came to light, Sam used it as an excuse to call a halt to the building. His stated reason was logical enough. It made no sense to continue with a speculative design when there was the possibility of learning the facts. Already it seemed likely that the 24 sides their design included should, in fact, be 20. What else might they find? This, to be sure, was before it became clear that further full excavation was unlikely to take place soon enough to be helpful.

The media accepted his statement, which neatly side-stepped the other harsher fact of life. By the end of 1989 the money had run out. The hiatus caused by the court case had brought the project to a point that Southwark Council had wasted so much of their taxpayers' money trying to achieve in vain. In March 1990 the work on the diaphragm wall finished. The contractors' machinery stayed on the site for a while, like giants resting, just in case something should turn up... Fund raising momentum had yet to pick up on either side of the Atlantic, partly because of a world economy drifting into the worst recession since World War II. After the Wall Street 'implosion' of October 1987 financial journalists were talking of a re-run of the

1929 Crash being imminent. It was no time be going around hat in hand to corporations now busy scratching together every last penny to make their bottom line. And besides, when asked, many potential donors said they felt that, if the project had been going to happen, it would surely have happened by now. In the UK particularly a common response was somewhat Irish in its logic: "I'd give you some money if I knew it was going to work". Those same people were less responsive to the counter argument that, if they gave some money, it *would* work. Others made it clear that the media squabbles over the Rose had created a 'plague on both their houses' resistance.

> *Our doubts are traitors,*
> *And make us lose the good we oft might win,*
> *By fearing to attempt.*
> *Measure for Measure*, Act I Sc. iv

1990 drifted aimlessly into 1991. With nothing else to do, it was open season for positioning papers discussing the various options. Suppose we offered Southwark the site back? "The sale of a long lease of a valuable site with the major capital expenditure which has been incurred on preparing excellent foundations for future construction of any kind" was one. "We might hope that this would produce enough money to pay off all our debts".

It was the responsible thing for a Board to consider but none of the alternatives was really a serious consideration. The only way forward was forward as far as Sam was concerned. He was positively Churchillian. He would fight in the flooded foundations. He would *never* surrender. Once again, he carried the day. He *might*, however, consider a major sponsorship – the 'Seagram's Globe', for example. But of offers of this kind came there none...

Board meetings began with Michael Perry (a senior Unilever executive brought in by Orr to chair the Board) scrutinising the accounts to be sure that the ISGC could legally continue to trade for the next month. Not only was there no money to build further, there was a debt to the banks to be considered.

> *...the bounded waters*
> *Should lift their bosoms higher than the shores,*
> *And make a sop of all this solid globe*
> *Troilus and Cressida*, Act I Sc. iii

Once again the site was empty. Somehow, it looked more forlorn than ever. London's least attractive swimming pool. At least the builders' paraphernalia had created the illusion of action and that illusion was one the project needed desperately. "A grand hole in the ground", one American donor grumbled, "not a grand concept at all". Twenty years on and the sum total of Sam's achievement looked like being a muddy hole holding a mountain of debt.

> *...bear it as our Roman actors do,*
> With *untired spirits.*
>
> *Julius Caesar*, Act II Sc. i

It was at this point that Sam gave what was perhaps his finest performance as an actor. In a situation where his back would have been against the wall – except that he didn't *own* a wall – he put on such a show of confidence and optimism that kept the media interested and, better still, at bay. The Board and the rest of those closest to the project lived in daily fear that some journalist somewhere would pick up a whiff of the *real* story about the Globe. One major piece of investigative reporting would almost certainly have pitched the whole enterprise into its own black hole. Instead, at regular intervals, there would be Sam giving yet another interview or photo opportunity, pointing dramatically in a hard hat on the site, clutching a bust of the Bard or doing something equally theatrical. Each time the content of the piece was identically and emptily euphoric but it was infinitely better than any alternative. All of us, again like Mr. Micawber, were waiting for something to turn up...

For Sam himself something already had.

Late in 1989, with work on the diaphragm wall irrevocably under way, he learned he had prostate cancer. It was news he kept to himself for most of the next four years. His colleagues knew nothing until the last few weeks of his life and he said nothing to his family until 1992.

It can be seen now that the knowledge affected everything he thought or did from that point on. It brought the horizon nearer and made action imperative. He worked but he no longer had time to wait. It made Sam even more – 'Sam'. Initially, at least, it did nothing to soften his attitude.

At a meeting of advisors, called together because they had not been involved with the project and could, therefore, discuss their perception of it objectively, Sam's replies to their questions about his plans were invariably firm but frequently impractical in the light of actual prospects. Yes, he fully intended this; no, he most definitely would never consider that. But on most occasions the "No" answer would be tempered by "Of course, *eventually* I might..." After an hour or so of this, one of the advisors, recognising a brick wall when he saw it and not caring much either way, remarked: "Sam, you *keep* saying 'eventually' – what makes you think you've *got* 'eventually'?"

I have a strong feeling that it was around this time that the touch of harsh practicality began to temper the Dream and led to its eventual realisation. Sam had no money and *he* knew he probably had little time. The price tag of the all-or-nothing complex was now up to about £24 million – some predicted more. One thing was sure, with every day that passed the price rose and the possibility receded. He eventually saw the sense in the argument some of us had been proposing for some time – break the project into component parts and cost it accordingly. Build the complex over time in 'manageable bits'.

How much for the concrete piazza on which the Globe would stand? £4 million. How much to build the great Globe itself? Another £4 million. Right, so we're now trying to raise £8 million instead of £24 million plus. That's a figure people can get their minds around. Build it and they will come. Let them *see* the Globe and they will believe the rest will follow... and so will the money. It was a version of the plan David Orr had envisaged after the court case and Sam now embraced it wholeheartedly. It was the only way, given his new and uncertain personal time frame, the Dream could possibly come to pass.

One person who was less than happy at the decision was Theo. As an architect he knew you didn't build this way. First you laid the foundations of the *whole* complex, then you built in sensible sequence. In building logic the Globe itself should be one of the last structures. In truth, he probably also feared that, once the Globe was standing, interest in and commitment to the rest of the complex could easily evaporate and it was the totality that interested him. The theatre was just part of it. But the persuasive arguments that had led Sam for so long had lost their potency – for reasons Theo was not to learn for some time to come.

> Hang out our banners on the outward walls;
> The cry is still, 'They come'
>
> *Macbeth*, Act V Sc. v

There was one ray of sunlight to break through those Stygian months and because it didn't really matter a jot – it mattered a lot as a symbol of what applied determination was still capable of achieving.

A banner with a strange device. In Autumn of 1991 American designer Gordon Schwontkowski's 30ft by 20ft banner projects a more confident message than many on the project actually felt at the time.

In 1989, through the Chicago branch, Sam had come across the work of a young man called Gordon Schwontkowski. Untrained as an artist, Schwontkowski had contributed a 10ft banner with Shakespeare's face to his local drama festival at Ripon College, Wisconsin. Sam contacted him. Could he, would he make another and bigger one to hang on the Bankside scaffolding as a defiant sign that something was happening? And while he was about it, could he make sure it would withstand the British weather?

It was an unlikely proposition to put to someone unless, like Sam, you made a habit of the unlikely. To his surprise, Schwontkowski, a supervisor with the local branch of UPS (United Parcel Service), agreed. In six weeks, working almost entirely at night, he undertook to deliver a 20ft x 30ft weatherproof banner using the Droeshout drawing of Shakespeare and the *Hamlet* quotation Sam selected – "This grave shall have a living monument". In fact, it took him ten weeks and 750 hours to paint the vinyl-coated nylon; it weighed

70 lbs and was valued at $30,000 when Schwontkowski's employers air-freighted it free of charge to an impatient Sam.

As it happened, the banner arrived in Southwark only hours after the remains of the original Globe had been discovered. It was unveiled on the 1990 Birthday with its proud creator present, along with the massed media and one hundred and fifty living descendants of Shakespeare. As the Mona Lisa face of the Bard smiled enigmatically across the river for the first time, one other face looked even happier. As the cameramen gave it their best shots, standing in the foreground of every picture, his yellow hard hat at a jaunty angle, was – guess who?

> His training such,
> That he may furnish and instruct great teachers.
> *Henry VIII*, Act I Sc. ii

One early investment was beginning to pay off. Because it wasn't dramatic, it tended to receive little public attention and was well into the bottom half of any board agenda but for many people it was one of the few realities of the whole project.

Patrick Spottiswoode dates the semi-official birth of Globe Education as a self-respecting 'department' from late 1989: "I knew we were in business when I was allowed to order a professionally-designed and printed programme – there was nothing more formal than that!" By this time, in fact, Spottiswoode already had several years of lectures and workshops under his belt. After the 'hiatus' of the court case, he'd been asked to return to run both the education activities and organise the sporadic Globe 'events' Sam deemed necessary to prove the project's continued existence and wellbeing. With both areas of activity taking off, he opted to concentrate on education.

Sam's interpretation of 'education' was a liberal one. Essentially, he wanted people of all ages to share the passion he felt for Shakespeare. In the truest sense of the word he wanted Shakespeare to be 'popular' again. Part of that could be achieved by convincing the people of Southwark that the theatre itself could have meaning in their daily lives but most of it would be a question of seeding the future.

From that point his instinct guided him. While he might scour the pages of printed scholarship and sit attentively at the feet of those who wrote them, he was perfectly well aware that the TV generation of children in Southwark would not. He would have to find a way to make Shakespeare come to life for them – hence his early insistence to Spottiswoode that in every manifestation of 'education' history must be made theatrical.

It was an instinct that often caused a *frisson* among the academics. Spottiswoode remembers a discussion on the subject of the Globe's future exhibition. Wouldn't it be great, said Sam, to have the first exhibit show Shakespeare sitting at his father's feet watching James Burbage's touring company giving a performance at Stratford and perhaps meeting the young Richard Burbage...? Maybe this was young Will's first taste of the theatre that was to beckon him from this rural backwater to the streets of London, where...

At which point one of the scholars present pointed out that there was, of course, no factual evidence for any such event or meeting. Spottiswoode recalls: "The man was correct but he'd missed the point. Sam, the actor/director, was 'envisioning' how things *should* have been, how the young Shakespeare's eyes *must* have been opened – just as his own had been... Sam yielded but you could see that he was slightly disappointed".

That same instinct guided him into other ways of arriving at the same destination and had done from the early days of the project. During those early 70's summer seasons he'd insisted on a childrens' cinema. With the help of Diana Devlin and a variety of scholars from London University he'd run summer schools and lecture series. The list of speakers read like an academic *Who's Who* and all of them were religiously recorded – often by Sam personally – for eventual inclusion in the Globe's audio-visual library. They were like academic vintage port – to be laid down for future generations. But then, so was the whole project...

> ...*since it is in my power*
> *To o'erthrow law, and in one self-born hour*
> *To plant and o'erwhelm custom.*
> Chorus, *The Winter's Tale*, Act IV

At the beginning of 1991, apart from a hole in the ground, all the project had to show for its efforts was a debt of some £2 million, which was beginning to resemble a hungry little bird with its beak open, requiring regular sustenance. There was a little money still trickling in but nothing like enough to service the debt. Any day now

– like Mr. Micawber – the Globe's expenses were going to exceed its income. At which point it could no longer legally trade.

The dilemma was that the bank debt took precedence over everything else. They had first call on any money that came in. They could also call in the debt whenever they liked but, then, that would sink the project and everybody would be a loser. Nor was the trickle enough to provide the kind of cash flow needed to pay a building contractor to do the work that might persuade more people to contribute. Things seemed to be at an impasse.

Fittingly, Theo was the architect of the solution. He was on his way home from another depressing Board meeting at which discussion had hovered around ground zero or lower. There must be something in the evening air around the Thames. It had spurred Sam into action on his stroll with brother Bill all those years ago and now it affected Theo as he passed the site.

His thought had the charm of one of those old Hollywood musicals where the hero turns to the rest of the group and says: "Why don't we do the show right here? We'll put it on *ourselves!*" What had suddenly clicked into place in his mind was that there were two aspects to the recession. While he couldn't afford to employ a full building crew, nor could a lot of other people. Dozens of qualified builders were sitting around idle. Why didn't he hire a site agent and hand pick a small group of tradesmen as direct employees, using them as and when money became available? Doing the job piecemeal in self-contained tranches was better than not doing it at all. He could use the building materials already donated in kind and the cash flow needed would be little more than the salaries of the workers. With a mountain of concrete to be built as the next task, there wouldn't be many trades to worry about – carpenters to build the shuttering, steel fixers to build the reinforcement and concreters to do the casting. It might just work!

In May Theo presented Self Build to the Board. Sensibly – since in Perry and Orr he was dealing with businessmen – he positioned it as a 5-year plan to build the Globe and the minimum amount of concrete needed to support it at a cost of £5 million. All that was needed was permission from the banks to use new income for the building rather than on paying off the debt. After months of careful negotiation permission was duly received. In December the Self Build Committee had its first meeting.

Theo secured the services of Eric Vassar and Ted Hampton, both recently retired from Lovells and familiar with the Globe site. They proceeded to hire a five-man team and supervised their work personally. Vassar took care of the logistics and Hampton the on-site work. Theoretically, it was a team suitable for a site 1/5th the size of the Globe's but it was all they could afford and, besides, when you're doing something you believe in, isn't one man supposed to have the strength of ten? There should be power to spare... Lovells helped with the site set up and donated a couple of portable toilets. With a telephone, a drawing table and some lock up boxes for tools they soon had a working site again.

As the money trickled in, the work crept on, almost imperceptibly at first, as the concrete foundations were laid that would underpin the whole structure. Gradually, Phase 2 took shape – the piazza which would hold the great Globe itself, standing higher than the original would have done so that it could have a nodding acquaintance with St. Paul's immediately across the river and so that, as the rest of London went about their business, they could see this new landmark rising.

For Theo this way of working was a dream come true: "What we're doing now is building the thing as if it were a pleasure not a business... Instead of having it run by bosses who turn up in their Jaguars, the three of us (Hampton, Vassar and himself) sit there being totally romantic about the building of it and we're getting it built in a very refreshing way... We must keep the 'romance'. On an old building site people used to take their kids on a Sunday morning to show them the building. It was a communal affair and we're just beginning to get that going again". With his small team – and remembering that Peter Street only had twenty – "We've managed to create the atmosphere of the way it was built in the first place".

> To show our simple skill
> That is the true beginning of our end.
>
> *A Midsummer Night's Dream*, Act V Sc. i

The second major event came in early 1992 with the decision to build the first two bays. (Discussed in more detail in Chapter 16) Sam was convinced that this visible manifestation was needed to help the general public and particularly potential donors piece out the project's imperfections by showing them what the Dream would actually *look* like.

The problem the fund raisers had had from the beginning was that people find it difficult to focus on futures; they are infinitely more attracted to the tangible. Time and again in trying to pin down the reason why there was reluctance to contribute they'd be faced with the argument that, well, the Royal Opera House is actually *there*, isn't it? And we have to make sure that's taken care of first, don't we? When you're competing for a share of the personal or the corporate purse, reasonably instant gratification takes some beating. To complicate matters even further, the arts are competing on the same playing field as some highly emotive *charities*. The money one earmarked for Great Ormond Street Childrens' Hospital, for instance, was lost to the Globe.

The bays were the second breakthrough the project needed. They would give the first physical shape to more than twenty years of whirling words. Standing 41ft high, they would be made with the hand-crafted joinery techniques used in the 16th century. Scholars could take them apart intellectually to their hearts' content but, more importantly, the public could see them and begin to feel the Dream.

They were costed out at $100,000 without the cladding and in no time word came across the Atlantic that sponsors had been found. In March Peter McCurdy, a builder specialising in the restoration of Elizabethan buildings was instructed to proceed. The bays would be built in his Greenham workshop and brought to the site for raising.

With an alacrity his predecessor, Peter Street, would have found admirable, McCurdy actually had four bays ready for the day in June when they were duly unveiled by Prince Edward. It was a day on which no one felt the need to cavil. No matter how long the journey had been – the media concluded – Old Sam Wanamaker is finally going to get his Globe...

> I do not like 'but yet', it does allay
> The good precedence; fie upon 'but yet'!
> *Antony and Cleopatra*, Act II Sc. v

'Old Sam' at last had achievement to add to his unquenchable optimism. What he didn't have was time. He badgered everyone who'd listen for more bays and for the first time his relationship with Theo was put under real strain. Squabbles had never counted. Shouting and table pounding were par for the course – but this was serious. For once their agendas distinctly differed.

Theo argued for a disciplined architectural approach now that Self Build finally had momentum. New money should go into proper foundations for the complex as a whole. To do anything else would add to costs later in the process. Did Sam want to build something that might fall down in a few years because it wasn't properly underpinned? Or rot, because there was inadequate drainage? We should do things properly. Yes, the project might take a decade or more to complete but that very slowness would help us to build beautifully, monumentally.

Sam would take that chance – besides, Theo was exaggerating. It was now perfectly clear to him that when people saw the shape of things to come, their imaginations were fired and their purse strings loosened. Couldn't Theo see that people wouldn't put money into concrete? Concrete wasn't sexy!

Sam's motives were mixed. He was the one who needed to see that Wooden 'O'. He also happened to be psychologically right, as far as the project's future was concerned.

The two bays became four (with plywood seating)... work on the piazza proceeded according to schedule and by The Birthday in 1993 a rudimentary stage was ready for Sir John Gielgud to dedicate and on which he spoke the first words within a Wooden 'O', "as yet skeletal but already functional". (*The Times*)

Then, as that same paper reported: "...Derek Jacobi, requesting a muse of fire, was joined by the assembled company. Simon Callow's crooked faker attested a million, Janet Suzman confined monarchies within the girdle of the walls, we pieced out Peter McEnery's imperfections with our thoughts; and the cavalry was invoked by

The Bremer Shakespeare Company's production of *Die Lustige Weiber Von Windsor*, the first performance in the embryonic Wooden 'O'. Designed by Barnes Vereker.

Felicity Kendal". All of it watched by a Cheshire Cat called Sam, sharing a corrugated iron shelter with Princess Michael of Kent to fend off the intermittent rain.

> *A noble troop of strangers;*
> *For so they seem; they've left their barge and landed;*
> *And hither make, as great ambassadors*
> *From foreign princes.*
>
> *Henry VIII*, Act I Sc. iv

Then came the inaugural performance – *Die Lustige Weiber von Windsor*. To some of those present the choice of a German company, the Bremer Shakespeare company, putting on a version of *The Merry Wives of Windsor* in German, cutting Shakespeare's twenty plus characters down to ten and having them played by five male actors, often in drag, might have seemed a touch idiosyncratic but there was method in Sam's apparent madness.

Apart from emphasising the fact that the Globe project had received infinitely more support abroad than it had from local theatrical circles, he'd chosen in Norbert Kentrup (Falstaff) and the Bremer Company a group of actors whose passion for Shakespeare remained untainted by undue reverence. The aim of their production, according to actor, Erik Rosbander, was "to discover the emotion behind the lines. Too often these days Shakespeare is just declaimed. The concentration is on the words, not on the emotion behind them". There was plenty of emotion in the way the Bremer actors threw themselves into their work, going off as one character, then coming back on as another. 'Authentic' it may not have been but enjoyable it certainly was and – as more than one person concluded – undoubtedly true to the spirit of the original stage.

Among other things, the production uncovered the layers of new meaning that any replication necessarily acquires. The all male cast would have been no surprise to Shakespeare; indeed, he would have been surprised by anything else. For today's audience the effect can easily seem uncomfortable and effete but the unselfconscious way the Bremer actors used the device served to make it something of a comment about contemporary gender stereotyping. By holding up the issue for inspection, they made us realise something we tend to overlook – namely that so many portrayals of women, including the "Wives", are simply projections of male fantasies. According to

Bremer actor, Christian Dieterle (who played Alice Ford): "Actors discover the feminine sides of their personalities". Whether this was apparent to the audience is a moot point but the sight of the Wives laden with Harrod's shopping bags was certainly appreciated, as was the way the cast coped – dare one say 'manfully'? – with the interruptions of passing jets, very much as one imagines Shakespeare's actors would have dealt with a noisy groundling.

The press were suitably impressed. "The Globe Rises from the Ashes", said *The European*, while *The Guardian* observed: "A Touch of Weimar at Globe Debut". But *The Times* ("Wilkommen and Welcome All") caught the moment best:

"The groundlings stood or squatted; those seated on bare planks huddled under umbrellas, the multi-coloured traverse drapes whisked back and forth, and the actors successfully competed with planes, helicopters and the chat of the Globe attendants. Despite weather and VIPs, it was an oddly homespun, intimate occasion, funny and rather moving. That, too, perhaps, was rather English".

Before the end of the play the sun shone fitfully through, illuminating the Globe stage for the first time in 349 years and causing Sam to observe: "I hope it's trying to tell us something".

I am in good name and fame with the very best
Henry IV (Pt.2), Act II Sc. iv

Success is often spelled out in little things.

Southwark had planned to rebuild the river walk between the South Bank complex and Tower Bridge and beyond. Now, in time for the 1993 Birthday they had completed the section between Blackfriars Bridge and Emerson Street, which they now re-christened – New Globe Walk. But the real proof that the project was well and truly on the map came when you could get into a London taxi and, when you asked for the Globe, the cabbie no longer scratched his head...

CHAPTER SIXTEEN

THE ARCHITECT'S TALE: PART TWO

(1987 – 1996)

> Creations of architecture, which being capable of no other
> life, and being not essentially composed of things pleasant
> in themselves – as music of sweet sounds or painting of
> fair clouds, but of inert substance – depend for their
> dignity and pleasurableness in the utmost degree, upon the
> vivid expression of the intellectual life which has been
> concerned with their production.
>
> John Ruskin, *Seven Lamps of Architecture*, "The Lamp of Life"

The hard part of Theo Crosby's task was to serve many masters. The Inigo Jones admittedly came with its own plans and the rest of the complex was a 'green fields' project from an architect's point of view, since it had no history. But the 'great Globe itself'...

There he would have to reconcile the competing theories of scholars and historians and balance the blandishments of theatricals, too, to 'improve' on the original.

As early as August 1981 he wrote: "I am in the process at the moment of re-examining the flats and Sam seems to want a bigger museum, and as soon as the theatre technicians get involved I know I am going to need a lot more space for workshops, lighting, offices, wardrobe mistresses, lavatories and rest rooms, tea bars and so on..." Nonetheless, he answered every communication with a courteous personal note.

Up to now he'd been able to hide his Globe work from his colleagues at Pentagram to a great extent – or at least, he thought he had. In fact, the project had already gained the joking reputation of being the longest-running charity job in the company's history. Now that building was about to start he needed a more formal working arrangement. So far the 'Globe team' had been just Theo and Edward Armitage, a contemporary of his from fledgling architect days. Over the years Armitage's strong practical sense had helped translate Theo's more ethereal ideas from drawing board to building site. Together they organised the Globe site during the summer of 1987.

Then, in December the 'green fields' came to him in the shape of Jon Greenfield, who was to become disciple, assistant and eventually torch bearer for the project: A graduate of Manchester University School of Architecture, Greenfield had worked on a variety of urban projects before his path crossed Theo's and he signed on as 'project architect' for the Globe. At the time the £18 million management contract looked straightforward enough.

Jon Greenfield, the young architect who began as Theo's assistant and then took charge of the project following his death. Pentagram

Greenfield recalls their first encounter vividly:

I later came to recognise Theo's way but my first impression was very startling. He was very tall, with a shock of curly white hair, and he had a confident charm that was overpowering to a young man. About half way through the interview he got up and walked out, asking me over his shoulder to start as soon as I could. I was left... not sure what to make of it all. The day after I received a charming letter. Theo was a very persuasive writer, and I have since seen many people become infected by some cause or other of his, or become a life long admirer, simply by receiving one of his well cast letters.

Thou wall, O wall! O sweet and lovely wall!
Show me thy chink...
A Midsummer Night's Dream, Act V Sc. i

By Christmas the existing buildings had been demolished and the site was clear. Six months later a company called Terresearch (the geotechnical subsidiary of Taylor Woodrow) began work on the diaphragm wall. ("Do we *have* to call it that?" a leading actress was heard to remark.) By the end of the year the work was done.

And then... nothing.

"Most curious of all", Greenfield noted in his journal, "when the operation had finished... there was nothing to see of the wall we had just built. A wall nearly 300 metres long, twenty odd metres high and 0.6 metres thick, costing the best part of a million pounds, completely hidden from view because the top of the wall was at ground level. The site looked much the same after Terresearch had finished as it had before they started... We had spent all the money the Globe had in the bank".

When there's nothing to see, it's hard to catch the fund-raising imagination and money was trickling in at a slower rate than the rain in that waterproof hole in the ground. Not to be deterred, Sam persuaded the Trustees to approach a consortium of ten European banks and borrow £2 million. At that time the target for the project was £18 million, so £2 million looked like a healthy contribution to the total cost. The only trouble was that building cost inflation at the time was running at roughly three times higher than the Retail Price Index. The money was literally melting in the hand and still the project wasn't paying its way...

On the strength of the loan Lovells were now appointed as contractors. Their representatives visited the site and made encouraging noises. When it was suggested that they think of this strange building with no roof as less of a theatre and more of a football stadium, the noises became even more encouraging. At least there was activity again.

In early 1989 Greenfield's journal records: "The first subcontract was to excavate the basement and to cast the main foundation raft slab. Building the concrete frame up to 'piazza level', just above street level, would follow. So, by the end of January 1989 the site was once again host to monster machinery, this time excavators and mucking away lorries. Again, the scale of the operation caught my fancy, if

Michael Perry and Sam celebrate the start of building in 1989.

nobody else's. Twenty-seven thousand cubic metres of ground had to be removed (the equivalent of nine thousand domestic skips). Mighty Meccano-like steel props had to be installed to hold up the diaphragm wall before the foundations could take the strain. Our enigmatic diaphragm wall, formed in the ground, was gradually brought into the light by the methodical excavations".

By one of those ironies that by now had become a feature of the Globe project the new foundations were being laid at precisely the same moment as the old foundations of the Rose were being uncovered next door.

Meanwhile, there were preliminary discussions with experts about oak frames; discussions about the preferability of offices to flats elsewhere on the complex. All in all, there was a great deal of talk. Talk, after all, was the one thing that was cheap. The fact remained that, although the work was undoubtedly going well, the money was going out on a regular basis and *still* nothing was coming in. "As the ground excavation works drew to a close", Greenfield noted, "it dawned on all of us, before we were officially told, that the site was going to have to shut down". And, indeed, in May 1990 Lovell's contract was suspended.

Here is a gentleman whom by chance I met.
The Taming of the Shrew, Act I Sc. ii

But, as in all the best stories, fortunes were soon reversed and perhaps the depths of 1990 had something to do with the revival of 1991. In the spring came the inspiration of Self Build and soon after the decision to build the two bays. The game was now very much afoot...

The idea of building a bay at all started as another happy happenstance. It wasn't even something that came out of one of the frequent Globe 'think tanks'. A man called Adrian Sanders happened to own an estate on the Sussex Weald and had the fancy to build an old style barn from his own timbers. With no particular knowledge of historic timber framing, he'd had his estate carpenter convert the trees to structural timber on his own saw bench and copy the design as best he could from an historic barn that was also on his land. At which point he saw the Globe's appeal for timber in a trade magazine and immediately contacted Sam in late 1991. Why didn't *he* build one of the bays in the same way as his contribution to the project?

Once the idea took root in Sam's mind, there was no dislodging it. Sam contacted Pentagram and as Greenfield recalls: "It was impossible not to be infected by the same joy..." Throughout 1989 the Pentagram team had been doing preliminary design work on the Globe's actual structure without going so far as to look for a contractor. Like everything else, that work had come to a frustrating stop in 1990 when the funds ran out. Greenfield himself had a tentative eye on a man called Peter McCurdy, as much out of general interest as looking for a specific builder for the Globe and during 1991 had visited two of the more important sites on which McCurdy had been involved.

Sanders was a name new to all of them. They decided to check him out and in January 1992 – with Self Build just beginning to stir into life – a small party that included Sam and Jon drove down to Sanders' estate. Not surprisingly, they found that, though building the barn at all was a considerable achievement, the workmanship was only an Elizabethan approximation and well below what the experts felt was needed for their reconstruction. Sanders took their comments in good part and, far from being put out, agreed to cast his eye over the drawings and schedule the Globe team came up with, so that they could assess the amount of timber that would be involved and some idea of the cost.

Sanders had fired their imaginations. This thing was not only possible – it was necessary. A week later Jon took Sam down to meet Peter McCurdy at his workshops at Stanford Dingley, near Greenham in Berks. "Part of a small band of reborn master carpenters", as Greenfield describes him, his special interest was the restoration of Elizabethan timber frame houses. Right away Sam had to admit that McCurdy's workmanship – in fact, his whole approach – was in a different league. To prove a point about the way Elizabethan timbers were hewn, McCurdy picked up a side axe and began to demonstrate by cutting wedges from a small round tree lying on a pair of trestles. One straight cut and another angled sent wedges flying out at his audience. The combination of energy and accuracy clearly impressed Sam deeply. Sanders would donate and cut the timber, but it would be under McCurdy's direction, and he would construct the experimental frame. The Third Design Musketeer had been recruited.

Before work could start, though, there was one more hurdle to be overcome. The Board had just managed to overcome a hurdle of its own in getting the banks to agree to allow Self Build. Nothing must be allowed to damage that fragile accord. At the Board presentation Sam was uncharacteristically nervous, Greenfield recalls, mounting too many arguments, which he repeated again and again. Luckily, Chairman Michael Perry could read Sam like a book by now and he also knew a good thing when he saw it. The design team left the meeting with *two* bays instead of one – two allowing for the most stable construction. They were to be ready for a June 17th unveiling.

Go you with me, and I will use your skill.
Much Ado About Nothing, Act I Sc. ii

From this point in early 1992 Greenfield and McCurdy began to work together as a seamless team and continued to do so until the Globe was finally built. Those first two bays, however, taught them the valuable lessons that could have been learned no other way. Building the bays at all meant that the academics had finally been pinned down, as far as dimensions were concerned. The time had come to turn the numbers into wood, thatch and plaster. Life must now be breathed into theory.

The two men set off on 'a major architectural trawl', visiting existing timber frame buildings of the relevant period all over the country to see how certain joins were designed, to measure and study the most minute details of construction. McCurdy was not a man about to produce 'his' version of an Elizabethan building, a modern interpretation prefabricated by modern methods. *His* Globe was to be the result of the continuation of the strict and careful traditional methods of his professional predecessors – a tradition he had meticulously schooled himself to relearn.

From February to May the two men visited major buildings of the relevant period – a practice they continued subsequently to verify further details of decoration. The Tower of London, Middle Temple Hall, Canonbury Tower, Charterhouse, these were just some of the buildings that were examined and annotated. English Heritage and the Museum of London both provided drawings and photographs. After all the sitting around, there was now much to be done in a short time.

McCurdy went out tree shopping. The New Forest, the Forest of Dean... wherever oaks still grew tall and straight. Seasoned oak is hard to work, whereas 'green' oak seasons in position. The trees were, therefore, chosen in the main while they were still growing. In Peter Street's day he would have taken the circular tree section and hewed it to a square, leaving the weaker sap wood in the corners of the square. In the course of time those corners would decay first, leaving the core solid. These main beams would then be rough hewn with a side axe and finished to a smooth surface with the long-handled adze. It would have been far too expensive for Peter McCurdy to have replicated that procedure. Instead, he persuaded the modern saw mills to cut the timbers in a special way under his direction.

To fit the pieces together involved hammering tapered oak pegs into holes slightly out of alignment, causing the pillars to pull together. All of which sounds a lot easier than it is.

There were options to be debated at every turn. Should the bays be $3^1/2$ storeys high (like a particular Holborn building they'd found) or should they follow the height described in the Fortune contract? Would this kind of joint work at this kind of angle? In April John Orrell arrived and joined the design team.

"Through it all", Jon recalls, "Theo was happy to let this research and design go on around him, keeping a weather eye on it but not attempting to direct it". Self Build was his project. The bays were Jon and Peter's...

The Globe under construction. *Drawing by June Everett*

You taught me language, and my profit on't
Is, I know how to curse.

The Tempest, Act I Sc. ii

While the work was going on, Sam – in typical fashion – was busy planning the 'theatre' of the June unveiling. It was to be a royal event and, therefore, spectacular. What about draping the bays with a large USAF parachute, which would be raised by a crane? The general consensus was that it would be asking for trouble. Greenfield was to claim that the debate exhausted more nervous energy than the building of the bays. He doesn't know to this day how the argument was finally resolved and the parachute abandoned without severing professional and personal relationships!

In a diary format column he wrote for *The Guardian* Sam publicly aired his private feelings of being misunderstood at every turn. The tongue was admittedly in the cheek but it didn't blur the clarity of the underlying message in his stream of consciousness ruminations:

...41 years a British resident and taxpayer and I'm still that US film-maker who plans to erect the replica Elizabethan theatre... All by himself, of course. Never mind the Shakespeare Globe Trust, a registered charity, never mind the distinguished roster of trustees and directors, chairmen of great banks and industries, never mind the armies of supporters worldwide. (Except the British Government – surprise, surprise)... Scrap the cliches: Shakespeare is good for you. Who cares? How do you compete with starving children, the popular heartrending Aids appeal and Elizabeth Taylor? Now the environment. God help us...

Having got that off his chest, he turns to the parachute:

A parachute? What do you mean – a parachute? Well, how else are you going to unveil two 41 ft high by 24 ft wide by 15 ft deep oak sections on the Globe site – by HRH Prince Edward – in front of 500 people? (The man is crazy) It's never been done before! What's wrong with balloons? And the water firemen, those jets in the sky look great and it's been done before! That's what I mean. Yes, but a parachute! It's too small anyway. I'll get a big one. It'll be too big. It'll snag on the edges of the bays and what happens if there's a wind? It's not safe. It's dangerous. Well, let's test it. There's no time... It's too costly, the crane and all... (God, he's stubborn) We've got a brass band, too... All I want is to create surprise and delight and great photo opportunities – something fresh and original. All I ask is to try it! (Silence) Ah, the hell with it. But don't call it an unveiling.

The day of the unveiling was clear and warm (as Sam had *known* it would be) but there was a breeze (as Jon had *said* there would be). But all of the arguments were forgotten in the wonder of the occasion. You couldn't be there and doubt that this – together with Self Build – was the true turning point of the whole project. Greenfield found himself quoting Churchill. Something about it being not the *end* or even the *beginning* of the end... but certainly the end of the beginning...

> I trust it will grow to a most prosperous perfection
> *Measure for Measure*, Act III Sc. i

Even before the bays were officially unveiled, fellow craftsmen and scholars had been allowed to inspect them. They had successfully survived the most critical scrutiny. But in the original conception that was only part of the point. The bays should be the equivalent of a 'show house', fully finished to give an accurate impression of what people could expect to see. By September they were thatched and impressive enough for even *Country Life* to publish a photograph.

During the process of fitting out the bays another bee had entered Sam's bonnet. At a building trade fair he'd come across a company that specialised in softwood moulding and turned balusters. So did several others but this one was called – *Richard Burbidge*. The coincidence was too great to bear; these people *had* to be involved. At which point the arch-rival, the Rose also turned out to be a latter-day ally. From a broken baluster found on the Rose site, Greenfield was able to reconstruct a model for the Globe's baluster, which Burbidge could produce. There the fitting out ended. While not complete – there was no plastering or seating – the bays had served their purpose. They complemented the Self Build programme and had significantly helped fund raising. Now the two programmes could work hand in hand. The two bays could take up their final location on the newly-completed concrete piazza. By April 1993 they would be joined by two more around a temporary stage and by the end of the year the four had become eight. There was no longer any room to doubt that the great Globe was finally rising.

❖

As a perfectionist, McCurdy fretted about certain aspects of the operation, such as the way the bays were originally arranged in pairs to flank the temporary stage for presentation purposes but he perfectly understood the publicity need for it. The traditional method of timber construction, he pointed out, was to prefabricate the flat frames and then pre-assemble them in the workshop, just to make sure everything fits. At that point the first frame goes on to the site, while the second remains as the template for the next bay and so on. As the bays are erected on site, you start at one point, then continue framing round the circle.

He considered his point conclusively proved when it was discovered that the first four bays, which had stood open to the elements for over a year, had altered dimensionally. Their stress patterns had changed to the point where it took a lot of time and effort to refit them when new bays came to be added. But while McCurdy was shaking his head, Sam simply saw another piece of the puzzle slotting into place.

A wisp of straw were worth a thousand crowns.
Henry VI (Pt.3), Act II Sc. ii

The first thatch to be used on a London building since the Great Fire of 1666.
Treated with a one inch plastic barrier, it made the Norfolk reeds fire-proof.

As the bays began their circular path, the thatching could begin.
There was less of a problem here. Although there had not been a
thatched building in the City of London since the Great Fire over
three hundred years before, thatch had remained a popular method
of roofing in parts of rural England, as it had since 500BC. And since
the thatch needs to be renewed every fifty years or so, as the ends rot
and gradually blow away, the art of the thatcher has never been lost.

Once the regulatory questions concerning safety had been
addressed, the question was – what *kind* of thatch? Straw or
water-reed thatch? Either would have been perfectly suitable but the
decision was made for them when the excavations of the Rose
revealed traces of water-reed, a flexible material that can be laid at a
steep angle. If anyone needed further confirmation, Shakespeare
himself provided it by having Gonzalo say in *The Tempest*: "His tears
run down his beard, like winter's drops from eaves of reed".

Norfolk water-reed then it was, fixed down with horizontal metal
rods and 9in thatching nails. Six thousand bundles of it would be
used before the teams of thatchers drawn from all over Britain had
finished their work in the spring of 1995. The only concession made
to the more nervous age we live in was a sprinkler (or sparge pipe)
system discreetly emerging from the thatch and the use of interleaved
fireboard together with a powerful fire retardant on the thatch itself
– nothing that would distract the eye.

There was one small problem no one had taken into their
calculations. Many of the thatchers came from the West Country,

where the height of their professional ambitions had been a thatched cottage roof. Now they found themselves perched high above London, working in rain or snow and often in high winds. "It was rather like mountaineering", one of them recalls, "We just had to cling on. Our crane driver stopped when the winds reached 60 miles per hour!"

As the thatching moved ahead, following close behind came the plasterers. The task they faced was to plaster 300 ft of wall to a height of 30 ft and to use some 250 tons of lime mortar in the process.

Once again there was meticulous attention to period detail and techniques. Vertical wooden staves were fixed to the huge green oak posts that form the skeleton of the Globe. Then – nailed horizontally across the staves, creating gaps of around an inch and a quarter – came the laths made from pliable green oak. The gaps are filled with the special plaster made of lime putty, coarse Chardstock sand and chopped goat hair ("lathe, lyme and haire") to form the base coat. (Originally, it would have been cow hair but, since long-haired cows are no longer with us, the goat came into his own.) While it's still wet, a second coat is applied, resulting in a textured finish, providing a good base for the limewash that coats the whole surface. Its other great advantage is its workability; it accommodates the building as it 'settles'.

No need to worry about the authenticity of this technique in terms of Shakespeare's time – it can be traced back to 2,400 BC. And with each ton of mortar needing eight litres of compressed goat 'cowhair' to bind it, a total of 2,000 litres were needed for the completed job.

And in case the job should appear to be too easy, there is a definite plastering 'season' that starts on Lady Day in March and ends on All Souls Day in November, so as to avoid frost and extreme heat. The sight of the team damping down the panels late into the summer evenings, and covering them from the sun during the day, would be enough to cause any DIY-er to think twice.

As the work went on, an element of Self Build was introduced here, too. Apprentices from Lambeth College began to be trained on site and gradually took over from the original plasterers.

> But qualify the fire's extreme rage,
> Lest it should burn above the bounds of reason.
> *The Two Gentlemen of Verona*, Act II Sc. vii

What the increasing number of visitors didn't see were the trials and tribulations Jon Greenfield suffered to get approval to use these old techniques that Peter Street had taken in his stride. It gave new meaning to 'getting your hands dirty'!

June saw him and Peter McCurdy at the Fire Research Station watching samples of their green oak burn for an anxious hour. On a hot summer's day they found themselves kneeling on a concrete base peering at what looked like a Sunday lunch someone had left in the oven. "We set to work scraping off the char, which was hard, dirty work. As we sweated, the charcoal became ingrained into our skin as we slowly revealed the unburnt timbers underneath... it took on an eroded appearance, like huge baulks of driftwood". When they measured the wood loss, they could afford to smile through their grime. The green oak was charring at a rate 25% slower than they'd anticipated...

This made it two in a row and by far the safer of the two. In March, Greenfield had taken part in a similar fire test for the walls. Lime mortar – once the building industry standard, hadn't been used in years and there was no available data on how it would perform in a fire. To satisfy the fire officers Greenfield had to prove his lime mortar – thanks, again, to Rockwool – would resist fire for an hour.

> To gild refined gold, to paint the lily,
> To throw a perfume on the violet,
> To smooth the ice, or add another hue
> Unto the rainbow...
> Is wasteful and ridiculous excess.
>
> *King John*, Act IV Sc. ii

On this March morning he found himself standing with a group on the cold side of a 10ft x 10ft oak and plaster section which formed one side of the test kiln. After about twenty minutes a loud crash told them that the plaster up to the laths had collapsed. Thirty minutes passed... forty-five... then the hour. They were home and dry. Out of interest they decided to see just how long it would last!! "Finally, at one hundred and seventy-three minutes a small circle of orange glow could be seen in one of the timber braces. The hole quickly enlarged and the test was stopped. We had wanted one hour and now had a certificate for just 'seven minutes short of three hours'". When they came to examine the sample, they discovered how far its original thickness of five inches had been reduced. When the test was stopped, they were standing just one lime plaster inch away from gas jets producing 1000°C of heat!

There was to be a small *crise* over cosmetics. There was a body of opinion that held the finished structure would have been plastered all over in Elizabethan times, giving it a matt white texture – a look far removed from the popular conception of half-beamed 'stockbroker's Tudor'. The theory being that plastering over the beams would protect them from the weather and so prolong their life. But what about all my wonderful beams, Sam cried, when that was suggested – no one will *see* them!

Luckily, the research Orrell, Greenfield and McCurdy had done by this time suggested that, rather than plastering, there was ample precedent for lime washing the timbers and just as much for doing nothing at all. Because the argument was evenly balanced – and to save Sam from cardiac arrest – they decided for the prettier option...

By the time of Sam's death at the end of 1993 all the structural decisions had been made and ratified at one of the series of Pentagram seminars organised by Andrew Gurr. As far as anyone could see, there was unlikely to be any new evidence forthcoming in the near future and, should something miraculously surface, they were fortunately dealing with the one kind of building that could be modified without too much trouble.

❖

The main item of unfinished business was the question of the interior decoration. There was a school of thought that argued for keeping the spare simplicity of the bare wood but the Authentics argued (rightly) that that just wasn't the way the Elizabethan theatres had looked. As Theo pointed out: "If you look at the buildings of the period, the popular ones are extremely wild and vulgar, a riot of crude plaster modelling and all brightly coloured". Greenfield agrees: "The Elizabethans were madmen for painting anything they could get a brush to". Both of them were concerned that the period fact denied the popular perception. Would the vivid decoration be a distraction for modern audiences? Or actors? Would it lend strength to the 'Disney' detractors? One thing they were fairly sure of. If they heeded the siren call to open with plain surfaces and paint them later, the work would never be done. In the event there were other priorities. Although the decisions were duly made, the work itself had to wait...

In early 1994 with construction now well under way, the team of Theo, Jon and John Orrell – with the addition of graphic designer, John Ronayne and Colin Sorenson (from the Museum of London) – got down to work to 'finesse' Theo's design...

In the earlier stages of design the question of decoration had received a low priority; there was so much else to settle first and most of it sparked controversy. Consequently, discussion on subjects like the design of the *frons scenae* had been sporadic. As early as 1981 Theo had prepared a series of alternative designs as a means of encouraging comment and discussion. His personal favourite was strongly Palladian in influence, formal and monumental. No, he agreed, it *couldn't* be strictly justified from contemporary sources but might one not assume that theatre art would be in advance of the tastes of time? Orrell demurred but felt it was at least a starting point and certainly several light years ahead of the 'Tudorbethan' conceits that so often passed for authentic Elizabethan design.

At this point Theo had not been converted to his belief in the 'wild and vulgar' colouring theory. His first thought on painting the interior was "A very chaste, classical light-painted scheme" but he was soon persuaded by Orrell that the original was almost certainly like the Swan, a wooden building elaborately disguised to look like stone, with *trompe d'oeil* effects and pillars made to replicate marble. De Witt describes the wooden pillars being painted so like marble as to "deceive even the most prying". Orrell produced ample evidence from other contemporary buildings and recommended that in addition, "all the balusters, rails and forward parts of the structure should seem to be of expensive coloured stone: the essence of the place was one of illusion".

We should hold day with the Antipodes...
The Merchant of Venice, Act V Sc. i

Discussion then moved to the stage hangings. The New Zealand branch of the ISGC in Wellington had volunteered to produce a set as their gift to the project. The hangings would be hung from a rod on copper rings and cover the central bay and the bays each side of it, allowing for a central opening. It was decided that the subject on the two inner curtains would be Hercules with his club on one side

HRH Prince Philip unveils the New Zealand stage hangings on 22nd April 1994. They took 500 women 10,000 hours, 50 metres of wool twill and £400,000 to complete.

and Atlas with the globe on the other. On the two outer curtains would be depictions of Venus and Adonis. John Ronayne provided the original designs, inspired by Flemish sources, and the consensus of opinion was that they should be executed in brightly-coloured red Doornick woven wool tapestry. Once the final design by New Zealand theatre designer, Raymond Boyce, was approved, the local lady volunteers got down to work. When it was unveiled by Prince Philip on the 1994 Birthday, it had taken 500 of them 10,000 hours, 50 metres of wool twill and cost £400,000. There was one design detail that most of the spectators missed – on the globe that weighed Atlas down, New Zealand was suddenly the centre of the known world!

The decision to build the two trial bays focused practical attention on a number of matters that could easily have lingered indefinitely in the realm of the theoretical. Theo now put Palladio firmly behind him and substituted Serlio. Serlio's *Architettura* had been an important work of reference for Renaissance designers and had much influenced Inigo Jones among others. While more relevant, to Orrell's eye the new designs were still too classical and not as 'colloquial' as he felt the Globe would have been. He urged Theo to be more colourful and finally made the sale. The next series of drawings teemed with life.

It was to be Theo's last contribution to the project. In February 1994 he was struck down with a serious aneurism. Confined to bed, he was the one face missing at Sam's memorial service that March. In the months of recuperation he remained actively involved. Jon Greenfield remembers: "I took *frons* drawings to the hospital, thinking he might have a gentle go at the designs. He approached them slowly

The New Zealands hangings (detail). Atlas bearing the Globe on his shoulders acts as a fitting symbol for the project. Note the positioning of New Zealand.

at first but became increasingly vigorous as his strength returned, corresponding frantically with John Orrell and Andy Gurr... Six or seven refinements were circulated, always with a plea for robust criticism. The last version was produced just two months before Theo died".

In September, just when everyone had determined that he was making a full recovery, Theo was knocked over by a cyclist. The shock caused a relapse and a few days later he died at the age of 69, just nine months after his old friend and sparring partner.

Those last few months, however, set the seal on how the interior would eventually look. The team continued to debate and decide the details of final execution, well knowing Theo's views.

The effect, they decided, should be dominated by the large figures carved into the two central posts at gallery level – the two Muses, Melpomene and Thalia. Melpomene (stage right) was identified in mythology with singing and tragedy; Thalia (stage left) with abundance and comedy. Muses were considered the inspiration of poets, their name deriving from the Greek word *mousa* or *memnon* – to think or remember. This was particularly appropriate, since ancient poetry was more often spoken and remembered than written down – very much as Shakespeare's actors had to remember their lines. Since the Muses were traditionally subservient to Apollo, he is depicted with his lyre between the Muses on the half storey above and between them.

On either side are Atlas, bearing the world on his shoulders and between the classical Gods and Goddesses – Mars/Ares (God of War), Minerva/Athena (Household Arts, Intelligence and Strategy in War), Venus/Aphrodite (Love, Giver of Beauty and Sexual Attraction) and Vulcan/Hephaestus (Metalwork and Craftsmanship). Theo had suggested six removable panels along the top of the frons depicting six of the Labours of Hercules. Subsequent discussion led Jon Greenfield to recommend doubling the number of panels, thus including all twelve Labours. Soon afterwards John Orrell came across a reference that had so far eluded his research. A Bishopsgate house dated 1600 had a plaster relief of Hercules supporting the Globe. Could it have been copied from the recently-opened playhouse? It became a model for one of the panels.

> ...look you, this brave o'erhanging firmament, this
> majestical roof fretted with golden fire...
>
> *Hamlet*, Act II Sc. ii

Then the group raised their eyes to the 'Heavens', the roof over the stage described in *Hamlet* as "this majestical roof fretted with golden fire" and here they came to a significant disagreement.

Orrell – a proponent of the Elizabethan stage as a direct descendent of the Roman – believed the roof should be treated as architecture, an Elizabethan 'echo' of the Roman coffered roof.

Ronayne opted for a single field painting of the sky as a kind of diagram of the cosmos. A 1594 description of the ceiling of an Elizabethan stage describes "above all was there the gay Clowdes... adorned with the heavenly firmament, and often spotted with golden...Stars". It would, of course, be divided into three by the two great beams that ran from the stage pillars back to the tiring house. After much discussion, a design incorporating a sunburst in the centre section, flanked by clouds on which astrological signs were superimposed was agreed. But even now, one suspects the debate is far from over.

While it continued, Greenfield moved on to work with specialists from the City & Guilds paint conservation course to decide on the pigment types and mixes and on the execution of the fine detail of the selected images.

When it came to the great columns that support the Heavens, Peter McCurdy was firm in his view that each of them should be cut, including the plinth, from a single baulk of timber. Finding a matched pair was one of the more difficult tasks he undertook but there they would stand, looking for all the world like pink marble – built to last an eternity.

❖

As the Globe neared completion, Greenfield in particular was concerned that Theo's vision should be realised in its entirety. Ruskin's "pleasure of the labour" must not be allowed to flag once the crown had its jewel. The Inigo Jones apart, the rest of the complex was more familiar and could easily seem anti-climatic. Greenfield was determined to maintain the momentum and, fortunately, the foundations for all the surrounding buildings were already in place.

Theo's desire had always been to create a total environment, built to relevant scale in relation to the dimensions of the Globe and giving the appearance of having grown up together. Greenfield has so organised the work that it can be completed in what he terms "virtually manageable portions", which can be manageably funded.

Each block is to be treated as "a different building from a different age: not what we so far recognise to be from our modern age and not from the Elizabethan age either". Theo's travels and studies had taught him not to fear architectural academia. Communities were living organisms. One age always looked back, took what it liked from previous ages and reinterpreted it. When the last touches have been added, the visitor will see a faithful replica of the Globe theatre, but he will sense something more. This is how it would have been if the Globe had never disappeared but had been embraced by the City's changing fabric.

As Greenfield sums it up: "Time will make it a virtual metaphor for the four hundred years since the first Globe was built". The present day Globe, built by Buro Happold (Structural Engineers) and Boyden & Co (Quantity Surveyors) is a fitting memorial for Sam and Theo who had the vision and the willpower to make it happen.

CHAPTER SEVENTEEN

THE ACTOR'S TALE

The actors are come hither, my Lord.

Polonius, *Hamlet*, Act II Sc. ii

NOTE: The interviews in this chapter were conducted while construction was in its early stages and represent individual projections of what the theatre should or would be like. The 'workshop season' of 1995 was to confirm some of those opinions and modify others – as related in Chapter 19.

When it comes to acting, we're inclined to think the 'star' system is a relatively recent phenomenon that reached and passed its peak in 1930s Hollywood. In fact, its origins go back much further than that and it was certainly alive, well and extremely active in Shakespearean theatre.

Just as in any group that's thrown together a natural leader will emerge, in a troupe of players certain actors will gravitate towards parts that suit their particular style. If their 'managers' have any sense, they will encourage the ones with talent to match their inclination and – a star is born.

In Shakespeare's day – and even before it – actors learned their craft the hard way, touring the length and breadth of the country when the Plague forced them out of the metropolis or simply because they had no permanent professional home. Playing in inn yards or sometimes on a temporary stage they erected themselves on the back of a wagon... occasionally by invitation in some noble's manor... very occasionally at court... always under the disapproving eye of authority. Carrying with them as their most valuable stock in trade a handful of plays, any of which they had to be prepared to put on at very short notice.

When Polonius announces to Hamlet that "The actors are come hither, my lord", he introduces them as:

The best actors in the world, either for tragedy, comedy, history, pastoral, pastoral-comical, historical-pastoral, tragical-historical, tragical-comical-historical-pastoral, scene individable, or poem unlimited: Seneca cannot be too heavy nor Plautus too light. For the law of writ and liberty, these are the only men.

Polonius's pomposity makes their 'credits' sound overblown but the records show that such a troupe would expect to perform all of the above.

Hamlet's reaction to the news of their arrival says much about the audience's expectation and anticipation of the familiar characters and stereotypes they could expect to see portrayed.

He that plays the king shall be welcome... the adventurous knight shall use his foil and target; the lover shall not sigh gratis; the humorous man shall end his part in peace; the clown shall make those laugh whose lungs are tickled o' the sere; and the lady shall say her mind freely...

(The line about 'playing the king' has a nice *double entendre* about it, now that we know Shakespeare the actor used to specialise in kingly roles and very probably played the Ghost of Hamlet's father in this very play.)

Today's provincial repertory theatre company – such as there are left – are probably the nearest equivalent to the Elizabethan troupe but can hardly come within touching distance. They consider themselves martyred by performing one play while rehearsing the next. Hamlet's players might easily be required to put on five different plays in the same week – from a repertoire of thirty or more. Clearly some short cuts were necessary, since there's no evidence that the Elizabethan actor had a higher IQ or a better memory than his modern equivalent!

All theatre is sharing... you share with the audience...
Sir Michael Hordern

Individual actors were only given their own parts to study – with two or three words preceding, so they would know when to speak. To help them check their entrances and their position in the play they could check the Platt (or Plot), a list of all the entrances and exits, which would be hung in the tiring house. In any case, to give a complete play to an individual actor was asking for trouble, since he'd be quite likely to take it to his next job, should he leave the company, and sell it to a rival impresario. Philip Henslowe was well known to pay a good price for a pirated text – and worry about legal complications later.

Such a practice calls for a certain mental agility – as was proved a couple of years ago when director, Patrick Tucker, gathered together a group of well-known West End actors and got them to replicate this Elizabethan method. Left alone on the stage with only their own 'prompt copies,' they frequently found themselves addressing an impassioned speech to the wrong character! Once they got into the swing of things, though, their performances took on an unusual energy. For Tucker – who works exclusively within the limitations imposed by the Shakespearean stage – the explanation was simple: "They were required to act rather than replicate a director's thesis".

Shakespeare's actors had to have their wits about them. Whether it was their colleagues on the stage or those other performers – the groundlings, they could never be sure of what might happen next. Not for them the old shoe comfort of the long run...

> As in a theatre, the eyes of men,
> After a well-graced actor leaves the stage,
> Are idly bent on him that enters next
>
> *Richard II*, Act V Sc. ii

Another practice, of course, was to write the parts for the special talents of particular actors – which is where the 'star' concept came in. Henslowe at the Rose could command the services of Edward Alleyn. He also had Christopher Marlowe on hand. The combination resulted in bravura parts created for Alleyn as the leads in Marlowe's *The Jew of Malta* and *Tamburlaine the Great*, both of which were continually revived and formed the playhouse's staple fare.

Later James Burbage and his Lord Chamberlain's Men developed their own star to rival – and eventually surpass Alleyn – in Burbage's son, Richard. For Richard it became Shakespeare's habit – as playwright-in-residence – to write the heroic parts with his lead actor in mind. The younger Burbage was the original *Richard III*, *Henry V*, *Macbeth*, *Othello*, *Hamlet* and *Lear*, among many others. For a time Alleyn and Burbage must have been comparable to Olivier and Gielgud, when they were competing in their very different styles to play the definitive classical roles – particularly Shakespeare – in the

1930s and 40s. Henslowe and Burbage Sr. meanwhile, were playing draft versions of Binkie Beaumont or Cameron Mackintosh...

Nor were the heroes the only stars. The crowds also flocked to see the leading comics. In the 1580s, for instance, Richard Tarleton must have been the Max Miller or Ken Dodd of his time, probably because of his doleful, long-faced appearance. It's said that he only had to peep through the hangings and the audience would be in fits of laughter. Like all the great funny men who followed him, he would either perform material written to fit his comic persona or adapt the text to fit his mannerisms. Audiences have always felt most comfortable knowing what to expect.

Comedian Richard Tarleton. The Max Miller or Ken Dodd of his time, it is said that he only had to peep through the hanging and the audience would be in fits of laughter. British Library

After Tarleton came Will Kempe, famous from the early 1590s. He was the original Falstaff and when Shakespeare had extended the character from *Henry IV* to *The Merry Wives of Windsor* – to please a Queen who expressed the desire to see 'Falstaff in love' – and finally killed him off in *Henry V*, Kempe was so associated with the role that other parts had to be created specifically for him to break the type-casting.

Kempe was followed by Robert Armin, apparently less robust and more melancholy in style than Kempe, who created Feste in *Twelfth Night* and the Fool in *King Lear*. All three men – and no doubt their lesser-regarded and remembered competitors developed their own styles and the plays they appeared in did well to take note of that fact of theatrical life. All of them were clearly consummate and subtle performers. They also had to be – by the nature of the staging – the first stand up comics, too, if they were to deal with the banter of the groundlings. Looked at this way, the past is suddenly much nearer.

All actors had to be nimble enough to shake a leg in the jig or dance that ended all plays. Audiences at contemporary productions of Shakespeare, who see the whole cast break into song and dance as a post-script to the play, are inclined to think this is a directorial affectation, designed to underline that what we have been watching was a form of 'popular theatre.' Whatever else the director may have been guilty of earlier in the evening in this respect, he is being true to a medieval tradition of maypole or Morris dancing that survived through Shakespearean theatre.

> Call forth your actors by the scroll
>
> *A Midsummer Night's Dream*, Act I Sc. ii

Although they learned to take it in their professional stride, the physical constraints of staging plays in an amphitheatre setting posed special problems. Quite apart from the sheer learning of lines – Burbage sometimes had to learn over 800 new lines a *day* – there was little enough time to block out movements and no directors as such to do the blocking. An actor could find himself marooned at the front of the thrust stage, unable to see when another character has entered, let alone who. A lot of Shakespearean entrances with their "Lo, here comes..." can be explained away as punctuational cues to give the incumbent actors time to collect their wits and remember the appropriate lines. Just as he wrote descriptions of places the audience couldn't see, he indicated the presence of temporarily invisible characters. A lot like radio drama, asking us to piece out imperfections with our thoughts...

Since the days of Shakespearean theatre, it could be argued, our actors have gone soft. One play at a time, the successful ones settling down into a 'run' of weeks or months... a little light film or TV work thrown in. It's perfectly possible to become a major star these days without a fraction of the on stage training a merely competent actor acquired in Shakespeare's day. And I use the word 'actor' without any fear of sexist reprisal, since there were no *actresses* in Shakespeare's day. The female parts were all played by boys – an acting tradition universal up to this time. The Greek and Roman theatres both used all male casts, as did the 'mystery' plays. And although women played in the masques at Court and great houses, it wasn't until the Restoration of the monarchy and the commercial theatre in 1660 that the profession of 'actress' was legitimised, when one Margaret Hughes was allowed to play the part of Desdemona. Until then the nearest a woman got to the stage was to collect the pennies at the door.

In addition to being given only your own part of the text, and never being quite sure who was on stage with you as the play progressed, your utterances of undying passion were delivered to a fresh-faced youth! In this regard at least, the new Globe will be less than authentic. Viola will be a girl disguised as a boy – not a boy *pretending* to be a girl disguised as a boy...

In many respects the Shakespearean theatre was more professionally demanding than anything we've seen since. The disciplines and the opportunities offered by the Globe's stage will provide new challenges for a generation of actors, many of them trained to project minimally to suit the intimacy of the film or TV camera. Will they be able to adapt their technique? In an age of less being more, what happens when you're called upon for more?

Brits don't think Americans can do Shakespeare...
Sam Wanamaker

But before we get to that, why did theatre folk – with a few honourable exceptions – do so little to help get the Globe built? To an actor a theatre – any theatre but especially a new theatre – spells jobs. But to an Actor it may have a lot to do with *whose* theatre...

For much of the twenty-five years it took to build the Globe the theatrical community was ambivalent – and part of it was downright negative towards 'Wanamaker's Globe'. Why him? Why 'that American', that 'super tourist'? Sam himself expressed again and again his own conviction. Just before his death he told an interviewer: "if someone like Peter Hall or Ian McKellen or Trevor Nunn had decided this was a good idea, it would have been built years ago with government funding. But I was an alien in more ways than one: I was not only a British alien, I was a London alien and a Southwark alien. The theatrical establishment has no truck with me at all... Brits don't think Americans can do Shakespeare". And he may have been right. It also upset him that some of the very biggest names were prepared to do little more than lend those names. Olivier, he would say, did more for the Rose from his death bed than he ever did as the Globe's President.

The trouble with Time is that it tends to etch certain patterns deeper, but totally obliterate others. It wasn't kind to the bubble of Sam's professional reputation. Many of the actors clustering around the Rose had never seen him on stage; to them he was simply that American who kept trying to build a Shakespearean Disneyland that was taking forever. It wasn't their fault but it was certainly Sam's bad luck that you had to be in your fifties to have had the opportunity to see him perform. Many of us who had would be inclined to agree with Michael Birkett – someone whose own theatrical credentials included collaboration with both Peter Hall and Peter Brook – that "Sam had more impact on English theatre than any non-English actor; he had energy that no one else could quite match", while as a director, "he was thoughtful and structure conscious – not a splash-and-paddle-a-foot-in-it director!"

Birkett believes that over the years the theatrical establishment's attitude to Sam and his project did mellow. "To begin with it was viewed as a visitor's quirk, rather than an establishment need and something of an impertinent intrusion... After a while they began to drop the – 'quirk' and admire the tenacity". Being British, many of them found it hard to come out and say so. Towards the end, Birkett feels: "it no longer seemed to them like a tourist endeavour – it was more like Schliemann at Troy!" An inspired individual had persevered and uncovered the past.

It wasn't as if Sam didn't know the players. As someone who'd been part of the theatrical scene since the early 1950's, he knew everybody – and that was part of the trouble, as far as many of them were concerned. Because they knew Sam, the one thing they were convinced of was that this was *his* project and that signing on meant being one of the supporting cast. There was nothing wrong with the concept of the actor-manager; indeed, in late Victorian and Edwardian times it had been a staple of West End theatre. But at least du Maurier and Alexander had their own company of players and a theatre to play in. All Sam had was a committee and a vision that kept evolving in the abstract. The Actors and the Directors came and went.

Some of them weren't too clear what it was for. After all, there was the National and the RSC – both close by – and, of course, there was Stratford. On top of that, Shakespeare was becoming no stranger to the West End, if the names above the title were big enough. And fringe theatre was thriving. What was the Globe going to be – a museum theatre? And "Won't it be terribly *un-com-for-table?*" Dame Maggie Smith was heard to enquire in her best Lady Bracknell voice.

Nonetheless, even the most rabid Rose supporters at the peak of Rose fever probably didn't see it as an either/or situation. Their allegiance was to the ruins of the real thing but rebuilding the Globe wasn't a bad thing either. Many of them managed to straddle the fence without too much physical or intellectual discomfort.

The one thing that few people in the theatrical community were prepared to put into words, if they happened to be supporters, was the question of who was to run the Globe, once it was built. Not the box office or the paper clips but who would be *artistically* responsible? They didn't ask because they all thought they knew the answer.

Sam always protested that he had no desire to be the Artistic Director of the Globe, once it was up and running but none of the Artistic Directorate he set up under the consummate chairmanship of Lord Birkett believed him. At the time of his death the directorate numbered 50, a group large enough to disagree on almost everything and far too big to agree on anything. It took a lot to disconcert Michael Birkett but even he had to admit to a little local difficulty: "You could never be *quite* sure who Sam had invited to be a member of the Directorate... He'd see some production that had impressed him and then say to So-and-So – 'Oh, you must be a member of our Artistic Directorate...'" Birkett, true to his family's judicial tradition, dealt with the evidence as presented. After all, fifty theatricals had *never* been known to turn up in one place at the same time!

> How many ages hence
> Shall this our lofty scene be acted over
> In states unborn and accents yet unknown!
> *Julius Caesar*, Act III Sc. i

"The theatre will teach us". That sums up the conviction of many of the actors and directors who look forward to using and being used by this unique space and it reflects their belief that no amount of academic theory can replace the experience of actually being there.

Sir Peter Hall's reaction is typical:

> My belief in the Globe project, paradoxically enough, increased markedly when the Rose was uncovered and I was able to stand on that stage and see how the auditorium worked... I had to realise that Shakespeare's theatre – which I'd been brought up to think of as a thrust stage, thrusting out – was much more a travel stage with a door on either side and the actors – travelling across the stage from one side to the other, a stage that had very deep proportions when you wanted that, and opened the inner stage. At the same time it could be a very intimate – almost a Japanese stage... None of us has ever worked on a stage like that... because it doesn't exist. I think we're going to find all sorts of new things... it's very exciting.

Birkett uses the analogy of the authentic instrument movement in music: "You knew what instruments were and were not available to Bach or to Beethoven and then you began to understand the particular 'sound world' the composers were inventing from... In Shakespeare's case I think you'll begin to sense the performance circumstance out of which the next play was written. When you've learned how to play Shakespeare as it must have been and drawn your conclusions from that, you'll have learned all sorts of lessons you can apply in other contexts..."

It's generally agreed that the effort the scholars have put into teasing out the 'geography' of the stage will prove to be invaluable to the performing of the plays and point to answers to questions that have long divided academic opinion. A feature of so many Elizabethan and Jacobean plays is not so much the sheer word count – we know they spoke the lines much faster than is today's practice – as the sheer number of *scenes*. Where do you stage them – inside, outside, upstairs, downstairs? Are they to be played consecutively, as printed, or – as seems increasingly likely – in an almost overlapping fashion, drawing the spectator's attention from one part of the stage to another with a speed rivalled only by a medium three hundred years in Shakespeare's future – the *cinema?* Many directors have a shrewd suspicion that this cinematic quality may well alter our perception of the relationship between scenes we think we know well, creating juxtapositions or counterpoint we'd never suspected and which the proscenium stage would not easily permit but which the multiple "stages" of the Globe will positively encourage.

In *The Empty Space* director, Peter Brook, argues that "...one of the greatest freedoms of the Elizabethan stage was the empty space. It gave opportunity to transport the audience through an unlimited succession of illusions, covering, if the playwright chose, the entire physical world. In an ideal relationship with the actor on a bare stage one would continually be passing from long shot to close, tracking or jumping in and out, and the planes often overlap. Compared with the cinema's mobility, the theatre once seemed ponderous and creaky, but the closer one moves towards the true nakedness of theatre, the closer one approaches a stage that has lightness and range far beyond film or television..."

"*Don't forget that before it was a text it was first a script...*"
Sam Wanamaker

Familiar speeches may take on a new meaning on that new/old stage. "To be or not to be..." suggests Birkett, "may become more conversational with Hamlet genuinely seeking advice... The Agincourt speech may become more intimate as well as patriotic... the theatre will tell us". Actor/director and Artistic Director, Mark Rylance agrees: "I would use the audience as my 'soldiers'".

Rylance experienced an approximation of what the Globe actor may have to contend with when he was performing *Hamlet* in New York. At a point he realised some of the audience were speaking the lines along with him. When he paused after "To be or not to be..." there were clear whispers of "...*that* is the question". Since it was impossible to ignore this contribution to the proceedings, he decided to acknowledge the presence of the audience by waiting for the whispering to die down and then repeating: "That is the question" in the tone of a response.

Birkett remembers Hall directing *Hamlet* on the Olivier stage in the early days of the National Theatre and discussing the nature of the soliloquy. Even then he was dissatisfied with the traditional depiction of the introvert isolated centre stage in a single spotlight. The soliloquy, he felt, was, in fact, the most *outward* speaking element of the play and not the most inward: "He felt the need to use the audience as the mirror – not the toe of your shoe". With the Globe "you may *have* to use the audience and, if you ignore it, you may fail..."

Something else it may tell us is to leave well alone. Playing Shakespeare over the centuries on every conceivable stage *except* the original has given editors and directors *carte blanche* to rearrange the original text to their heart's content, as they devised what he must have meant or should have meant. Scenes that didn't seem to play easily on a conventional stage would be cut or transposed. Shakespeare's original stage directions would be largely ignored, if they didn't fit the new 'concept'.

The justification has always had a certain simplistic logic to it. What do we do when folio and quarto don't agree? For some of the plays there *isn't* an 'original' text. In any case, Shakespeare never transcribed his own text, so the versions we have got aren't exactly Holy Writ... or Holy Will.

The resulting performances would inevitably fade, but the lasting damage was to the *text*. Every playwright lives in fear of the annotated prompt copy becoming the 'official' text without his knowledge but the damage to Shakespeare has arguably been more insidious. Qualifying footnotes apart, the 'edited' version becomes *the* version and the rearranged stage directions become accepted pointers for the next generation of performers.

Perhaps that doesn't matter. We have, after all, come to regard Shakespeare as a subject for interpretation, since he came down to us divorced from his context. But now that context is restored, perhaps it's time to drown the book *we've* constructed from his words and go back to the one he wrote – directions and all.

When my cue comes, call me, and I will answer
A Midsummer Night's Dream, Act IV Sc. i

We may then find that those brief cues are clues that would be all the shorthand needed by a troupe of players so used to each other that little needed to be spelled out. The analogy of a football team in which each player instinctively knows where to find another, sight unseen, is not as naive as it may first sound. Ensemble acting that flowed uninterrupted across and around the several acting areas that might be in use at any one time may prove to have a lot in common with a fast moving game.

Because of the pressures of time, Shakespeare's actors can barely have had time to read a new play through even once, let alone rehearse it in the modern sense. Patrick Tucker is in no doubt as to the implications: "Shakespeare, who had been an actor himself, would have written for the actors to find stage business and character from their own text, for there was no time for them to get it from anywhere else. He understood their problems, and so put mood, character and even moves into their individual speeches. Everything the actor needed to know about his character was in his lines, and his lines only". He was also physically present, more often than not, to correct actors who missed the point...

To pursue the sporting analogy a little further, we have grown used to witnessing the event on television in the same way that a stage director focuses our attention. We see what we are shown, whereas the spectator at the actual event has the freedom to scan the rest of the field and perhaps be the first to spot the player anticipating a move yet to happen but which will prove decisive. Shakespeare's theatre may be like that and we would do well to set tidied-up texts and latterday thinking to one side for a time, and re-examine what the original text has to say.

One example serves to indicate the possibilities. Macbeth on stage with Lennox after the Cauldron scene hears the news that Macduff has fled to England and launches into a twelve line speech expressing his intentions. Most editors have chosen to indicate this as an aside, because of its revelatory nature and have Macbeth address only the last two lines to Lennox. Yet the 'aside' is not indicated by Shakespeare. Supposing Macbeth has either forgotten Lennox was there in the heat of the moment or else didn't care what he heard. Supposing he was actually boasting for Lennox's benefit? Any of these possibilities says something about Macbeth's character that is not normally built into the reading we are given.

The Globe provides the opportunity for a back to basics approach and, as long as we leave our preconceptions with the gatherers... more often than not, one suspects the theatre will tell us.

...in all the play
There is not one word apt, one player fitted
A Midsummer Night's Dream, Act V Sc. i

The theatre will also tell us whether we have actors with the technique to take advantage of the new context. Peter Hall feels "today there are probably thirty or forty actors who can do what is necessary. Not more. That's because there's been a marked decline in the experience of Shakespeare... Shakespeare's not taught very much in drama schools and it's certainly not taught very *well* in drama schools. Most actors don't do any Shakespeare..."

Actor, Ralph Fiennes is more optimistic than Hall. He believes there is no lack of "daring or passion" among the younger generation of actors; on the contrary, he senses great "energy". What is missing in contemporary theatre is the requisite level of "language awareness". "The plays just aren't being written that will encourage linguistic debate". To that degree he agrees with Hall that there is a lack of preparedness to deal with the verbal complexities of Shakespeare.

Fiennes welcomes the intimacy he feels the Globe stage will provide. "The good actor, by being aware of his audience, will adapt to his space. I've always felt that studio spaces, for instance, were kind to an actor. And the great thing about Shakespeare, of course, is his *own* adaptability. He can tolerate the grandiose and survive the highly minimal in the way of performance. I feel the naturalistic style many actors have developed as a result of working so much in film or TV is likely to work perfectly well on that stage. I know many people doubt that – but we shall see".

> ...you must either be directed by some that take upon
> them to know, or to take upon yourself that which I
> am sure you do not know...
>
> *Cymbeline*, Act V Sc. iv

Mark Rylance is optimistic that the Globe will help provide an opportunity for actors to take back control of their own destiny. "There has been a great separation since directors like Peter Brook and later John Barton became gurus and teachers. Although, to be fair, we have learned more about Shakespearean production from them in the last few years than in the previous three hundred. Actors have become removed... they go to work for a company on an idea that a particular director is going to teach them, which is quite different from working on a play. Younger actors no longer talk to elder actors and receive the tradition; that 'tradition' has been broken. Actors have abdicated responsibility for the planning stage that takes place before rehearsal. They must take more responsibility for the whole, working *with* not merely *for* the director. Unless they do so, unless they take on board that they're part of a live event and that you can't present the same thing time after time, they'll end up not talking to anyone but to an *image* of someone... It has a lot to do with the theatre becoming considered a middle class or a suppressive medium, as opposed to the revolutionary medium it *should* be".

Rylance is hopeful that the Globe will help change things. "In Shakespeare's day a leading actor with a vision – like Burbage or Alleyn – led his team". He recalls the power of the RSC's production of *Nicholas Nickleby*. "Great work comes out of the kind of ensemble playing that happened in that production. Trevor Nunn probably thought it was all to do with his vision but it was much *more* to do with the fact that this group of actors had played together for many years by this time; it came out of that confidence in each other – just as it did with Shakespeare's players". A revolutionary thought occurs to him "Maybe the *actors* should choose the *director?*"

"The actor's responsibility will be very much increased in this new theatre because of the limitation of technical devices available and a lot of performers may come up bare on that stage... It's going to take an increased belief, a very accurate focus and strong characterisation – by that I mean belief in the character you're playing. You're not going to be able to 'signpost' things with sets and lights. The light we're going to need is the illumination of Shakespeare's insights. It's going to rely much more on the spirit and the relationships between the players – an exciting prospect to me but not to everyone". None of this can be expected to happen overnight and Rylance hopes to see a group of young actors who are prepared to devote a few years to the project to develop this sort of ensemble playing: "This must be an actors' theatre".

❖

Standing on the Rose stage gave Peter Hall a strong sense of increased possibilities for the actor:

> It was a space on which you can shout or whisper. The horror of modern Shakespearean production is that we either play in theatres that are too big, so that we have to bellow, or we do 'chamber Shakespeare' in the studio tradition in which the full resonance and sensuality of the voice can't be used. Shakespeare obviously demanded the whole range of the voice from shouting to whispering.

The Globe, he felt, would create an intimacy between actor and audience that had no equivalent in the modern theatre.

> The idea that the Swan at Stratford is Elizabethan theatre is absolutely not true. The Swan's a lovely building but the stage is like a diving

board. It's very dramatic to walk to the end of it but there's nothing you can do except dive off it. And in the Swan you have to walk back again!

The Globe will be quite different – as the Rose was. The relationship between actor and audience will be intensely personal and will create different disciplines... I mean, once you consider that he played to three thousand people tightly jammed together in broad daylight, you realise why there are no pauses in Shakespeare, why the text has a kind of muscular grip on the audience. You have to keep their attention. It's public speaking. It's public acting...

Hall believes the physical space will help unravel the clues that are there in the text:

The essence of Shakespeare is preserving the blank verse line. And Shakespeare tells you... if you know how to look – when to go fast, when to go slow, when to pause, when to come in on cue. When to be emotional and when not. When to be antithetical. When to be prosaic. It's there, it's in the writing. It's like music. And very few actors know how to do that.

> Speak the speech, I pray you, as I pronounced
> it to you, trippingly on the tongue...
> *Hamlet*, Act III Sc. ii

There's also the question of *speed*. The constraints of conventional theatre cause most Shakespearean productions to be cut – some to a considerable degree. This is partly due to the need for scene changes, the removal of bulky props and, of course, the obligatory 15 minute interval.

As far as we can tell, until something like 1610 there were no significant breaks between scenes. From about that time the fashion in the hall theatres to have brief pauses or musical interludes became increasingly popular in public theatres but for most of his career Shakespeare would have seen his plays performed without interruption. As Iden Payne, the American actor/director who did so much for Stratford, once noted: "The fundamental quality of a Shakespearean performance should be complete fluidity of action". He might well have added "and continuity of speech".

"If you speak the lines", Peter Hall insists, "it is perfectly true you can get through most of Shakespeare's plays in two to two and a half hours". When he says this, he is talking about the plays *as* written. "If you don't observe the original structure... if you chop up the lines, then you can easily put 25 to 30 minutes on the playing time". Actor Tim Piggott-Smith confirms this. Touring with Hall's company in the late 1980's, he experienced his closest approximation to what the Globe will offer. Following Hall's direction to "speak the lines", he remembers: "We were certainly following Hamlet's advice to the Players to speak the speech trippingly on the tongue but when we played the Tokyo Globe, we found we'd taken fifteen minutes off the performance – and that was entirely due to that uncluttered open space!" The experience told him what the actor at the original Globe must have felt every day of his working life: "You can't expect to hold the attention of all those closely-packed people for over two hours until you're filling every second". He'd discovered for himself the truth in Hall's observations. "The audience runs after the play, rather than trudges".

There's clearly a balance to be struck here. Trevor Nunn feels that if we went back in the proverbial time machine and saw Burbage and Co., "we wouldn't understand a word of what they were talking about" – because of the dialect and the speed of delivery. Hall feels sure that Shakespeare's contemporaries never managed to play *Hamlet* in a couple of hours. "I've done it in 3 1/2 hours at absolutely breakneck speed. You couldn't speak it quicker – so I'm sure the 'two hours' traffic of our stage' is a slight bit of public relations". On the other hand, it might simply mean that the traffic on the stage *started* at two o'clock. In any case, what do we mean by truly *authentic*? As Sir Anthony Hopkins argues, there will have to be compromise, "if certain techniques jar. Otherwise you'd play the whole of Shakespeare in a sort of Warwickshire burr, because that's roughly how they spoke – in fact, very close to how *American* is spoken today!"

The interval poses perhaps the larger problem. Shakespeare's audience neither expected or needed one and today's academic opinion is firmly against one. The groundlings were free to move about during the performance and did so. Their physical needs were amply taken care of by the various vendors who wandered amongst them selling food and drink. With that as his context, Shakespeare had no need to construct a play that built to a dramatic first act curtain. There were no *curtains*, and there was no need for a dramatic break. The modern director, restaging the plays in a conventional theatre, has to contrive one – often by rearranging the action. The new Globe will do away with that need and, by doing so, allow us to find meanings that have been lost due to these self-created constraints. A performance will be different from seeing a play anywhere else; it will also, as scholar Alan Dessen reminds us, "keep in mind the pivotal role of the playgoer's imagination in the unspoken contract assumed between the original players and their audience".

> *...after all comparisons of truth,*
> *As truth's authentic author to be cited.*
> *Troilus and Cressida*, Act III Sc. ii

To be or not to be – 'authentic'?

Peter Hall takes a strictly purist line: "I must say, I'm worried whether the thing will be pure enough, because I don't trust directors and designers to leave well enough alone... I really, really wouldn't *add*. It seems to me that the great thing about the Globe project and Sam's vision was that it should be completely rigorous. You can have visitors from other places coming and doing *Comedy of Errors* on motor bikes, if that's what they want to do – but they should do it somewhere else. The Globe should use itself in a completely puritan sense".

Kenneth Branagh comes up with precisely the same image in describing what worries him about the way the theatre is to be used: "If the place is pulled about too much, if it turns into 'Ye Olde' pots-of-ale, ·busty wenches atmosphere or, alternatively, if somebody brings in motorbike Shakespeare, it'll be a disaster... I don't need a motorbike to make Shakespeare interesting and I don't think our audiences do, either".

Rylance takes a less conservative view. "I think it's very likely that the techniques of the proscenium theatre may have misled us over the years about Shakespeare's intentions. I'm coming round to saying that it's going to be well worthwhile experimenting with the limitations Shakespeare worked with – as well as the benefits, because there *are* benefits... I'd use this as my start point... As someone who also directs, I know how tempting it is to look for a director's effect, because then you feel more confident, having thought of it. "*Now* we'll be all right". It's easy to stop thinking and you can't afford that..."

I charge thee,
Whate'er thou hear'st or see'st, stand all aloof,
And do not interrupt me in my course.

Romeo and Juliet, Act V Sc. iii

Rylance is one of the few people who can claim to have experienced a little of the immediacy of the Elizabethan theatre – however accidentally. In the summer of 1991 he and his company, Phoebus Cart, staged *The Tempest* on the site, improvising their movements around the builders' debris amidst thunder and lightning that might have been commissioned for the play. Well into things and with his audience duly rapt, Rylance found himself with an unexpected theatrical contribution.

Actor/director Mark Rylance is named designate Artistic Director on August 1st 1995. *Rose Smith*

The back of the Globe site happens to abut on to the cheque clearing depot of the Midland Bank. The hour is late and the security man decides it's time to put out the dustbins. He opens the back door on the spectacle of strange looking people illuminated by lightning and cavorting around the concrete ruins. "Oh, bugger it!" he offers before shutting the door firmly. Rylance and his fellow actors took it in their stride. A Japanese tourist, who was following the text, began to turn the pages feverishly...

The present feeling is that there will be a number of carefully-designated productions that attempt to adhere as closely as possible to what would appear to have been the original staging conditions. With that goes the realisation that, however close that approximation may be, the one thing no one can replicate is the Elizabethan *audience*. Whatever control is exercised over what happens on the stage itself, how can you 'direct' a modern audience to behave with the instinctive manners of four hundred years ago without making them impossibly self-conscious? The separate elements of performance will have to find their own balance.

Rylance's overriding concern today is that any production should help reveal more of Shakespeare's meaning and "release the language". Going back to origins is only one way, however, important. "Authenticity is certainly a purpose but not the *prime* purpose. I believe it should have a place in those first seasons – indeed, in every season – but the function of Shakespeare's plays is to develop the human consciousness through the performance and the experience of these strange tales. Authenticity is nothing unless it's authenticity that reveals better methods of doing things, that helps the plays function and work in new and unexpected ways... It would be sad if it became a purist house. I'm all for people trying what they want on that stage, as long as they realise that this is a new kind of stage. If they want to interpret, they'll have to figure out new ways of interpreting. There's absolutely no point in building sets; they must do it minimally".

"It's important the Globe is not a museum, that it relates to the modern day. To my mind that's the purpose of building it. It's a tool – and a better tool than any other theatre in this country – to discover not only the practices of that age but to discover more about what that extraordinary man Shakespeare had to say about our human character that will do something for today... If the academic world is going to come in without an open mind, high handedly – as I feel some are – it won't be a happy marriage. Because that's essentially what it is – the beginning of a closer marriage than other theatres have between actual practitioners and the academic world. It's going to be a tempestuous marriage with no possibility of divorce. It's a Wooden 'O' – and we're all climbing into it!"

I will hear that play;
For never anything can be amiss,
When simpleness and duty tender it.

A Midsummer Night's Dream, Act V Sc. i

Sam grew to look beyond the discoveries about Shakespeare's original intentions to future possibilities for theatre in general: "I believe the effect of seeing work in this space will influence modern production and modern playwriting". "If you write for this space", Rylance points out, "you will necessarily look at the people who wrote for it". Joe Orton, he recalls, studied Beaumont and Fletcher for structure. "If we're lucky, the theatre will provide an impetus for *new* plays, perhaps even for another Shakespeare". Michael Birkett agrees: "It's taken us a long time to realise that the Globe is not just to do with reinventing the past... There are theatrical discoveries to be made here that can't be discovered in any other way..."

By the time the Globe opened the Bremer Company was only one of several companies that had commissioned new plays for its unique stage.

CHAPTER EIGHTEEN

WE'LL HEAR A PLAY
(1993 – 1996)

It is a Holy Grail, a dream, an ambition I will have
spent one quarter of my life trying to fulfil.

Sam Wanamaker

Now do I long to hear...
...whom to thank,
Besides the Gods, for this great miracle.

Pericles, Act V Sc. iii

To say that Sam never lived to see his Dream fulfilled is not strictly true. That gusty April day in 1993 was his personal opening night – even though it took place on a wet afternoon and not a word of Shakespeare's original language was uttered by the German actors on that temporary stage. Piecing out the imperfections with his thoughts was no problem at all. He knew that in all probability this was the nearest he would get. And perhaps the audience that gave him a standing ovation sensed something, too.

He wore his left arm in a sling. He was suffering, he told everyone, from a frozen shoulder and you believed him. In fact, the cancer was spreading fast. Earlier treatment had failed to arrest it and his face was beginning to look gaunt. But then, people said, that was the accumulated strain showing, surely? By now he was a man playing on memory, taking each event as it came. A fund-raising trip to the Far East early in the year was almost too much for him and his apprehensive preparation for it was the first time his longtime assistant, Marina Blodget, realised just how ill he was.

From then on, she saw the technique that went into each 'performance'. The smile summoned up to be there on time and anticipate the reaction... the gritted teeth to mask the pain when anyone accidentally jogged the 'frozen shoulder'. "He was," she remembers, "the bravest man I've ever known!"

In July he was invested with the CBE – an honorary title because of his American citizenship – to go with the Benjamin Franklin

Sam Wanamaker, CBE. Heritage minister Peter Brooke presents Sam with his
honorary award 1993.

Medal he'd been awarded a couple of years earlier for his
contribution to Anglo-American relations. In an ideal scenario one
would have waited until the opening performance and then knighted
him on the stage of the Globe but those who decide these things had
come to realise that there was no time for that.

When he was asked where he wanted to receive the award and
have the reception, he gave an Anglo-American reply that was also
typically 'Sam' – "I'll have the award in London, where I did all the
work and I'll have the party in America, where I might get some
more money".

There was also a curious serenity about him at this time. In
September there was a ceremony on the site to unveil the latest bay
– the sixth – sponsored by Glaxo. My wife and I walked up to the
site with a leading industrialist who had reluctantly contributed small
change at best to the project. The geography was such that you
walked though builders' paraphernalia until suddenly you emerged
on the site itself in the early evening sunshine. You could literally
hear his breath being taken away. The sight was, indeed, everything
that Sam had painted so often with his words – majestic and hopeful.
For the rest of the evening I could hear my industrialist friend telling
one group or another how, of course, *he'd* been behind this thing from
the beginning.

At one of the last public appearances Sam unveils the bay donated by Glaxo. With him is John Hignett, Chairman of the ISGC Board and a Glaxo executive (1993)
David Rogers and David Jones

Sam for once wasn't mingling and pressing the flesh and with his arm in the by now familiar sling, he was anxious not to have anyone press him. His hair was noticeably thinner, the character lines in his face etched by now and I realised that it was the first time I'd thought of him in connection with the word 'frail'. But when the bay had been declared open and it was his turn to speak, all of that dropped away.

The passion was still there but he spoke quietly, elegiacally about how far we'd come, what remained to be done. He spoke of the future but of a future that was somehow ours rather than his. He envisioned the generations to come that would accept what we had done as part of their birthright. I'd heard him speak many times, so the words were familiar. Often in the past, I'd thought he hadn't known when to stop, when he was starting to oversell. Today, everything came together. It wasn't a speech; it was a benediction.

On this sort of occasion you often leave in the knowledge that you won't see the person again – in fact, I never did – but today wasn't one of those occasions. If you can't imagine the conclusion, you can't see the signs and you knew Sam was indestructible. Besides, the job wasn't finished yet.

> *The sun will set, before I shall discharge*
> *What I must strive to do.*
>
> Ferdinand, *The Tempest*, Act III Sc. i

But for him it was. For a few more weeks he kept up the pretence. The phone calls were, if anything, more frequent and the passion even more urgent. He would still summon up the energy to visit the site as often as possible, pressing the button that released his self-administered pain killers more and more often. What was happening was now obvious but nobody 'noticed'. Only a handful of people were taken into his confidence. Michael Perry, now Chairman of the Trustees, was one. In his Christmas card to him Sam wrote: "Mike – you will make it happen. Sorry I won't be with you to share the celebrations – but I've been celebrating anyway!" And in a message to the readers of the Globe newsletter, which appeared posthumously, he expressed a similar sentiment: "You have dreamed this dream with me until now, but you must finish it". To his brother, Bill, who flew from Los Angeles to spend the final days with him, he confided: "When I'm gone, this will all be finished much faster".

On Saturday, December 18th with his family at his bedside Sam died. He was 74.

The tributes poured in and the sub-editors had a field day with lines they must have been saving for years. "Saviour of the Globe Takes Final Curtain" (*The Observer*), "Yes, They'll Play It Again, Sam" (*Western Morning News*); "Shakespeare Crusader Dies" (*The Mail on Sunday*). *The People*, realising its readers knew Zoë better than Sam because of her recent TV work, led with "TV Zoë's Dad Dies" but the *Yorkshire Post* used a line which turned up again and again in the obituaries: "Globe Dream Lives On".

And as the world returned to the new year reality of 1994, there was a palpable sense that this was true. Sam's death flushed out a great deal of guilt in people who had been half-hearted or sporadic in their recent support. This thing was now so close – well, we've got to do it for Sam. He suddenly had more friends than he would ever have counted in life.

Building went on apace. Visitors to the Birthday unveiling of the New Zealand hangings were amazed to find themselves walking not simply on to a piazza with a few token bays but actually into the Wooden 'O' – 13 bays complete with galleries and even some thatching. Imaginations took flight. Today – the hangings. Tomorrow – why *not* "the vasty fields of France?"

❖

Another bequest that wasn't in Sam's will was Globe Education. He died knowing that at the present rate of progress, by the time the Globe opened it would be providing lectures, workshops and courses for 25,000 people a year and that its efforts would be spread not just locally but nationally and, increasingly, internationally – which was precisely the brief he'd given Spottiswoode in the first place. "I was grateful and slightly surprised", Patrick said later, "that he'd restricted himself to the planet and not included the entire solar system!"

By the time the Globe opened he calculated that he would have taught over 60,000 students personally and the department as a whole some 100,000. In 1995/6 alone there were 22,000 and the bookings for 1996/7 showed an increase of another three thousand. The word was indeed going forth.

No matter what some of Southwark's so-called 'leaders' many have thought over the years, the community itself had learned to appreciate the depth and sincerity of Sam's personal commitment. Children from Southwark schools had always been allowed to visit the Museum free and would be given special dispensation at the temporary exhibition. When the Globe opens, 75 local school children will be admitted as Groundlings free of charge at every performance.

In the year of Sam's death a project called *Tackling Shakespeare* was initiated in which children from seven Southwark schools and members of the local Millwall FC soccer team joined in workshops run by Globe tutors. The idea was to contrast popular culture now with popular culture in Shakespeare's time and to encourage Southwark children to 'train' and rehearse for a performance in the Cockpit at the end of the term. The students were then taken to a Shakespeare performance and a match at The Den, Millwall's home ground.

Sam was a great believer in the actor being an integral part of the society in which he lived. *Tackling Shakespeare* simply reversed the principle, as far as the kids were concerned. The 1993 exercise was further developed in succeeding years with projects like *Upon This Bank*, which explored other cross-curricular activities that related the Globe to the community, both then and now.

And despite the prognostications of many conventional educationists, young Southwark responded. *They* didn't find Shakespeare one bit boring, when he was set in this kind of context.

Nothing would have warmed the Wanamaker heart more than to have seen a particular performance in April 1995 of the 'Scottish play'. Students of Tuke, a Special Needs school for the learning-impaired, unaware that the play was a dusty old 'classic', reinvented the doings of Macbeth in a spirited version combining music, dance and tableaux that moved many of its audience to tears.

> *I don't believe that people in the theatre should*
> *be isolated from the society in which they live.*
>
> Sam Wanamaker

In pursuit of Sam's injunction that the Globe should be "a stage for the world," in 1993/94 the international *Hamlet* project linked A-level students from all over England with their contemporaries in Poland, Denmark and Germany. Under the guidance of workshop teams from Globe Education which visited the schools involved, the students studied four film versions of the play, exchanged their observations with each other by means of video reports and each school then contributed a "theatrical piece based on the play" at a series of eleven national festivals. In all, over 3,000 students took part and the winners of the national festivals took part in two international festivals – the first in Bremen, due to the connection with the Bremer Company, the second on the Globe site. Once again, Shakespeare emerged newly-minted; no one caught a whiff of 'museum theatre' here. As the festival's motto proclaimed: "One touch of Shakespeare and the whole world is kin".

Students taking part in The Hamlet Project (1994). *Rose Smith*

Not content simply to bring Shakespeare up to date, there was in every sense an investment in the future in the shape of "Globelink" – a scheme in which participating schools contributed to the actual building of the Globe.

Some 350 Globelink schools from 30 countries, in fact, paid the £100,000 cost of the 'heavens' by means of £200 'time capsules' buried in a special vault beneath the centre point of the theatre. "Bury your school to raise the heavens", was the intriguing invitation. Each capsule contains memorabilia chosen by the children themselves. When future archaeologists come to disinter them, they'll find such items as signed programmes from school Shakespeare performances, a tape of advertising jingles, a piece of the Berlin wall, a current school science curriculum, a list of youth words and meanings, pebbles from the Rocky Mountains – enough material to fund a thicket of theses about the way we lived then!

To raise the money in the first place demonstrates the imagination of the children and their activities have been Shakespeare-inspired, ranging from costume design competitions to a performance of *A Comedie of Errors*, entirely faithful to the First Folio, and a performance of *Hamlet* in mime.

The 'link' helps forge a chain between past and future in the same way that Shakespeare's words managed to do. Which is why the quotation used to summarise the scheme is apt. Taken from *Henry VIII*, it reads: "Our children's children shall see this and bless Heaven".

❖

A London schoolteacher summed up the attitude that was beginning to prevail outside official circles in day to day London at least, when she wrote in a letter to the *Evening Standard*:

> It is difficult to understand why a Government which insists that all children learn Shakespeare has put nothing into the project. My pupils are puzzled that it has taken an American to attempt the reconstruction of Shakespeare's theatre, so lovingly and accurately, in the part of London where he spent his creative life.

Another correspondent pointed out acidly that, "since Shakespeare's vocabulary can be proved to consist of some 30,000 words – 2,000 of which he introduced to the language – whereas the average 'educated' person today has been estimated to be able to summon up five and a half thousand at best, it seems reasonable to try and make up a little of that leeway".

> *The dearest friend to me, the kindest man,*
> *The best-condition'd and unwearied spirit*
> *In doing courtesies...*
> *The Merchant of Venice*, Act III Sc. ii

Only two clouds marred the view in 1994. One was Theo's illness. In February he'd been taken to hospital with a ruptured aorta that required nine hours of major surgery. During the spring and summer, though, he appeared to be making a good recovery.

The other was the fact that, with the best will in the world – and even if pennies tumbled in quantity from heaven – there was no way Peter McCurdy and his team could complete their work in time for a 1995 opening. Once again, the date would have to be put back but for once, there were compensations. This time no one could reasonably doubt that the Globe *would* open and meanwhile, the decision had already been taken to 'market' the site. As work continued, visitors could come and see for themselves both the theatre and an 'embryo' exhibition housed in the undercroft. And come they did in their thousands. In that first full year more than 100,000 of them came, saw the Globe and its temporary exhibitions, bought their souvenirs – and then went home to tell their friends. The Globe was once again firmly on London's map.

1996 would now be the official opening – June 14th, 1996 – with 1995 devoted to finishing the major work and putting on a 'workshop season'.

And then on September 12th Theo died. The card read: "A Light has Gone Out". In many ways his death was more of a shock than Sam's. When you've got past the upset of a friend or relation being seriously ill and determined that they're recovering, your attention tends to be distracted. This wasn't supposed to happen. To have one of the heroes die before the curtain goes up is tragic enough. To lose two is bad theatre. But, as with Sam's death, it spurred the understudies to even greater efforts. Theo's vision would live – Jon Greenfield and Peter McCurdy would see to that.

At his memorial service someone was heard to whisper: "His *name* always intrigued me, so I looked it up. Did you know it's the Greek word for 'god'?"

CHAPTER NINETEEN

THE THEATRE WILL TELL US...
The Workshop Season of 1995

By the summer of 1995 the Globe was two-thirds complete after four years and some £4 million of self-building. The surrounding bays were in place, plastered and thatched. The lowest gallery level had its five rows of bench seats, although the two upper galleries had to make do with a single row of makeshift benches. The yard was appropriately raked but lacked the final coating of hazelnut clinker finish. The stage was a temporary plywood structure, not the oak that it would be, as was the tiring house frame, attached to the scaffolding. Plywood also had to be used for the stage columns. It was a theatre of illusion for the time being but a functioning playhouse, nonetheless.

For more than a year now the structure had been a London landmark. To anyone travelling by river or standing on the opposite shore it already looked finished and the steady stream of people going to and fro added to the impression. Posters beckoned in public places. Radio commercials caught the ear and the media discovered – slightly to their surprise – that it *was* going to happen after all and rearranged their adjectives. "Troubled" and "beleaguered" were replaced by "determined", "triumphant" and "reborn". In July the Globe emerged from its crysallis as the scaffolding came down.

In August the Royal Mint issued a special set of postage stamps commemorating Bankside. Five separate 25p stamps showed The Swan (1595), The Rose (1592), the First Globe (1599) – loosely based on the Visscher drawing, The Second Globe (1614) and The Hope (1613). Sharp eyes – and a magnifying glass – revealed some familiar figures in the crowds surrounding the playhouses. On a platform Dr. (John) Dee, the famous Elizabethan savant, addressed the populace; elsewhere you could find Prospero and Caliban, Hamlet, Bottom and on a hillock, quill and manuscript in hand, the Bard himself. The whole was the witty work of C. Walter Hodges.

...there we may rehearse more obscenely and courageously.

A Midsummer Night's Dream, Act I Sc. ii

It had been decided that, while work continued in late summer, there would be a short 'workshop season'. *Not* an opening – definitely not an opening – but an opportunity for a handful of actors and directors to try out some of the theories on Shakespearean theatre that had been so far confined to learned dissertations or crude physical approximations. Time to start to learn that unique stage, time to begin to find out what the theatre had to teach.

By way of prologue, in April Andrew Gurr and Globe Education organised a series of seminars under the general title of 'Within *This Wooden 'O''*. A number of academics took this last public opportunity to put down their personal markers on what lessons they felt might be learned, what questions they most wanted answered. By the time most of them met again at the official opening a certain amount of theory would have either been rewritten or confirmed into fact.

Gurr tried the novel experiment of 'polling' the assembled academics on certain aspects of 'authenticity' in performance.

"Should there be *intervals?*" brought a three-to-one "NO", for instance. "Should obsolete in-jokes – depending on the names of the original actors, for instance – be cut?" Only a quarter were in favour of this kind of editing. Where should the acting 'focus' be – upstage in front of the *frons* with the entry doors close by or at the centre of the main thrust stage 'enclosed' by the galleries and audience, the area known as the platea? Despite the prediction of a former stage manager of the National, the vote was 10-1 in favour of the *platea*.

More controversial was the question of whether the female roles should be played exclusively by boys. On this there was a 50-50 split, though there was a clear majority on the question: "Should the ladies onstage wear masks, as they traditionally would have done when outdoors?"In fact, this discussion went further and there was general agreement that the staging should also extend to the male actors wearing appropriate hats, to kings wearing crowns, dukes coronets, etc.

There was a small preference (22-21) for 'authentic posters' of the 'Come see the evil Jew get his comeuppance' type and against the idea of evening performances with artificial daylight.

Yes, it would be worth attempting to 're-authenticise' original pronunciation at least once but since (a) it would be very difficult to know what was being said and (b) it would be even more difficult to know if it was being said *correctly*, once would probably be enough!

In summarising the debate, Andrew Gurr was realistic in assessing the conclusions of a group that consisted largely of academics. The actors who finally set foot on the Globe stage would have their own priorities and preferences. (In that he spoke truer than he knew.) But whatever *they* chose to do, he reminded the group, in the off-season – from October to April every year – the theatre would be the province of Globe Education and then the experiments could really start...

The theatre will tell us...
Michael Birkett

In July 1995, when the final arrangements for the workshop season were being completed, one of the last big pieces of the puzzle dropped into place. For some months now the media stories had revealed a consistent sub-text. Whatever else they might be covering, they had unanimously come to admit that this thing was as good as done. "This embattled project" had become in *The Times* – "the superb re-creation..." In its small way it was a conversion on the Road to Bankside...

Another sign of media acceptance was the frequency of – "Who's going to *run* the place and what will be the first play?" Mark Rylance was the answer to the first and, as Artistic Director, he would decide the second.

Chosen after a lengthy series of interviews, the 35-year old Rylance came to the job with excellent credentials. Trained at the Royal Academy of Dramatic Art, he had played leading roles with the RSC and won critical respect for his unconventional interpretations of some of the classic Shakespearean roles, including an insecure, stubborn, droopy-moustached Ulsterman in the role of Benedick in *Much Ado*. "Every new appearance becomes an event", wrote the *Daily Mail* critic of one of his performances, "He is a taker of risks. A lone honer of his art. A charismatic presence, possessed of a vivid intelligence".

When the official announcement was made on August 1st, there was general consensus that the appointment was a good one – youth tempered by experience was at the helm and what the Globe had here was a man if not for all seasons, at least for some seasons to come. Sir Peter Hall spoke of his "metaphysical talent for putting Elizabethan concerns into the modern world". In his 'global vision' at the press conference Rylance announced that he would be putting together a 32 member company over the next three years, "a core repertory group who will devote themselves to exploring this space for a few years". He didn't intend to limit the company's repertoire to the Bard, although that would clearly be the top priority. He hoped to attempt morality plays and Greek and Roman drama to discover what Shakespeare and his contemporaries looked at and were influenced by. He would also be working with contemporary writers.

His ambition was to create "a sensual theatre", a theatre that would "mix the high classical Greek and Roman form with the very common and grounded form of a bear-baiting pit or a courtyard or a bordello or a circus or a carnival... If you come and just want to actually enjoy the sunshine or the rain, then you can come and relax, no problem. If you come with your head and your heart and your body and your soul, then I'm going to be providing something for all that breadth of human activity here. High words, but those are my hopes".

In a passage that caught the attention of most of the next day's papers, he added that he hoped that modern audiences would also experiment with the uninhibited behaviour of their ancestors. "I can think of nothing more delightful. I'd be happy for people to throw things and shout... It's marvellously close to a bear pit or an arena. The actors will share the same space as us, as we tame our own inner beasts, our lions, foxes and badgers, our own feelings of malice and lust".

It was as much of a performance as a press conference...

> ...the voices of the players came most clear
> and pleasant to the ears of the lookers on.
>
> John Dee's translation of Vitruvius

Shakespeare's Globe and the Bankside theatres (1995). Royal Mail

AUGUST 12TH

"I want the group this side to look at the text you've been given to see what Lady Macduff says about *herself*... then this group to find out what is said *about* her... then the group over there to tell me what it tells you about the *plot* of the play. It's the only scene in which she appears..."

Artistic Director Designate, Mark Rylance was conducting an afternoon workshop. Several hundred people fanned themselves with the text in the relative 80° shade of the galleries. Down in the yard on this most untypical British summer day the 'groundlings' sat rather than stood. On a cooler day they might have indulged Rylance by talking back and moving around but today it was just too hot for all that. Light dresses mingled with tank tops and T-shirts, elegant straw hats with head coverings improvised from knotted handkerchieves. The crowd might well have puzzled Shakespeare. The playhouse certainly would not.

The main part of the structure was complete, the galleries in place. Only the prefabricated plywood stage and tiring house had the appearance of a temporary tooth filling that would be duly fixed on the next visit. None of which mattered, because the building was alive! The architect's drawings and the artists' impressions failed to convey the intimacy of the place. Sitting there, you were immediately aware of the rest of the audience in your peripheral vision in a way that conventional theatre seating doesn't permit. The actors on the stage – even this solitary actor – merely completed this human 'O'. As Theo and John Orrell had predicted with their experiment all those years ago, only the stage was truly shaded, its light cool and even.

There was a wholeness, a completeness about the occasion that was hard to define but which made Rylance's title – "360 Degrees in Character Playing in Shakespeare" – particularly appropriate. Standing alone on the plywood stage, youthful in baggy shorts and vivid sneakers, he could easily have been a groundling himself, anxious to express his opinion. The audience, self-conscious to begin with and not knowing what was expected from them, were warming to him and entering into the spirit of the occasion, calling out to him and to other members of the audience with whose views they disagreed.

At one point a number of them stood and crowded around the front of the stage. Rylance backed away in pretended fear. "Now I feel threatened". He was joking but the reaction was instinctive. The tactility of the relationship with the audience was something even experienced actors would have to work hard to get used to. As the afternoon wore on the rapport began to build and the audience to enter into the spirit of the occasion.

"Hey", Rylance said laughing, "it's a bit like a game show, isn't it?" The audience laughed with him. *Now* they knew where they were, these New Elizabethans...

...this unworthy scaffold...

Henry V, Prologue

SEPTEMBER 10TH

Rainy Sunday was the backdrop for the last of the workshop sessions and the contrast with Mark Rylance's sunny afternoon could hardly have been more dramatic. Even though clouds of another kind had been gathering in the intervening weeks.

The 'house' was packed for the first time, ensuring as accurate an acoustic as the structure in its present state would allow. Around the foot of the temporary stage swirled the groundlings, adding a slightly unauthentic touch in their colourful plastic capes and hoods.

Enter Sir Peter Hall, arguably the most prominent director of Shakespeare of his generation. For the last two years he had been a Trustee of the Globe project, a late convert to the cause. What would *he* have to say?

What Hall said was spoken clearly, as he walked slowly down to the front of the stage. In his view the present stage was wrong in several important respects, which he proceeded to enumerate. When he'd finished, he turned to face the people sitting to the right and by now behind him. They hadn't heard much of that, had they? They loudly agreed that they had not.

That was one of the problems and Hall had neatly dramatised what other, less skilled performers had been feeling as one workshop followed another.

The soliloquy had always been a theatrical device that fascinated him and more than once he had gone on record as saying that he believed that the spotlit introspection we are used to was untrue to the spirit of Shakespearean performance. Given the design of the stage and the proximity of the audience, he was now convinced, the actor would have had to take that audience into his confidence, which would mean moving around the stage, so as to face them all in turn. There could be little involvement with a character who kept his back to you and whose words you couldn't hear! So what was preventing the actors at the new Globe from doing just that? The stage itself, Sir Peter argued.

It was just too big. The 'thrust' of the stage takes the actor too far forward to be able to command the audience: too many of them are to the side or behind him. The stage of the Rose, by comparison, had a shallow curve.

Then – like many of the previous players – he was troubled by the pillars that supported the heavens. They were also too big, too far forward and too far out, making it difficult for actors to negotiate them – an impediment rather than an assistance. They invalidated, he felt, the side stages and the forestage almost entirely.

He argued for reconsideration of the design of the 'inner stage'. The present version would certainly never permit the concealment of Othello's bed or a royal throne. He quoted the example of the Rose again, where the entrance doors were not inside the pillars but outside them, thus allowing an army to "walk in from one door, walk round the outer stage, round the pillars and exit the other side". Which also left you with "a clearly defined central playing area".

In Hall's mind was always the impression he had carried away after standing on the space of the Rose's excavated stage. He had "felt the auditorium". He did not 'feel' the Globe stage in its present form and wrote to Sir Michael Perry, Chairman of the Globe trustees: "I personally would find it very difficult to stage a Shakespeare play on the space... and in no sense would I find it a liberation". Other actors and directors, both professional and amateur, expressed variations on the same theme but said essentially the same things with less articulacy, before going on to add that, nonetheless, they had found the theatre itself unique and exciting. Julian Glover described it as "fantastic, atmospheric, eager and welcoming".

> ...now I am cabin'd, cribb'd, confined, bound in
> To saucy doubts and fears.
>
> *Macbeth*, Act III Sc. iv

The season consisted of forty-five workshops and, going in, it was known that, in assessing it, allowances would have to be made for the unfinished state of the structure. The plywood in the stage area did nothing for the acoustics, while the plywood flooring of the two upper galleries actively amplified every footstep. The floor level of the pit was three inches lower than it would be – causing the groundlings to get a crick in the neck – and lacked the final surface material. A lot of the sound went straight into the ground.

Several modern theatrical precepts were put in question from the first performance. Audiences filing in instinctively made for what we now consider the 'best seats' – the lower gallery immediately facing the stage – yet the design of the theatre means that these are the seats *furthest* from the stage. Shakespearean audiences knew better. The 'best seats' were in the Lords' Room above and behind the stage, providing the actors are in motion, and after that the two 'wings' of the gallery.

The problem was that too few of the actors *did* move about. There was fretting without much strutting. Many of them spoke their lines into the texts they were carrying and played them almost exclusively to the front row of the 'stalls', where most of the audience were clustered. When it was suggested that they were too often drawn lemming-like to the front of the stage and tried to use the pillars as they would the familiar proscenium arch, a reason frequently given was that the gap between them and that front row drained them of '*energy*'. Certainly, very few had yet mastered the technique of playing to the sides of the theatre and their understandable preoccupation with the text prevented the intimacy to be gained from eye contact with the audience.

Even so, every now and again the stage showed flashes of its possibilities. Yes, it would require a more physical style of acting. Movement worked and made the occasional lack of it a powerful dramatic contrast. Intimacy worked when two characters spoke their lines facing each over. Gesture worked but in terms of the subtlety of body language, not the grand scale – just as speech didn't require volume as much as pitch and clarity. Julian Glover noted: "Verse speaking with special observation of line endings is essential and the serious study of this technique a priority... no one can saunter on to the stage, but must 'enter', and when on it, be much on the move, and employ physical gesture to reinforce his argument (a much laughed-at method today)".

In short, many of the things that didn't work pointed clearly towards what things would – and originally had. Which is precisely what a workshop is for. While understanding the concerns the 'theatricals' had, one wonders whether some of them weren't to some degree prompted by a desire to adapt the theatre to their hard-learned techniques rather than adapt their techniques to a new and challenging space? Sam had always said that modern actors would have a problem learning how to adapt. Had he been there to see the workshops, he would undoubtedly have said it again...

Understandably, the academics were not particularly understanding. It had taken them fifteen years to come to an agreed design and they were naturally fearful that any changes would crack the fragile surface of that accord and re-open the debate. The academic "black hole" across which the two sides were now peering at each other was the lack of hard evidence with regard to the stage of the Globe. Admittedly, there was a crude drawing of the stage of the Swan, detailed contracts for the Fortune and the Hope (but no drawings) and the excavation of the Rose but all they proved was that there was no *one* design for an Elizabethan or Jacobean theatre. The Globe's adopted stage design was an educated inference – a fact Peter Hall was quick to mention: "The actual scholastic facts... are so vague and contradictory that almost anybody can make them mean anything".

In many ways the situation was a repeat of the one Theo had faced when the theatricals had tried to influence his earlier drawings but at that stage there was no real time pressure. Now there was a real structure to debate and one still capable of modification. The actors, who felt they had barely been consulted in the past, now considered that in an area open to interpretation, the interpretation of those who had to make the space *work* should be given priority. It was their turn.

It was decided to try one further experiment. On Sunday, October 6th one final workshop would be staged to put all the key comments to the test. Decisions had to be made...

Being a pragmatist, Jon Greenfield was coming around to the view that it might make very good sense to *keep* the stage temporary for the opening season. Modify it – but don't finish it. After all this time, what was wrong with a little more learning?

This is the third time; I hope good luck lies in odd numbers.
The Merry Wives of Windsor, Act V Sc. i

OCTOBER 4TH

A small group of us stood looking down into another hole in the Bankside ground.

Mark Rylance – the head he'd recently shaved for his controversial Macbeth covered with an exotic headband; Jon Greenfield, looking relieved to be occupied for a few moments with something that couldn't possibly be used to reinterpret the design of the Globe stage; Patrick Spottiswoode, Chief Executive, Michael Holden and myself. Around us, looking ridiculously young, trudged the team of archaeologists from the Museum of London in muddy gumboots and yellow hard hats. Holding back a little were the supporting cast – "someone from the Council" and two besuited young men keeping an eye on the interests of the landlords, Legal and General (who owned the freehold) and their lease holders, Chelsfield plc.

A derelict building in Bear Gardens had recently been demolished and now – in the light of the Rose and Globe episodes – even gumboots had to walk on all sorts of eggshells. Nobody had any hope of developing a site in this part of the world until the archaeologists had had their say. This time nobody was arguing.

As we gathered round, a thin-faced young archaeologist tried to explain in layman-ese what was happening in that muddy hole. It was like looking at a slice of birthday cake made up of different layers. There a layer of red brick, sitting on top of another of yellow Victorian brick... rubble as filler... concrete... more brick. It was hard to realise that each of those layers had once been the bedrock on which several generations had built their lives, unaware of even more generations beneath their feet.

What had they found, Greenfield asked? Any *glass*? Quite a bit, as it happened. One of the other archaeologists produced a cardboard tray in which their finds to date were carefully laid out. Clay pipes, animal bones and a whole pile of beautiful coloured glass fragments, almost Venetian in their delicacy. On the site, Greenfield explained, had once stood the famous Bear Gardens Glasshouse, which in 1703 advertised "Looking Glass Plates blown from the smallest size upwards to 90 inches, with proportional Breadths, of lively colour, free from Bladders, Veins and Foulness, incident to the large plates hitherto sold". On the evidence in the cardboard tray, the advertisement did not lie.

So we were in the right spot. The question was – what else? The birthday cake was exposed down to the 17th Century, the period that mattered to us. "Any – *beams?*" Holden asked, apparently casually. Well, yes, there seemed to be a part of a beam but they couldn't quite see yet. From their description it seemed that it might be in roughly the right place. Mark Rylance made more notes on his clipboard.

The coloured glass was fine but that wasn't what had brought us here. It was that beam – or at least the possibility of it. What might be under all those layers and – if the Rose and Globe excavations were anything to go by – *safely* under them was the Hope, the last of the great Jacobean playhouses – the completion of the Bankside quartet of the Rose, the Globe and the Swan.

Once again you felt the presence of Philip Henslowe in the Globe story...

Once the original Globe began to take away Henslowe's business at the adjacent Rose, he moved north of the river to his specially-commissioned Fortune. Somehow, being away from the bustle of Bankside bothered him and he determined to return to it. The Rose had long since closed (1606), so he had to build again, renting the old Swan in the meantime.

In 1613 he had the idea of pulling down the decrepit old Bear Garden and erecting in its place a structure that could be used as both a playhouse and a bear-baiting pit. The theatre, he instructed the builder, should be "of such large compass, form, wideness, and height as the playhouse called the Swan". The stage must be able to be "carried and taken away", while the heavens must be built "all over the said stage, to be borne or carried without any posts or supporters to be fixed or set upon the said stage" – a line which, had they read it, would have made many a late twentieth century theatrical nod knowingly.

When the Hope opened its doors at the end of 1613 its resident troupe were the Lady Elizabeth's Men who, at least to begin with, played thirteen days out of fourteen – the odd day being devoted to the baiting. Despite that, the ambiance was apparently a little distinctive or gamey, to say the least – a fact Ben Jonson refers to in *Bartholomew Fair* (1614), a play he wrote for the Hope. Apart from Jonson, major writers like Massinger and Fletcher also wrote for Henslowe.

The Hope was Henslowe's last toss of the dice. Even so, the pull of the Globe was stronger. After he died in 1616, his interest passed to his son-in-law and partner, the former actor, Edward Alleyn but

Alleyn lacked his father-in-law's flair and interest. By 1620 or so the place had largely reverted to bear-baiting and by the 1630s it had even taken back the old name of Bear Garden. This particular hope did not spring eternal...

> Ajax: ...Who shall answer him?
> Achilles: I know not: it is put to lottery...
> *Troilus and Cressida*, Act II Sc. i

OCTOBER 16TH

For all the intellectual support and emotional sympathy he elicited, the one thing that eluded Sam in his lifetime was – money. Time and again the project shuddered to a halt as funds ran out and he would have to execute a tap dance on his imaginary stage to distract the supporters from the lack of any real action.

After his death the trickle of contributions increased without ever approaching a flood. Part of this was the 'guilt factor'. We really did mean to get around to this while Sam was alive – look, the cheque's in the post... A more persuasive factor was the visible state of the project. Bays were in place; the Wooden 'O' was taking shape in front of even the most sceptical eyes. Progress was steady but slow. Building could only take place when funds were available and delays were the norm.

Nonetheless, the hard and often thankless spadework put in by the core team – augmented by the appointment in early 1994 of Michael Holden as Chief Executive – was beginning to pay off. Between 1994 and 1996 more than £2 million had been raised from private and corporate sources; the number of visitors to the site was running at a rate of 150,000 a year; the temporary exhibition was not only drawing the crowds but winning design awards. Wonder of wonders, the operation was almost self-sufficient before the theatre was even officially open! As Michael Holden put it – "Sam's cohorts have multiplied and gone forth indeed!"

By the spring of 1995 the nagging question began to be heard. Was the summer of 1996 really realistic after all? The public relations implications of yet another delay were horrific. Well, forget about the decorations for now but surely we can finish the *structure*, can't we? *Can't* we? Even that was becoming increasingly doubtful as the year wore on. The workshop season bought a little breathing space in some ways. After all, you couldn't expect to do as much building when people were actually using the place... And there was always the Lottery.

For many years country after country and state after US state had found a lottery a useful way of raising extra cash by capitalising on the public's desire to have a flutter. Buy a ticket for a nominal amount and – who knew? – when that weekly draw was made, *you* might find yourself made for life. In a sense it was a tax on the gambling instinct. For years the UK stood aloof from this vulgar 'continental' habit but in 1993 the National Lottery Act became law. Honour and face were saved by the provision that much of the money so raised should be donated to worthwhile causes in the arts and charities. And the sum of money available was not insignificant. In 1995 alone the Arts Council had £300 million to bestow.

One of the first applications the authorities received was from the Shakespeare's Globe project. It was one of many and would receive due and lengthy consideration from the Government-appointed committee or quango, chaired by Lord Gowrie. File it, forget it, don't count on it was the advice the Globe team gave themselves. The project hadn't found favour in high places in the past. Why should things be any different this time, even though it's obvious that it was past the point of return? And when The Royal Opera House was awarded £55 million, a sum the popular press considered "excessive" and "elitist" ("It's Tutu Much", screamed *The Sun*), the committee's priorities seemed clear. As far as the Globe's application was concerned, they needed a few more facts and would get back to us around September. Fingers were firmly crossed and everyone went back to work.

> ...here, afore Heaven,
> I ratify this my rich gift.
>> *The Tempest*, Act IV Sc. i

Just before the Lottery witching hour came a pleasant surprise. From the day he persuaded Gordon Getty, heir to the Getty oil fortune, to become involved, Sam had said repeatedly and publicly that, "I told Gordon I would never ask him for money". At the same time, he made it clear that, should Gordon choose to *offer*... In 1987 at the Ground Breaking ceremony Getty did offer in what he called "The Getty Challenge". If the Globe could raise £9 million from their own sources – and he wasn't about to put any conditions on

Gordon Getty, whose generous 'challenge' was finally met. (1995) *Marina Blodget*

those sources – then he would top it up with £1 million of his own. At the time £9 million seemed as far away as the horizon. It was something you'd get to when you got to it – maybe. Like the Lottery application some years later, it was put in the back of the mind.

But in early September it was pulled firmly forward. Jerry Link's sums showed that the magical £9 million target could now be claimed. He duly claimed and Getty was as good as his word. Link thought his only problem now was whether to announce the good news before or after the Lottery decision. In the event, the Lottery committee preempted him by announcing on September 18th that they were deferring their decision for another month. They needed a little more information and reassurance in one or two areas.

The press immediately anticipated the worst. *The Independent* headlined their coverage: "Lottery Fund Snub for 'Disneyland' Globe", although at the very end of the piece it did have the grace to quote Lord Gowrie, the Arts Council chairman, as saying that the project was "an inspiring and important vision".

This time there was no point in being stoical. Now it was count the days until October 13th, when the decision was promised. Nothing could stop the project now but the timing was still on a knife edge. The Getty money was just about enough to complete the main structure – and the Americans were adamant that it should be used for that and nothing else. The trouble was that nothing would be left over to start on the next phase – the exhibition and the Inigo Jones – and there were rumours that it was the next phase that particularly concerned the Lottery people. After all, they couldn't influence the design of the theatre, nor could they do much about the Inigo Jones, where the actual plans existed. But the rest of the complex existed only on paper and in the heads of the architects. And wasn't it a well-known fact that pipers liked to call some of the tunes?

There was one other piece of good news and that was about the albatross of the money owed to the banks. Seeing the project so well advanced, the consortium agreed to convert the debt to equity, so that the money became virtually a loan and the Trustees could sleep more easily than they had in years.

Perhaps the extra month served a 'cooling off' purpose in the end. Perhaps the strength of the media reaction also played a part. Perhaps everybody got a little too tense with so much at stake. There was almost a sense of anti-climax – leavened with just a touch of delightful hysteria – when Chief Executive, Michael Holden received the phone call to tell him that the application had been successful and would be confirmed at a press conference on the following Monday, October 16th. There would be very few conditions and the bottom line read – £12.4 million.

That amount of money would complete the Globe and the Inigo Jones, tidy up the piazza and build several of the surrounding buildings, such as the office block and box office. A further £6 million would be needed to build the exhibition in the undercroft and that would now be the fund-raising target. Lovell's contract could now be re-activated and the self build team incorporated into it with Ted Hampton acting as both 'conscience' and Clerk of Works.

It's doubtful if many of those who read the news realised the two underlying ironies in the outcome.

Overnight the Globe had crossed a line from outcast to Establishment. Receiving the Lottery money put the project into the camp of the Royal Opera House and now Sadler's Wells (£30 million) and made it the legitimate target of the 'anti-arts' brigade. "This money is going to arty-farty types", trumpeted MP Terry Dicks (Tory: Hayes and Harlington) in the House of Commons. He chose to paraphrase 'elitist' but the word hung in the air.

Virginia Bottomley, the National Heritage Secretary, was ready for him: "As far as London is concerned, there are flagship institutions which affect tourism and our national pride. There is a misunderstanding that the lottery money goes to ballet dancers and bassoon players". Then she delivered the *coup de grâce*: "It goes to brickies and electricians because the construction industry benefits from the money".

But there was one more twist to the story. The Lottery money was not, strictly speaking, the Government's, taken in the normal way from the citizen taxpayer's pocket. This was a tithe paid by the man in the street as the fee he paid to gamble. In a very real sense the people were giving Sam the theatre he'd so much wanted to give to them...

❖

As the year turned, the debate over the stage continued. The academics, Orrell and Gurr v. the actors. In essence, the issues boiled down to three. The size and shape of the stage; should the stage be fully covered or not (which involved the position of the pillars); the position of the entrances in the *frons*. All of these issues had to be decided by a February deadline, if even a temporary structure was to be ready for the 1996 events.

The stage decision turned out to be relatively straightforward. John Orrell's view prevailed. The stage would have been a 44ft by 25ft rectangle and the evidence of the Red Lion and the Fortune contract gave the argument a strong underpinning.

The question of stage covering proved more controversial. Orrell argued that the Fortune and Hope contracts referred to covers over the stage, though the wording of those documents is still open to other interpretation. Additionally, the evidence of the Rose indicates there must have been a cover over the whole stage to cause a 'drip line' that created erosion in the yard floor. On this there was less unanimity.

The columns, of course, were the main bone of contention and here the actors were unanimous in rejecting the Workshop Season layout, where the columns had been placed 5ft 6ins from the sides of the stage, giving a separation of 33ft. That particular layout had not been arrived at arbitrarily but only after extensive research into contemporary Elizabethan structures that followed the 'vernacular' tradition, in which the invention of new forms was firmly rooted in past solutions with invention kept to the minimum.

Orrell proposed an elegant solution that broke the deadlock. The Globe, he argued, was not an ordinary Elizabethan playhouse but a most extraordinary one in almost every way and significantly different from the other surviving examples. By qualifying the vernacular, so to speak, it would be possible to argue the case for a somewhat greater cantilever than the original 5ft 6in. The agreed new cantilever would now be 8ft 3in – meaning that the columns would now be set 8ft 3in back from both the front edge of the stage and from the sides, giving a new column separation of 27ft 6in. Although the actors had originally wanted 12ft from the front of the stage and 9ft 6in from the sides, Mark Rylance felt the compromise was sufficient. The 1996 season would be the test and there would still be time for further discussion before the commitment of the 1997 gala opening.

In any case, the new projection gave the actors a bonus, since the 27ft 6in column spacing pushes the doors in the *frons* outside the columns, increasing the separation from 22ft to 33ft. Peter McCurdy and his team at last had something to build...

❖

In January Mark Rylance officially took up his new job and immediately announced his plans for the year or so ahead. On the June date building would stop for the day, while Founders and 'family' celebrated the miracle of being here at all. The Globelink schools would dedicate the 'heavens', a bust of Sam would be unveiled and on the stage – temporary or no – there would be an 'entertainment'.

Meanwhile, he was busy putting together the nucleus of what would be his resident troupe. Following the Founders' Day event, there would be a Prologue season when, in late August, they would perform *The Two Gentlemen of Verona* in the great Globe itself. The following year – in June – would see a week of gala festivities prior to the anniversary of Sam's birthday.

For now sits Expectation in the air
Henry V, Act II Chorus

CHAPTER 20

THE RAINMAKER'S TALE
(Concluded)

And one man in his time plays many parts,
His acts being seven ages.
As You Like It, Act II Sc.vii

There were many Sams. Talk to the number of people I've interviewed for this book and, when I read my notes back, I was reading descriptions of several distinct and different characters.

Sam polarised people; on different occasions he could even polarise the *same* person. There were no shades of intermediate grey with him. You were either on his side or you were not. And I suspect all visionaries have that in common. The City on the Hill – or whatever form your personal Dream takes – shines so brightly that it dazzles and prevents you from seeing clearly who and what lies on the road taking you there. It's not calculated to make you the easiest of travelling companions. And Sam, particularly towards the end, was a man in a hurry.

I have had a most rare vision
A Midsummer Night's Dream, Act IV, Sc. i

I don't think there's any doubt that he was a visionary, although these days the word is much diminished by casual usage. While other people peered and prodded at the difficulties involved in building a theoretical theatre, he saw its social as well as its cultural benefits; while some were busy arguing the political case for a handful of over-priced council houses, he could envision the revitalisation of an entire community that would be triggered by his putting this first symbolic piece in place.

Not just *any* piece. The finest library or museum wouldn't do it. It had to be a *theatre*. A theatre, after all, existed to draw from people and their lives, enhance what it found, then give it back. And to be standing on the very ground where a theatre had done just that must be meant.

The Liverpool experiment in the 1950's had shown him that putting on a show was only part of the theatrical experience in the life of a community. The faces of the children at some of the early Globe events confirmed it all over again.

His original vision went much further, though most of those who worked with him in later years saw only the Globe complex and many of them felt *that* was too ambitious. Yet those with memories long enough to remember Sam in the 1960's knew that his original scheme prefigured what would happen to the whole redevelopment of the South Bank, long before the property developers crossed the bridges with their cheque books. Many of them feel that Sam's much-maligned shoe boxes might have been a more acceptable solution than the higgledy-piggledy arrangement commercial happenstance has handed us.

For much of the journey the sheer size of his vision was a burden to him. Even in its scaled-down version he was pursuing the art of the possible instead of the ideal. No wonder he was constantly improvising and embellishing the Globe project, often to the consternation of his loyal supporters, who thought they knew which way they were pointing, until Sam's vision shifted a degree or two!

It always seemed to me that there was a cultural problem there, too. Wasn't it George Bernard Shaw who wrote of the British and the Americans being "divided by a common language"? However long he had lived among them, Sam couldn't be expected to *think* like a Brit. *De facto*, if he had, he would have achieved nothing like as much as he did. It was British *attitude* as well as language that impeded him. In America a project like the Globe would have been completed in no time at all. Sam knew that. Some foundation or corporation would have come along. Even in Europe he wouldn't have had this kind of problem. Look at the Pompidou Centre in Paris. As it was, he had the bad luck to run into a mean streak that's begun to surface more and more in the British character of being unwilling to embrace an idea that comes from someone and particularly somewhere else. And then never quite coming out and saying so. It suited too many people for too long to dismiss Sam and his ideas as being too 'American' with all that that implied. Yet at the end of the day it became clear that only an American could have got the thing done.

> *I expected it all to happen very quickly, spring up in two or*
> *three years... Or I probably wouldn't have started it...*
>
> Sam Wanamaker

The Globe cost Sam a great deal, as visions often do. From the 1960's he mortgaged his career to it, taking work that would pay him as much as possible for as little commitment of time. "I've got to go off and earn some money," he would say to explain one of his occasional disappearances. Without the Globe, what would he have been? It's anybody's guess but I can see him as an Anglo-American Jason Robards, getting good reviews for the occasional 'classic' part and filling in with more commercial fare, as happened to Olivier and others in later years.

Ironically, if Sam had remained a major active theatrical figure with the Globe as his 'hobby'. he would probably have succeeded sooner. We Brits like amateurs; we distrust people who take serious things seriously.

It would have been good to see Sam's Lear or Prospero. There were those who felt they *had* − without benefit of stage. Before there was even a temporary plank of a stage, the Globe gave Sam free rein to play an entire range of *ad hoc* roles. Charm, anger, camaraderie, outrage, betrayal, sorrow, injured innocence... you could see all of them, often within seconds of each other. It's often occurred to me that the consummate actor suffers one terrible drawback from which the rest of us are fortunately spared. How do you know when an actor has stopped *acting?* Does even *he* know? Is Alec Guinness, so quiet and unassuming in private interview, *acting* quiet and unassuming? Was Sam in his sudden outbursts angry or acting anger? And was the equally sudden over-optimism, the sunshine that inevitably followed the storm, real or theatrically apt? We can all have our theories but we shall never know − except to know that it made you want to stay around to see how the plot turned out.

❖

The manner put some people off; there are no two ways about that. One colleague likened him to Orson Welles as being a "flawed director of himself" and even daughter Zoë feels "He needed a director − and he knew that". I'm not so sure. If the performance had been more modulated, better adapted to individual and audience, we'd have 'learned' him and known where we stood and we might have even taken him for granted. It was the predictable unpredictability that made him dangerous and prevented you from ever taking your eye off him. Perhaps the clue lies in the self-knowledge he showed in an interview, when he admitted that "It was once wisely said of me, 'You seem to bring out the beast or best in people,' and, with a faint glimmer of a blush and a shy downcast glance, I must admit my chief talent appears to be that of provoking controversy".

> ... when he speaks,
> The air, a charter'd libertine, is still,
> And the mute wonder lurketh in men's ears,
> To steal his sweet and honey'd sentences
>
> Henry V, Act I Sc.i

I think he was wrong – or perhaps he was just acting again. I think Sam's chief talent was his power to *move* people. Like the classical orators, there are those who can make us listen to what they have to say and a very few who make us want to do something about it.

Sam was one of the few. Words that he'd used countless times seemed to possess him and would flow out in new configurations of passion. If he really believes in it this much and wants it this badly (you found yourself thinking), we can't stop *now*. Then you forgot the irritations of his impossible self-imposed deadlines and the frustration of seeing the empty eyes of the non-believers as you mentioned the Globe *again*... because how often in this life do you met someone so sure of what they're doing?

Towards the end there was a sad grandeur about him. There was no more time for frills and trappings. Day by day the Dream must have become clearer and brighter to him and he made it clearer to us. Yes, there would be a theatre but more than a theatre – more even that the most famous theatre the world had ever known. At the heart of Sam's Dream was the belief that, given the means and the place, people will come together to celebrate the truth of what they have in common and that the thoughts and words of this singular man, William Shakespeare, embodying his own 'vision', can reach out across time and culture to become an international language. Once put down your Wooden 'O' and you can turn the world on its axis...

So may a thousand actions, once afoot,
End in one purpose...

Canterbury, Henry V, Act I Sc. ii

On June 14th 1996 – which happens to be Sam's birthday – nearly four hundred years after Shakespeare and his fellow actors created the Globe from the relics of the Theatre and almost fifty years since Sam's first fateful walk along Bankside, the words of Shakespeare will be heard once again in their original setting. To make that happen one man did, indeed, play many parts. But the part he played that I shall always remember is to be found nowhere in Shakespeare. To me he was the irrepressible Don Quixote with the rest of us an endless retinue of Sancho Panzas.

Which is why, when on that June afternoon that first audience is listening to the sound of applause, to some of us it will be the sound of windmills falling...

❖

But release me from my bands
With the help of your good hands.
Gentle breath of yours my sails
Must fill, or else my project fails,
Which was to please. Now I want
Spirits to enforce, art to enchant;
And my ending is despair,
Unless I be reliev'd by prayer,
Which pierces so that it assaults
Mercy itself and frees all faults.
As you from crimes would pardon'd be,
Let your indulgence set me free.

Prospero's Epilogue, The Tempest

David Hockney 'Queen Elizabeth & Shakespeare'. 1979, crayon 17 x 21 inches
©David Hockney

CHAPTER 21

'PROLOGUE' POSTSCRIPT

Founder's Day June 14th, 1996

> To perform an act
> Whereof what's past is prologue
> *The Tempest*, Act II Sc.i

The sun that had so often eluded Sam came to pay its respects that June day and stayed for the rest of the summer.

The Globe 'family' were there – all those who had given money or time or both, answered phones, stuffed envelopes and, in one way or another, kept the faith all this time. They weren't here to hear a play or see a show; they were here to see each other and to celebrate the fact of being there at all. You can't measure joy but on that day you could touch it.

They smiled when the black clad children from Globelink schools around the world threaded their way through the standing Groundlings, bearing their golden zodiac banners and balloons... They laughed when host Mark Rylance produced an armful of bulging folders which, he claimed, contained the names of the thousands of people who had been involved over the past thirty years – all of whom he proposed to name... They laughed even louder when Prince Philip, indicating the wooden 'O', recalled that one of the oak beams had come from Windsor Great Park. "I don't know which one it is," he added, "but if it falls down, it will be that one!" ... and a few moments later all rose as one, when he unveiled the bronze bust of Sam, head resting on hand and smiling enigmatically, as well he might.

Everyone knew it would have been his 77th birthday – but few realised that his ashes were safely buried beneath the stage. Henceforth, *every* birthday would be Founder's Day. In every sense, he was here.

Prologue Season: August 21st, 1996

> I cannot find words to express the good fortune that
> my generation of actors have had thrust upon them ...
> Not Garrick, Kean, Irving, Ellen Terry, Booth, Walter
> Hampden, Olivier or countless others have had the
> opportunity to play the theatre Shakespeare had in his
> mind's eye.
>
> Mark Rylance

The stage had been modified from the previous year but it was still a temporary structure. Playing on it professionally for a full month would provide ample opportunity to test out some of the theories in practice, even if no one expected all the arguments to be resolved.

Temporary decorations brought the jewel box to life and stunned many of the 'first night' audience who came with monotones in mind. Even those of us who knew what to expect found ourselves transfixed by a bright colour here, a detail there. Around and behind the 'marble' pillars stretched the stage covered with rushes.

Many thought the choice of the Prologue play a strange one. *The Two Gentlemen of Verona* (1594) is usually considered one of Shakespeare's apprentice works, which was precisely why Rylance chose it. "My objective in this Prologue year," he wrote to the Board, "is to establish a relationship between the actors and the audience, no more." To do this, he felt, he should avoid one of the 'classics' and offer instead a piece that few of the audience would know. *Two Gentlemen* also happened to have within it "many seeds of later work in character, theme and stagecraft, including use of the balcony, a forest and rapid changes of location." While the cast could learn valuable lessons, the audience could see something that didn't arrive complete with excess critical baggage. It proved a wise choice. To make the piece even more accessible, Rylance – who also played Proteus, one of the two 'gentlemen' – dressed the cast in contemporary clothes. Without making it a 'modern' statement, audiences could relate to a couple sitting at a cafe table, for instance, or carrying ordinary luggage.

Hamlet claimed there was 'providence in the fall of a sparrow' and it would be hard to recall a major event in the Globe's thirty year history without an element of the accidental. During the previous evening's public dress rehearsal – at which the Groundlings were admitted, in true Elizabethan tradition, for one penny – actor George Innes must have been paying undue attention to the American theatrical injunction to "Break a leg!" – because, shinning down a rope from the balcony, he did just that. Consequently, the opening performance found a hasty rearrangement of minor parts and sometime actor, Mel Cobb – who had been peacefully occupied as a plasterer – making an unscheduled appearance as the Landlord. Later Rylance joked to reporters about the Elizabethans being famous for having short rehearsal times – "But one *day*?"

In the event, the first public performance was an opening night. The packed house was well met by daylight, then, as the sky darkened, the lighting slowly came up, so subtly that few of the audience even noticed, so taken were they with the events on stage.

Particularly telling were the reactions of the Groundlings, paying their £5 to stand around the stage for the next two and a half hours. Would they respond or would they be self-conscious? From the outset it was quite clear that they were here to have a good time. "Like an intimate Albert Hall during the Proms," as someone described it.

The dog broke the ice, so to speak. When stand up comic relief, Launce appeared with Crab – an elongated, lugubrious mutt – those nearest the front of the stage began to pat him and you could feel the audience's collective hope that all that sniffing at the stage pillars

Mark Rylance as Proteus in *The Two Gentlemen of Verona*. John Tramper

315

might presage a 'christening' – which on more than one subsequent occasion it did.

Then, when Proteus plots treachery, there were cries of – "Go on, son!" answered by countercries of – "No, you rotten devil!" The spurned Julia, comparing herself to her rival, Sylvia, was greeted with a loud "Meeow!"

As I left, I heard a young couple behind me commenting on the evening. "It was great," he said, "I understood everything that was going on. And you don't usually get that with Shakespeare." In his curtain speech Mark Rylance thanked "the two men who made it possible - Mr. W.S. and Mr. S.W." Both of them would have felt the young man's verdict justified their joint enterprise.

I do now let loose my opinion; hold it no longer
The Tempest Act II Sc.ii

The critics were near unanimous in their praise and even those who came to jeer could scarce forebear to cheer. "Triumph of the Will", said Michael Billington in *The Guardian*, "Global Warming: New Theatre Restores Old Vigour to Bard" *Evening Standard*; "Shakespeare Comes Home" *Daily Telegraph*; and perhaps as encouraging as any – "A Great Night Out for a Fiver" (Benedict Nightingale in *The Times*). The consensus was that the Globe had avoided the Scylla of museum theatre and the Charybdis of Disneyfication. "Speaking as a critic," Nightingale concluded, "I know there is fun and excitement ahead."

There was also some immediate gratification. The four week season was attended by over 40,000 people, roughly 94% of capacity. And to prove that the project wasn't to be dominated by theatrical performance, Globe Education played host to a record 36,000 students during the year, while the European Federation of Associations of Tourism Journalists named the Globe "the best attraction in Europe" by awarding it their European Tourism Initiative Golden Star Award. As the year ended – three years after Sam's death – even he would have had difficulty, looking at the summer's crowds and now the hordes of builders moving in for their winter's blitz, remembering that hole full of Bankside mud.

But leaving the reviews, the box office receipts and the other details aside, the very fact that there was something to celebrate was the true wonder that cried out for attention before succeeding generations (rightly) took it for granted. Perhaps James Wood *(in The Observer)* got closest to it when he wrote that "The Globe represents precisely the naive, clumsy, ordinary reverence that most troubles the cultural materialists, and encourages their special condescension. For the Globe is a triumph of excessive love."

❖

I foretold you then what would ensue
Troilus and Cressida Act IV Sc.v

Reflecting on the four week season, Mark Rylance likened the experience of playing in the Globe to "getting on a horse, never really having ridden before, and then have it gallop away with you... We experienced such a force of energy in the space from the architecture and the audience as I have never felt in proscenium or thrust theatres or even in outdoor spaces. It wasn't to do with the novelty; it was entirely to do with a new relationship – the empowerment of the audience."

"There's a whole new level of communication with the audience, particularly in the yard, and a totally different kind of contact between the members of the audience. They can *see* each other. You're standing next to people and they're talking during the play, just as they do at a football match."

"Now, to be honest, much of the communication is pantomimic but it has the seeds of powerful stuff. I remember our director, Jack Shepherd, coming to me at the interval on the opening night. He was enthused by the audience reaction but he wondered where it was going; he'd never seen anything like it. I told him not to worry. I said: "We're beginners. We must learn to shape it." What we were finding was that the narrative of play was not in the control of the players but shared between the audience and the actors."

"What we have to learn are the ways Burbage and others developed – ways of encouraging audience reaction and ways of pulling it back. As the run progressed, I found myself doing just that, particularly in the second half. I'd begin by playing to the audience as my conscience. I'd take them into my confidence as to what I was about to do, so they were behind me. Then, when I began to be duplicitous and when they started to boo and hiss, I'd turn to them – "What's your problem?""

"The whole genius of the play – which playing it this way reveals – lies in taking people along in what they think is a light comedy of wit – nothing serious is going to happen. Then, suddenly, they're taken to a forest and there's a wild boar on the stage about to rape a young woman – and they're a party to it. They've gone along with it!"

He contrasts the Globe experience with what has become traditional theatrical practice.

"We tend to aim for an ideal performance, which is rehearsed and polished and set – and then repeated night after night with the same effect. But that *isn't* the ideal. The ideal is for the performance to grow and for things to be discovered, something new every night. We have to let go of the idea of controlling the reaction. The audience should be free to react in different ways. This is what is making some directors nervous about the space, this loss of control. They don't have their usual tools of lighting and scenery. Instead, they have to work with the energy of the play..."

Two Gentlemen is painted in broad brush strokes and is not particularly well known by its audience. What happens when this new audience involvement meets one of the more 'serious' plays?

"Again, we must ask ourselves how Burbage did it! My feeling is that when you decide to 'go inside', as with a soliloquy, you must imagine the 'distracted globe' – the phrase Hamlet used to describe his mind after seeing the Ghost – imagine having fifteen hundred people sitting round the inside edges of your cranium. If you go out to them fairly, willing to put the questions to them and willing to take their responses, I believe they will play fair with you. One small example occurred in *Two Gentlemen*. When Valentine asked Julia to forgive me and take me back, the audience shouted out – "Don't do it, Julia!" And I'm thinking – "My God, if she doesn't have me back, this is what it feels like to have a mob around you who might take justice into their own hands! So my pleading as a character was greatly motivated! And she took me back as she never had before, in defiance of their merciless justice. In that way *the audience is shaping the narrative*."

There was learning about the configuration of the stage. This year's positioning of the pillars will be replicated, together with the rest of the stage, in the permanent building for the 1997 opening ... "There are still those who maintain the pillars are not quite right but until and unless we get incontrovertible evidence, we can't say that. It's probable the stage will be changed in time but only as a result of hard archaeological evidence. I feel we must go through the ritual of opening and then play on it for a while to build our own body of evidence through experience.

The *frons scenae* and the 'Heavens'. *Richard Kalina*

"We now have a better understanding of the central space. The debate we've been having is – is the *frons scenae* the back of the stage or should we consider that to be the back of the Lords' Room, which is *behind* the *frons*? At the moment two-thirds of the stage is visible and one third is hidden. I have now come to believe – by playing on it – that we should regard the *frons scenae* as a 'face' with a 'mind' or hidden space behind it. The stage at the moment is a rectangle but, consider it as part of a greater totality, and it becomes a square. Now, you don't consider that hidden space a *playing* area but you encourage the audience to imagine it's alive and that things are happening back there – Prospero's cell, Rosalind's glade and so on. It's not an inner stage but a 'discovery' space, a mental space – like a rood screen in a cathedral. It opens up lots of possibilities."

The biggest drawback or disappointment with the theatre? "The fact that, even when the place was packed to capacity, people were unwilling to come down the *sides* of the stage. The stage is said to have three fronts but it doesn't; it has an extended front centre. And once the majority of the people are in front of you, as an actor you are drawn to that front space. We'll have to think our way around that."

"The only other thing was a problem with the acoustics of the lower gallery – the upper two galleries were fine. People sitting there got too much 'information'; there were too many surfaces with sound bouncing back. We think cloth at the back of the lower gallery will deal with that."

"Over all, I couldn't be happier. We're novices but we've learned so much already in those few short weeks. The geometry and the thought behind the architecture is much more sophisticated than any proscenium theatre... yet it comes across as a welcoming space, where there isn't someone at the top of the table and someone at the bottom."

As the new year turned, there was – as the saying goes – good news and bad news.

❖

And monarchs to behold the swelling scene!
Henry V Prologue

January 8th, 1997

PRESS RELEASE

"Buckingham Palace announced today that Her Majesty the Queen will celebrate the opening of Shakespeare's Globe Theatre on Thursday 12 June, 1997. She will be accompanied by His Royal Highness Prince Philip, Patron of the Shakespeare Globe Trust.

Her Majesty will attend a specially devised celebration for the completion of Shakespeare's Globe – a performance of Triumphes and Mirth. This event will be the highlight of a two week 'Festival of Firsts'.

❖

March 1997

Lord, what fools these mortals be!
A Midsummer Night's Dream Act III Sc.ii

Snatching defeat out of the jaws of victory, the Conservative government in its death throes decides to allow the new owners of Anchor Terrace to build flats inside the protected shell that covers a significant part of the original Globe site. Southwark Council grants planning permission and also agrees to a further block elsewhere on the site. The decision, it is said, is non-negotiable – despite the fact that it is the polar opposite of the understanding reached in 1989 at the time of the original excavation. Nor had there been any discussion with the interested academic or theatrical parties before the decision was arrived at.

Realization dawns that eight years on, far from consolidating progress, some things are moving backwards. The Rose at least, is protected but the Globe is to be erased by a couple of casual strokes of the bureaucratic pen. While the Globe supporters gather their thoughts and their arguments to present to the new Labour government, the line that comes to mind is... *Lord. what fools these mortals be!*

Richard Kalina

THIS WOODEN 'O'

ENVOI

"**I** could write for ever and never pin down the complex, multi-talented, beautiful human being who was my husband, Sam – a man who was always ahead of his time; first, last and always a man of the theatre, which was his life's force. I'm delighted that his friend and collaborator, Barry Day, has done it for me. He shared Sam's vision that one day the Globe would once again become "The Glorie of the Banke". And now it has... "

Charlotte Wanamaker

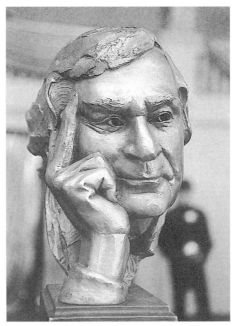

Bronze bust of Sam by Gerald Laing. *Richard Kalina*

BIBLIOGRAPHY

ADAMS, Joseph Quincey - *Shakespearean Playhouses* (Peter Smith, 1917)

BARTON, John - *Playing Shakespeare* (Methuen, 1984)

BECKERMAN, Bernard - *Shakespeare at the Globe (1599-1609)* (Macmillan 1962)

BERRY, Herbert - *Shakespeare's Playhouses* (AMS Press, 1987)

BRAINES, W. W. - *The Site of the Globe Playhouse, Southwark* (Hodder & Stoughton with LCC - 1924)

BROOK, Peter - *The Empty Space* - (Penguin, 1990)

BROWN, John Russell - *Shakespeare & His Theatre*, illustrated by David Gentleman (Lothrop, Lee & Shepard Book, 1982)

BURTON, S. H. - *Shakespeare's Life and Stage* (Chambers, 1989)

CROSBY, Theo - *How to Play the Environment Game* (Penguin, 1973)

ECCLES, Christine - *The Rose Theatre* (Nick Hern Books, 1990)

GURR, Andrew - *The Shakespearean Stage* (Cambridge University Press, 1980)

GURR, Andrew - *Playgoing in Shakespeare's London* (Cambridge University Press, 1987)

GURR, Andrew & ORRELL, John - *Rebuilding Shakespeare's Globe* (Weidenfeld & Nicolson, 1989)

HARWOOD, Ronald - *All the World's a Stage* (Secker & Warburg/BBC, 1984)

HILDY, Franklin (Ed.) - *New Issues in the Reconstruction of Shakespeare's Globe: Theatre Proceedings of the Conference Held at the University of Georgia, February 16th-18th, 1990.* Presentations by Franklin Hildy, C. Walter Hodges, Julian Bowsher and Simon Blatherwick, Andrew Gurr, Allan C. Dessen, Hugh Richmond and John L. Styan (Peter Lang [New York], 1990)

HODGES, C. Walter - *The Globe Restored: A Study of Elizabethan Theatre* (Ernest Benn, 1953)

HODGES, C. Walter - *Shakespeare's Theatre* (Oxford University Press, 1964)

HODGES, C. Walter - *Shakespeare's Second Globe: The Missing Monument* (Oxford University Press, 1973)

HODGES, C. Walter (Ed.) - *The Third Globe: Symposium for the Recon-struction of the Globe Playhouse*, with S. Schoenbaum and Leonard Leone (Wayne State University, 1979)

JACKSON, RUSSELL & SMALLWOOD, Robert (Eds.) - *Players of Shakespeare (1 & 2)* (Cambridge University Press, 1988)

ORRELL, John - *The Quest for Shakespeare's Globe* (Cambridge University Press, 1983)

ORRELL, John - *The Theatres of Inigo Jones & John Webb* (Cambridge University Press, 1985)

ORRELL, John & GURR, Andrew - *Rebuilding Shakespeare's Globe* (Weidenfeld & Nicolson, 1989)

PAYNE, Ben Iden - *A Life in a Wooden O: Memoirs of the Theatre* (Yale University Press, 1977)

REDGRAVE, Michael - *The Actor's Ways and Means* (Theatre Arts Books, 1953)

REDGRAVE, Michael - *Mask or Face* (Heinemann, 1958)

REDGRAVE, Vanessa - *Autobiography* (Random House, 1994)

RICHARDSON, Tony - *The Long Distance Runner: An Autobiography* (Morrow, 1993)

RUSKIN, John - *The Seven Lamps of Architecture* (Century, 1988)

SCHOENBAUM, S. - *Shakespeare, The Globe and the World* (Volger Shakespeare Library & Oxford University Press, 1979)

SMITH, Warren D. - *Shakespeare's Playhouse Practice: A Handbook* (University Press of New England, 1976)

STYAN, J. L. - *Shakespeare's Stagecraft* (Cambridge University Press, 1967)

THOMSON, Peter - *Shakespeare's Theatre* (Routledge & Kegan Paul, 1983)

WHANSLOW, H. W. - *The Bankside Stage Book* (Wells Garner, Darton)

WICKHAM, Glynne - *Early English Stages 1300-1600* (3 Vols) (Routledge & Kegan Paul) (1959/1963)

WITTKOWER, Rudolph - *Architectural Principles in the Age of Humanism* (Dent)

YATES, Frances A. - *Theatre of the World* (Routledge & Kegan Paul, 1969)

Picture/Photographic Credits/Permissions

We are grateful to the following for permission to include their material listed below: David Gentleman, David Hockney, June Everett, Pentagram. It has not been possible in every instance to trace the source and copyright owners of certain photographs and illustrations, despite our best efforts. Should that information become known to us we would be pleased to include it in any subsequent edition of this book.

Dustjacket - Marc Aspland, *The Times*
Frontispiece - Tom Doust
xv - Tom Boulting
xvi - Edinburgh University Library
3 - David Gentleman
5 - Map. C Redwood, 1916
9 - By Permission of the Trustees of Dulwich Picture Gallery
13 - Courtesy Guildhall Library, Corporation of London
19 - Tokyo Globe
23 - Will Kempe Dancing a Jig from his Account of Dance from London to Norwich 1600 - By permission of the British Library
25 - Special Collections Department of the University of Arizona Libraries
26 - Dominik Klimowski
43 - Bill Wanamaker
44 - The Raymond Mander & Joe Mitchenson Theatre Collection
46 - Charlotte Wanamaker
52 - Charlotte Wanamaker
58 - Mander Mitchenson
64 - Keith Michell's Modern Dress *Hamlet* (1972)
66 - June Everett
88 - (Andrew Gurr) - Peter Whyte; (John Orrell) - Wendy Orrell
91 - By Permission of the British Museum
96 - Pentagram
101 - The Provost and Fellows of Worcester College, Oxford
105 - Bibliotheck der Rijksuniversiteit Netherlands
107 - Courtesy the Royal Library, Stockholm, Maps and Prints Department (De La Gardie Collection)
108 - Topographical Glass from John Bates - The Mysteryes of Nature and Art 1634 - By Permission of the British Library
120 - The Cockpit Playhouse, Bear Gardens Museum
124 - Globe Bankside Development Plan model - 1971 - S. Wanamaker, T. Crosby, Sir O. Arup
131 - Pentagram
132 - Pentagram
134-135 - Pentagram
176 - Ann Ward
179 - Sam Wanamaker with road sweepers - 1986
185 - By Permission of the Trustees of Dulwich Picture Gallery
202 - June Everett
220 - Pentagram
222-223 - Dennis Bailey, by permission of Pentagram
227 - Pentagram
232 - Schwontkowski Banner
238 - Bremer Shakespeare Company
242 - Pentagram
244 - Michael Perry and Sam Wanamaker - 1989
248 - June Everett
251 - Thatcher at work
256 - Richard Kalina
257 - New Zealand hangings - Atlas detail
264 - British Library
278 - Rose Smith
282 - Sam Wanamaker and Peter Brooke - CBE award
283 - David Rogers and David Jones
286 - Rose Smith
293 - Royal Mail
303 - Marina Blodget
312 - David Hockney
315 - John Tramper.
319, 321, 323 - Richard Kalina.

INDEX